DIMENSIONS OF CHANGE

DIMENSIONS
OF
CHANGE

Problems and Issues
of American
Colonial History

EDITED BY

Lawrence H. Leder
LEHIGH UNIVERSITY

BURGESS PUBLISHING COMPANY • MINNEAPOLIS, MINNESOTA

Contents

LAWRENCE H. LEDER

The Mix of Institutional and Ideological Change

COMPOSED OF ESSAYS specifically written for this book, to-gether with some major source materials on which the individual authors based their essays, this volume offers students and teach-ers an opportunity to explore the scholarly mind as it probes each of five different phases of early American experience. Thus it offers not only an understanding of what history is, but, most important, of how historians work. It further demonstrates the essential nature of history itself — no study can ever be com-pletely comprehensive or eternally definitive. The historical past has an infinite richness and variety, just as does the human ex-perience itself.

Early American history exemplifies that richness and variety as much as any other chronological segment. The issues that moti-vated men, that determined what they considered important, and that shaped their responses to the challenges of life were multi-dimensional, and the historian must contend with this variety while simultaneously relating the issues in an orderly and mean-ingful fashion. Thus these essays deal with five aspects of colonial life, but each author realizes that his essay represents merely one of the many dimensions that he could utilize.

John M. Bumsted explores the nature of colonial religion, a major force in the life of colonial Americans. Modern students sometimes overlook the vital significance of this factor, since our society places less emphasis on it than did earlier ones. Yet, seventeenth- and eighteenth-century Americans found in religion an explanation of a vast and terrifying unknown, a rationale for something which otherwise seemed inexplicable. Accustomed as the late twentieth century is to space exploration — although we remain awed by the immensity of the firmament and intrigued by what might lie beyond our own solar system — men in the seventeenth and eighteenth centuries felt a similar emotion as they confronted the vast continents of the Americas. They saw a wilderness, fruitful but dangerous, immense but mysterious, challenging but awesome, and they realized that something or someone mightier than themselves had produced it. Brought up in the medieval religious tradition, they naturally turned to God for faith, hope, and strength to meet the challenges presented to them by the untamed wilderness.

However, the American environment had an impact on men's understanding and appreciation of God, and more so on their institutionalization of religion than on their doctrinal and theological issues. The transfer of European religions to America created new problems for traditional churches, ranging from the practical application of Puritanism's ideas about church and society to establishment of an episcopally-oriented Church of England without its traditional hierarchy. Americans adapted themselves and their religious institutions to the New World, an adaptation that reached its climax in the Great Awakening of the late 1730s and the 1740s. From this emerged an American tradition which included religious fragmentation, lay control, a decline in ministerial authority, an increasingly personalized faith, and techniques of disputation which provided Americans with models for their later disagreements with their mother country.

Imperial economic development as described by James G. Lydon also had its impact upon colonial life. The English had a national economic policy in mind by the seventeenth century, and they intended somehow to fit their New World possessions into that policy. From rather simple beginnings and a concern with the accumulation of bullion reserves, English mercantilism became increasingly sophisticated and emphasized the profits of complex trade patterns. However, England suffered a disadvantage in comparison to those states that controlled trade with more highly developed areas such as the Near East and Asia. The lands acquired by England contained an indigenous population which did not produce finished products of an exotic and therefore intrinsically valuable nature. America offered raw materials, particularly foodstuffs and other agricultural products. As Europe's economy changed, these raw materials took on added importance, and thus England's American possessions gained in value.

Among American products to which mercantilists gave increasing attention were tobacco, furs, fish, and sugar. Exploitation of these required a large resident population in the colonies, rather than mere trading posts, and this in turn created new problems of control for the mother country. England utilized various techniques, ranging from corporate colonies to proprietary grants and finally to royal colonies in an effort to control and coordinate the economic development of its empire. It also created an administrative agency to oversee mercantilist policy. By 1696 this had developed into the Board of Trade, which supervised the enforcement of various trade laws and regulations.

The earliest trade regulations involved tobacco, but soon they included other commodities as their production reached significant volume. Colonials could ship sugar, cotton, indigo, and dyewoods only to England, from whence English merchants might reexport them at a profit to themselves and the nation. As colonial populations expanded, England faced the threat of manufacturing competition from its possessions, and it responded by a series of statutes intended to hamper or prohibit colonial production of certain finished goods. Among the items whose manufacture in the colonies English mercantilists restricted were woollen cloth, hats, and ironware; some argued against permitting shipbuilding in America, but England never limited that activity because it proved beneficial to the empire as a whole.

English mercantilists further controlled the empire by directing its trade patterns, not only requiring that certain commodities go directly to England, but also flatly prohibiting some commerce, such as that with the foreign West Indies which threatened English investments in sugar production in their own West Indies islands. Indeed, by the mid-eighteenth century, out of a welter of laws and regulations seemingly adopted with little rhyme or reason, there emerged a coherent policy which treated the empire as an economic whole, assigning a specific role to each of its parts, and giving English authorities the responsibility of preventing usurpation by one element of the functions of another.

Prior to the mid-eighteenth century, the system worked moderately well. Permissiveness, evasion, and laxity marked the enforcement of trade regulations, and grievances existed, but both England and its colonies prospered. Once England had defeated France in the Seven Years War, it reviewed the costs of an empire, including military and naval protection, diplomacy, bureaucratic administration, and the floating of a large public debt. This led to demands within England for a tightening-up of its imperial administration, for a more effective control of the colonial economy in order to enhance the mother country's profits. A greater centralization of authority and a more restrictive approach to mercantilism than before developed after 1763. However, by this time the North American mainland colonies were maturing and seeking new and expanded economic opportunities. In essence, they had started to develop their own mercantilism which placed them increasingly in competition with the mother country. As England first tightened up existing controls and then instituted new ones, a storm of protest arose in the colonies.

In part, Americans' increasing sophistication by the mid-eighteenth century came about in conjunction with their increasing involvement in scientific developments. As Roy N. Lokken has indicated, a direct relationship existed between science and commerce throughout the seventeenth and eighteenth centuries. Practical sciences such as navigation, cartography, botany, and zoology received a marked stimulus from overseas exploration, the discovery of new lands, and the rapid expansion of trade.

The blossoming of scientific endeavors in western society fitted well with its religious concepts, for it opened still wider the wonders of God's universe, and it reinforced Christianity's assumptions about divine providence. The Newtonian universe, conceived as a great machine or clock, functioned in accord with natural laws created by God and describable in mathematical terms. From this grew a rationalistic impulse in religion. Once religion and science came to terms with one another, science itself became secularized. Those engaged in scientific activity in the eighteenth century increasingly avoided the philosophical and especially the religious implications of their work.

Most scientists in eighteenth-century America were amateur rather than professional, and their primary occupations ranged the gamut, including high government positions. As scientific endeavors rapidly expanded by the mid-eighteenth century, there occurred a marked trend toward the institutionalization of science, and by the 1760s scientific societies existed in most major American towns. Often concerned with practical applications of new knowledge, these societies and their members communicated with one another, offered premiums for new inventions and applications, and endeavored to expand America's industrial technology. Moreover, these scientists participated in an international natural history circle which added a cosmopolitan flavor to American society.

Nascent scientific endeavor in the colonies stimulated two developments which played an important part in bringing on the rupture with England. Not only did it make American society more cosmopolitan and stimulate intercolonial communication among the intellectual leadership, but it gave the colonials an optimistic outlook on their future and their ability to improve men's lot. In looking at Europe they saw science fettered by the decadence of monarchial tyranny and aristocratic corruption. In looking at their own republicanism, Americans saw a brilliant future for science and themselves. The optimism stimulated by science had a most important impact on colonial attitudes.

American attitudes toward political thought, as described in my essay entitled "Colonial Political Thought," also reflected optimism. Although colonials relied heavily on political ideas which had originated in England, they markedly modified them during a century of relative freedom of action. Colonials viewed government as a necessary evil and insisted on keeping it to a minimum. They expected government to control men's base instincts, not to create new opportunities. They constantly sought a harmonious balance in government, a system of checks and balances which would prevent action rather than facilitate it.

Too busy carving a civilization out of the wilderness, Americans did not devote themselves intensively to abstract political speculation, but they did discuss their expectations from government, particularly when pressed to it by periodic crises. They explored the nature of the British constitution — which not only governed them, but also became their ideal — and they analyzed the nature of the constitution in each colony. Their deliberations always had a pragmatic purpose; they sought to limit authority and to block unwanted intrusions of power, whether from England or from royal or proprietary officials in the colony. This became the focus of almost every Anglo-American dispute in the eighteenth century.

In their efforts to understand the British system of government and to stipulate the rightful limits upon its authority over them, Americans badly misconstrued the entire situation. Since no one in England took these speculations seriously, no one contradicted the colonials. This had its later ramifications as the Americans insisted on the reality of the fanciful myth they had constructed. And the myth's constant reiteration in the colonies gave it a vitality which would eventually make it impossible for Englishmen to challenge it without destroying the whole fabric of empire.

Utilizing the Glorious Revolution of 1688-89 as their touchstone, Americans created a situation in which they enjoyed greater liberty than any other colonial people and possibly than most Europeans of the time. The Glorious Revolution — or, as they often phrased it, "the late happy revolution" — provided a pattern whereby the colonials could defend themselves against the evils which had plagued seventeenth-century England. Thus they fought against executive authoritarianism, attempts to weaken popular legislatures, efforts to give real power to hand-picked governor's councils, as well as any exercise of authority by Crown officials. All of these signified a departure from the balanced ideal, however chimerical, which Americans found in the Revolution Settlement.

Once the English found the energy to challenge American misconceptions about government and empire, they let loose a nascent hysteria which had earlier remained in check. What Americans had once viewed as the bastion of good government suddenly became infected by all sorts of devils, beginning with Chancellor of the Exchequer George Grenville and ending with King George III himself. Yet the British had made their intentions known very clearly in the Declaratory Act of 1766, a document which Americans deliberately ignored because it so completely contradicted their assumptions if not their conceits. The failure of the colonials to face reality and their insistence upon their self-constructed myth kept them from understanding the true nature of the British Empire and from appreciating the fact that its locus of authority rested in London, not in a series of colonial towns.

For all groups in America, the accelerating controversies with Britain from 1763 to the early 1770s posed serious dilemmas, but for none did it challenge their basic allegiance. Misunderstandings could be cleared up, conflicts could be resolved, and rationality could return to the empire — or so almost every American believed until late 1775. By then, as Miles L. Bradbury suggests, a number of colonials began to realize the inevitability of conflict between England and its colonies and began to decide whether they would support the American or the British position. By July of 1776, no American could turn away from that decision. The moment of truth had arrived, and it was a traumatic one for many in the colonies.

Americans had traditionally and unquestioningly given their allegiance to Britain and the Crown. Indeed, they gloried in being Englishmen, and not even the changes in British policies in the 1760s altered that fact. No sharp division existed between Whig and Loyalist, and many who later rejected the new United States found just as much dissatisfaction with British policies at this time as did those who became leading rebels. After 1773, however, the line between Whig and Loyalist began to sharpen, and the passage of the Coercive Acts — or, as American rebels labeled them, the Intolerable Acts — most clearly widened the cleavage.

Those who valued their allegiance to the Crown above all else began to find themselves politically isolated. They could not accept the actions of the First Continental Congress, including the Continental Association and the extra-legal machinery to enforce it, the replacement of royal authority by Whig committees, and the harassment of those who would not actively and openly condemn British policies. As the Whigs became increasingly militant, the gap between them and the future Loyalists widened. Many who chose to remain with the king did so at great cost to themselves, and they most often did so on an individual basis and for personal reasons.

Clearly, both the Whigs and Loyalists looked upon themselves as patriots. The real issue centered about the locus of patriotism, with the Loyalists refusing to transfer their allegiance to a new entity while the Whigs did so. Many Loyalists understood the deficiencies of British rule, but they could not believe these deficiencies to be so great as to warrant the abandonment of nearly 175 years of tradition. Maintenance of the *status quo* overrode all other considerations for a number of Americans, regardless of their station in life. Both sides in the American Revolution firmly believed that they fought for America; they simply disagreed over the nature of the America that they envisioned for the future. Since fate favored the Whigs, the Loyalists found themselves displaced, disgraced in their homeland, and buried in oblivion by the historians of the revolution, while their opponents found themselves in possession of a new nation.

The irony of the situation lay in the fact that English and

colonial leaders entered the 1760s with a certain amount of good will toward one another. However, good will alone soon proved inadequate. Continuance of England's North American empire had hinged upon the capacity of its leaders to understand the institutional and ideological changes which they had permitted and sometimes encouraged in the colonies. Yet, their understanding of these changes was sharply circumscribed by communications techniques which had not improved significantly since the days of Sir Walter Raleigh. The sinews which had bound the fledgling Jamestown and Plymouth settlements to England in the 1620s could not tie the populous thirteen colonies to the mother country in the 1770s. Thus the disturbances which led to the American Revolution stemmed from a basic failure of colonials and Englishmen to understand one another's needs and to communicate adequately. Just as George III did not appreciate the carefully wrought institutional and ideological constructs of his American subjects, so too they did not understand those of Georgian England.

JOHN M. BUMSTED

Religion in Colonial Life

An UNDERSTANDING of early America must begin with two
inescapable facts: it was a new land, and it was settled with some
very old ideas. A totally new environment — a new landscape,
a different climate, unfamiliar flora and fauna, a native population never fully comprehended — and the challenges inherent in
establishing a civilization in a howling wilderness 3,000 miles
from "home" created an impact which twentieth-century man can
understand only intellectually, at least until space travel provides
him with a comparable experience.

The leaders, if not the rank-and-file, of the Europeans who
crossed the Atlantic in the seventeenth century appreciated the
vistas opened for experimentation and innovation by the "New
World." But not even the most imaginative and creative of them
could escape their own upbringing and traditions. In the American wilderness the colonists had a new vessel into which they
could pour anything, but they had only ingredients prepared in
Europe, mainly in England. Even the consciously "new" was, in
the last analysis, little more than a reaction against the old. Genuine innovation in early America existed less in carefully designed
efforts to be different than in long-term results of generations
fitting European patterns to the new environment. The real impact of the wilderness occurred in a gradual and subtle shift in

ideas and institutions, which ultimately produced arrangements quite distinct from those of Europe. Religion affords a prime example of the process at work.

The basic changes in the patterns of colonial religious life occurred less in formal theology and metaphysics than in new institutional arrangements. Despite an impressive colonial output of religious writings, mostly by New England Puritan divines, America did not produce an original and influential philosopher and theologian until the mid-eighteenth century, when Jonathan Edwards achieved some international reputation. And even Edwards made his contribution through brilliant analyses of the American phenomena of evangelical pietism and revivalism.

The first generation of Puritans included some first-rate theologians in John Cotton and Thomas Hooker, but their experiences were largely European and they cast their doctrinal formulations in European terms. Nevertheless, Cotton and especially Hooker had to translate a European theology into terms compatible with American experience. This resulted in works such as Hooker's *The Summe of Church Discipline,* devoted to practical political problems of founding and running Puritan churches in the New World.

While Puritan divines in England wrestled with doctrinal questions, which resulted in the Westminster Confession of 1648, Puritan divines in America characteristically produced the Cambridge Platform, which accepted the doctrinal foundation of the Westminster Confession, but moved on to create a written constitution for church government. American Puritans never really moved beyond the doctrinal statements of the Westminster Confession and its successor, the Savoy Confession; American Anglicans accepted unquestioningly the 39 Articles and the Book of Common Prayer; American Quakers relied heavily on the writings of George Fox, English founder of the Society of Friends. However, all churches in America moved to their own destinies by altering, usually subtly, occasionally bluntly, the bases of church organization and institutional power. This had doctrinal significance, however unaltered the creeds might remain.

For all churches, the transfer from Europe to America created new and in some cases unexpected problems. New England Puritans were challenged to take a theology and doctrine formulated in England but never really put into practice and make it work. Anglicans faced the basic difficulty of governing an episcopally-organized church without resident bishops. Quakers and a variety of other European sects needed to readjust from open persecution to a situation of relative toleration. Out of a multiplicity of churches, colonies, and experiences, three general problem areas stand out: defining new relationships of church and state, ultimately resolved by the principle of pluralism; adjusting church organization to suit the new institutional needs of the American environment, ultimately settled by lay domination sometimes verging on internal democracy; providing for spiritual needs of a population caught in an unfamiliar set of experiences, eventually settled by adoption of evangelicalism and an ethic of individual pietism. In the final elaboration of all these solutions, the mid-eighteenth-century religious revival known as the "Great Awakening" proved critical.

Almost without exception, the Englishmen who founded the British North American colonies accepted the partnership between church and state, in which all members of the body politic theoretically belonged to the single state church, supported it financially, and accepted its regulation in matters of faith and morals as enforced by the state's police power. The Protestant Reformation had not broken the church-state link, but had merely shifted the balance of power so that the state more visibly dominated the church (Erastianism). In England, the state assumed that loyalty to the monarch (the Supreme Governor of the Church of England) and support of Anglicanism were synonymous, and "true Englishmen" could worship in no other church.

While many of the first settlers in America dissented from the Church of England, few sought to separate church and state. To some extent, Roman Catholics who settled Maryland tried to break the usual church-state relationship, but only to the extent of tolerating their worship within an Anglican establishment. The Pilgrims in Plymouth Colony at first attempted to keep the state out of religious matters. They implicitly feared the danger articulated by Roger Williams, founder of Rhode Island, that connection of church and state permitted the corrupt state to dominate the "saints" in ecclesiastical matters. But when pressed, Plymouth established its religion as the colony's state church. Most Puritan founders of New England insisted that they remained Anglicans, seeking only a more purified church, and they sought to restore the church to a pre-Erastian independence of the state. However, they did not question the linkage of church and state, and many observers then and later have labelled their system a theocracy.

Besides Williams and a handful of religious fanatics in New England (most of whom ended up in Rhode Island), only the Quakers in the seventeenth century really pressed for toleration. And throughout the colonial period, technical church establishments remained in most British North American colonies. In the southern and West Indian colonies, the Church of England was "by law established." In most of New England, Puritan Congregationalism was the state church, although Anglicanism was more or less established in New Hampshire, and Rhode Island was the home of "soul liberty." In the middle colonies of New York and New Jersey the Anglican church was established, but in Pennsylvania a genuine disestablishment of religion existed.

Although most settlers accepted European assumptions about church establishment, their churches and leaders found the American situation quite different from that of the Old World. Some groups, especially the Puritans and to some extent the Quakers, ceased to be dissenting outsiders and became dominant insiders, with some curious results. Other groups — Anglicans in some colonies, Presbyterians and Lutherans in all colonies — ceased to receive state favor and competed on the open marketplace. All churches in North America faced competition and lived with relative practical toleration. For some churches accustomed to public support and for others which had developed an ethic accepting persecution, this produced difficulties.

The Puritans who settled New England offered perhaps the clearest example of the change from persecuted to persecutor. While it may seem peculiar that a people accustomed to harassment and imprisonment should employ these tactics on others, most Puritans believed that theirs was the *only* true church. As Nathaniel Ward ("The Simple Cobler of Aggawam") put it in 1645, "He that is willing to tolerate any Religion, or discrepant way of Religion, besides his own, unless it be in matters meerly indifferent, either doubts of his own, or is not sincere in it." The Puritans moved to New England to establish the proper spiritual and ecclesiastical values, and they would not permit any threat to their endeavours. Nevertheless, Puritans held that certain matters such as marriage and divorce, which had been monopolies of the courts of the Church of England, were purely civil matters and not under church control.

By the end of the seventeenth century, pressures from the mother country had forced Puritan New England to accept toleration for Protestants, although Massachusetts Bay and Connecticut continued to collect tax monies from all citizens for support of their Puritan (or Congregational) churches, and the state in the colonial period never ceased its financial and administrative support for Congregationalism. The vast bulk of the population favored such an arrangement. However, the shift to toleration did clearly separate political privileges from church membership, and this represented a considerable change from the situation then prevailing in England. Historians still debate the degree to which the Puritan colonies in practice had ever successfully restricted citizenship to church members.

The situation in Quaker Pennsylvania is particularly interesting in terms of the changes produced by a move to America. Pennsylvania was founded with the most liberal notions of religious toleration and of separation of church and state of any American colony. Nevertheless, William Penn clearly intended it as a Quaker refuge, and he meant to have Quakers (whose religious ethic included not only toleration but pacifism) as its political leaders. The openness of the colony's government, as well as its fertile lands, brought thousands of non-Quakers to Pennsylvania, and almost from its inception the Friends had difficulty maintaining their dominance. Equally distressing was the coincidence of Pennsylvania's founding and the beginning of large-scale warfare in North America between English, French, Spanish, and their various Indian allies. Quaker pacifism proved a far more tenable position when Friends were a small persecuted minority of a non-pacifistic population than when as political leaders they faced the problem of survival in North America. Many Quaker leaders ultimately compromised their religious principles, while others, who maintained notions of peace and friendship (particularly with Indians) in the face of the harsh realities of continental warfare, eventually withdrew from positions of leadership.

For other churches, particularly those of non-British origin, toleration and competition brought different problems. Dutch Reformed churches in the middle colonies became a principal bulwark of the Dutch language and customs against the dominant values of British North America, and the various German churches served the same defensive function. Leaders of churches of ethnic minorities soon discovered that maintaining strict standards of behavior and discipline among their members merely produced apostasy, frequently to competing English-speaking churches. Standards and operating assumptions worked out in Europe simply did not apply in North America.

For most Americans, toleration of religious beliefs other than their own was more a matter of necessity than of principle. In New England, the Church of England complained continually of its disabilities and pressed for toleration, while in Virginia Anglicanism strained to preserve its religious monopoly against small bands of Presbyterians, Quakers, and Baptists. Moreover, toleration and separation of church and state were hardly identical notions. Puritan Massachusetts might tolerate Baptists and Anglicans, for example, but the state still employed its whole mechanism in the service of Congregationalism. Finally, most colonies extended toleration only to Protestants, frequently by specific charter restrictions supported by public opinion. Only Pennsylvania extended full citizenship to Roman Catholics and Jews; even liberal Rhode Island did not recognize "Papists." Nevertheless, acceptance of dissenting religious beliefs had been achieved in North America by the early eighteenth century, and no colony maintained a monolithic state church. All Americans accepted the possible distinction between political citizenship and religious membership in a particular state church — and most could agree that civil as well as ecclesiastical authority could fulfill certain functions monopolized by religion in much of Europe, such as education. Good citizenship did not depend upon being a particular kind of Christian, and tacit acceptance of this constituted the basic principle of pluralism which became fundamental to religious development in North America. The multiplicity of religious groups made religious conformity an impossibility.

If the conditions of settlement in America created a tendency toward pluralism, so too did they develop a movement toward both local and lay control of religious institutions which frequently tended toward democracy. The North American environment — both natural and man-made — needed new institutional structures within which churches could reasonably operate. America, 3,000 miles from Europe, had relatively vast spaces and a scattered population. This made tight centralized supervision of particular churches difficult and even produced problems within local churches servicing an enormous geographical area. Even for state-supported churches, financial support came almost entirely from local parishioners, which led them to demand a voice in the expenditure of the revenue. Churches which relied on voluntary contributions obviously faced similar demands. Collecting taxes from the general population for support of the church, particularly in Puritan New England, posed some serious difficulties in defining church membership. How could taxpayers be excluded on doctrinal grounds from the church they supported? Absence of large ecclesiastical endowments and the tenuous support provided by the state, combined with general colonial economic limitations, restricted the establishment of institutions of higher learning for the training of clergymen in the accepted European fashion. These factors led toward local autonomy in church organization and toward lay control rather than clerical domination within the local church.

The Atlantic Ocean barred any European attempt to control American institutions, whether churches or governments. Nevertheless, many denominations tried to maintain an international centralization, often more fictional than factual. Perhaps the outstanding feature of the attempts was the reluctance of colonials to drop the fiction despite its failure to meet their needs.

The Anglican Church developed in seventeenth-century America without any direct episcopal supervision beyond a tenuous link with the Bishop of London. Despite the obvious anomoly of an episcopal church without a resident bishop, American Anglicans did not demand one until late in the colonial period. The Dutch Reformed churches faced a difficult situation as a result of the assertion of control by the Classis of Amsterdam. They had difficulty in resolving disputes and misunderstandings because of communication problems, and candidates for the ministry had to make the long and dangerous journey to The Netherlands for ordination. As early as 1706, local ministers complained about the problem, but not until 1735 did the Amsterdam Classis approve the concept of a local judicatory, and not until 1747 did one begin meeting. Before that time, certain Reformed ministers had ordained candidates without proper authority, and establishment of a coetus (a voluntary meeting of ministers with limited authority) split the denomination between those who sought to keep "the Dutch way" and those who favored local autonomy. In most cases, establishment of American supervisory bodies with some authority occurred only after it had become clearly evident that the authority of the European body was bankrupt and being ignored; local supervision was preferable to anarchy. Not until the 1750s did all major American denominations have their own jurisdictional authorities.

While the ocean made international centralization impossible, America's sheer size made centralization within a single colony extremely difficult. Puritanism had come to America with a theory of local congregational autonomy, and it devoted most of its efforts to creating some framework of centralization. The Cambridge Platform of 1648 devoted considerable attention to the relationships between autonomous churches, and the Saybrook Platform of 1708 in Connecticut consciously attempted to force central control on independent congregations. However, those denominations which began with congregational autonomy, such as Puritanism and various German pietistic groups, had less adjustments to make than did those which in Europe had been centralized in presbyteries, consistories, or dioceses. Whatever the major jurisdictional unit in Europe, the basic unit in America was invariably local. For most churches this did not require new institutions of ecclesiastical government, but it did require a shift in emphasis. The parish vestry was an important unit of the Church of England in the mother country, but it became the principal instrument of Anglican church government in the colonies.

Once Americans had accepted local, autonomous government of churches, the question arose of who should do the governing. Even those churches founded on congregational autonomy had not, for the most part, also accepted lay dominance in their government. A ministry ordained of God, specially chosen and educated, expected in the colonies — as in Europe — to dominate the congregations. New England Puritanism attempted to maintain what one minister called "a silent democracy in the face of a speaking aristocracy," but in New England, as elsewhere, the democracy refused to remain silent. As the Lutheran leader Henry Muhlenberg complained, "it is easier to be a cowherd or a shepherd in many places in Germany than to be a preacher here, where every peasant wants to act the part of a patron of the parish, for which he has neither the intelligence nor the skill." The levelling experience of American church government both elevated the layman and lowered the clergyman.

The gradual decline of the minister's position was closely related to his difficulty in maintaining a superior education over that of his congregation. In Europe, a host of long-established universities trained clergymen, educating them in the complex medieval systems of logic and assuring their fluency in a variety of classical and oriental languages. Seventeenth-century America had only Harvard College for most of the period. Education in Europe for Americans was expensive and difficult; the transatlantic journey was arduous and difficult. As a result, America,

especially outside New England, had to recruit its clergymen in
Europe. These emigrants did not understand the ways of the
New World and lost authority while learning them. Theodorus
Frelinghuysen, the leading Dutch Reformed minister of the eighteenth century, was European born and educated, fluent in Latin,
Greek, Hebrew, Aramaic, Syriac, and Rabbinic Hebrew. His arrival in New Jersey in 1720 provoked decades of dispute within
and without his congregation as he attempted to impose European
standards. In addition to the problems of education, many denominations could not ordain their clergy locally. This often led, particularly within southern Anglicanism, to clergymen who served
churches without ecclesiastical ordination and investiture, and
who therefore found themselves at the mercy of their congregations for their continued employment. Not surprisingly, clerical
authority lasted longer in New England, which produced high-
quality native-born and educated clergymen.

A decline in status is frequently two-sided. While few ministers
in America matched the stature and attainments of early Puritan
clergymen like John Cotton and Thomas Hooker, the American
congregations had a generally higher educational level and socio-
economic position than did those of Europe. The entire thrust of
American society was away from the privilege of caste represented by the European clergyman. Threats from the laity to the
minister's position mirrored the conditions of American society.
Whichever laymen tended to dominate secular society also tended
to dominate the churches. Merchants frequently controlled urban
churches; self-perpetuating oligarchies of planters organized in
vestries ran churches in the plantation South; larger bodies of
relatively equal farmers and artisans governed churches in more
open rural farming and frontier communities.

Central to lay control in all churches was localized domination
over ministerial appointment and localized financial support of
the church. In no colony did the state contribute direct financial
support; instead, even for established churches, it merely authorized local collection of tax monies for ecclesiastical expenses.
Churches had no large endowments controlled by private agencies
outside the local area, and few Americans could afford to become
patrons of churches as did European princes and noblemen. Clergymen of all American denominations were painfully aware that
funds for their salaries and church maintenance came from their
local congregations, either through taxes or private contributions.

And a contributor naturally felt, as one Massachusetts man put it in the early eighteenth century, that he should have "all the Benefit of his money."

Closely related to financial support was church membership. This presented no problem for American churches such as the Anglican, which had its European origins in a national church situation. By their very nature, national churches included the entire population in their membership, avoiding doctrines which demanded superior spiritual attainments of church members. Most American denominations had begun in reaction to national churches, however, and had established particular tests for church membership, such as evidences of experience of conversion. Transference to America of a church with high qualifications for membership created no difficulties as long as it maintained itself by private support and a purely voluntary membership.

The Puritan churches in New England ran into extraordinary difficulties, however, by combining high membership qualifications with state support and ecclesiastical monopoly. It was one thing to insist upon "converted Christians" as prospective church members in England, where Puritanism had operated on the fringes of society as a purely voluntary church. In New England, however, the Puritan churches depended on ecclesiastical taxes collected from the entire population, and freemanship and full political citizenship depended upon church membership. Not surprisingly, pressures in New England sought to lower the standards for membership. This resulted in the tortured reasoning of a Synod of 1662, authorizing what amounted to a new category of church membership for children of those baptized but not themselves converted. Not all Puritans approved of the halfway covenant, as it became called, and other ministers, led by Solomon Stoddard of Northampton, favored opening the doors of church membership to the entire community. For the most part, opposition to the halfway covenant came from laymen, who insisted on maintaining the old standards and who produced many debates within the churches. Lay power prevented many clergymen from instituting halfway practices in their churches. Nevertheless, adoption of the halfway covenant and pressures from England to separate membership in the body politic from membership in the church preserved the exclusive nature of Puritan church membership, but at considerable cost to the original intentions of New England's founders.

By the early eighteenth century, the elevated status of the

American clergyman was clearly in jeopardy, while the authority of the layman was not only on the rise, but in most churches visibly dominant. Not all local churches operated on a democratic basis of "one man, one vote," but many, especially in New England, certainly did. Ministers of all denominations bewailed their loss of authority and their inability to insist upon high Christian standards of conduct and comportment for their congregations. The New World had shifted the balance of power in churches to the layman, and there, despite valiant efforts at reform, it remained.

If American conditions required new definitions of church-state relations and ecclesiastical government, so too did they produce a population with new spiritual needs. For the most part, Old World churches dealt with a geographically and socially stable population. The religious message necessary under such circumstances reassured the individual of the church's presence at various stages of his life: birth, marriage, and death. It provided spiritual solace for clearly defined strata of society (such as the peasant, the gentry, the urban merchant) in everyday life and during constantly recurring catastrophes such as pestilence, drought, and war. The European approach had always assured individuals, whose lot in life was fixed from birth, of the predictable nature of their earthly existence, however "nasty, brutish, and short." And more important, most Europeans had their place and knew it. In North America, a mobile population, in both a geographical and social sense, had the needs of an open pioneer society rather than those of a closed stable one. The New World added personal insecurity into life on earth, partly through new and unfamiliar threats such as Indian raids and climatic conditions, but more significantly through sudden changes in circumstance which might come to any individual. Opportunity also leads to failure; a society undergoing rapid change and flux created new levels of personal insecurity which modern psychologists usually label "anxiety" and "alienation."

The very move to America from the Old World meant entering into the unknown, and as the colonial population expanded from the seacoast into the interior, the psychological problems of settlement became even more intense. Instead of facing a world of familiar difficulties – even catastrophes – supported by family, friends, and church, the American pioneer moved into the unknown separated by an ocean from his relatives, unacquainted with those settling with him, and often isolated on his individual

farmstead or plantation from easy intercourse with others ex-
periencing similar problems. Under such circumstances, the pioneer not only needed spiritual support and reassurance, which his
isolated condition made it difficult for religion to provide, but he
also required more than sacramental celebrations, ethical advice,
and a rational discussion of salvation. Instead, he needed emotional support which he could not get through a constant church
attendance because his location and situation denied him that
opportunity. The wilderness was as new an experience for religion as it was for the pioneer, and relief for anxiety and alienation was relatively slow in coming.

Some European denominations — English Puritanism and
Quakerism, for example — had developed in response to Old World
problems which differed more in degree than in kind from the
American experience, and these faiths brought to the colonies an
emotionally comforting and reassuring spiritual message. To a
great extent, this explains the success enjoyed by early settlers
under conditions of hardship in New England and Pennsylvania.
But by the early eighteenth century, both Puritanism and Quakerism had lost sight of their earlier insistence on an immediate
religion of heart and spirit, although scattered ministers such as
Jonathan Edwards continued to emphasize these points. Continental emigrants, especially from areas deeply affected by the
Thirty Years War, imported a religious posture born of wartime
conditions of uncertainty and hardship, stressing direct reassurance of God's presence and support through experiences of conversion and communion with the Supreme Being. By the 1730s, an
indigenous American religion stressing a personally meaningful
relationship of the individual to God (usually called pietism)
joined forces with the continental emigrants and a new movement
of spiritual regeneration in English urban areas led by the
brothers Wesley and by George Whitefield. The merger between
indigenous and emigrant pietism occurred first in New Jersey,
where the native-born and educated Presbyterian minister Gilbert
Tennent collaborated with the Westphalian-born and educated
Theodorus Frelinghuysen. Both men leaped to the side of the
great itinerant Anglican preacher George Whitefield when he arrived in the middle colonies in 1739.

The collaboration of native American and Old World forces
produced a spontaneous outburst of spiritual concern in the early
1740s known in the colonies as the "Great Awakening." The times
were ripe for such an occasion. The decade of the 1730s had added

an increasing sense of unresolved problems and growing tensions to the constant change and uncertainty in America. The American dream of peace, prosperity, and opportunity to advance seemed particularly threatened. As usually happens under such circumstances, a movement came along which fed upon the perceptions of problems and tensions, and which offered a solution to them.

The colonials certainly faced many difficulties. An increasingly tense international crisis worried Americans. A war, which began in 1739 between England and Spain, threatened to draw France into the conflict. That would lead to increased Indian raids, recruiting of soldiers, impressment of seamen, and threats for some areas of armed invasion. An economic crisis also existed. Easily available land in seacoast regions seemed to be vanishing rapidly, the international crisis reduced opportunities for movement to exposed frontiers, and the absence of an adequate medium of exchange limited the American economy and led in most colonies to demands for paper currency. Opposition to paper money by the ruling classes produced open statements of class conflict, such as that of the Boston town meeting, which declared that the townsmen would not "have our Bread & Water measured out to Us by those who Riot in Luxury & Wantonness on our Sweat & Toil and be told perhaps by them that we are too happy, because we are not reduced to Eat Grass with the Cattle." Finally, a wave of epidemics, which struck many parts of the colonies in the 1730s, represented a new experience; never before in America had such large numbers of people been wiped out so suddenly by communicable disease, never had life in the colonies seemed so transitory.

In an age in which religion still mattered, the movement which fed upon and responded to the people's needs was spread by the clergy and was spiritual in its emphasis. George Whitefield in 1740 brought and publicized new techniques of emotional appeal to the general population. Unlike parish ministers, who lived with their flocks for years and taught the ethical and moral values of Christianity, Whitefield itinerated from place to place, preaching solely to the immediate needs of his audiences for spiritual reassurance and security. A magnificent and practised public orator, Whitefield understood how to manipulate crowd reaction and excitement to his purposes, and whatever the complexities of life which produced attentive listeners, Whitefield reduced the issue to simple terms — you must be saved — and he cut through complicated theological and ecclesiastical jargon to explain how to become saved — accept Christ in your heart. Wherever possible,

Whitefield attempted to attract the support of the local clergy
to add legitimacy to his presence. Jonathan Edwards's wife Sarah
summed up Whitefield's appeal in a letter to her brother:

He makes less of the doctrines than our American preachers generally
do, and aims more at affecting the heart. He is a born orator. You have
already heard of his deep-toned, yet clear and melodious voice. It is perfect music. It is wonderful to see what a spell he casts over an audience
by proclaiming the simplest truths of the Bible. I have seen upwards of
a thousand people hang on his words with breathless silence, broken
only by an occasional half-suppressed sob. He impresses the ignorant,
and not less the half-educated and the refined.

His own ego obviously fed by success on the grand scale, Whitefield stuck mainly to the cities of colonial America, where large
crowds would gather to respond to his performances.

But colonial clergymen quickly discovered the obvious merits of
Whitefield's techniques, and scores of itinerants, mostly younger
men, joined the handful who had long worked in the wilderness
to bring the message of pietism to America's rural communities.
Many ministers recognized the spiritual, institutional, and practical benefits of revivalism. The population was obviously ready,
and large numbers previously hostile or indifferent to religion
might join the churches. Spiritually renewed and grateful to those
who had touched their hearts, laymen might hopefully cease their
endless insistence on controlling ecclesiastical institutions, and
the status and power of the ministry would be improved. By 1743,
the urban and northern rural phases of the revival had ended.
Because southern rural settlement was much more scattered, revivalism had not yet significantly affected that region. Two general currents remained: a constantly expanding backcountry
revival which continued unabated throughout the eighteenth century and a substantial debate over the meaning and value of
revival which produced an enormous controversial literature and
contributed to schisms and divisions within most denominations
of colonial America.

Clergymen in America almost unanimously favored revival during its early phases from 1740 to 1742. But by 1743, mutterings of
clerical discontent burst into open opposition. Critics objected to
certain "abuses" which they felt dangerously questioned the
divine authority, especially "enthusiasm," itinerancy, censorious-
ness, and antinomianism. Complaints centered around the intru-
sion into parishes of itinerant evangelists without the consent of
the settled minister. Such intrusions frequently resulted in an

overly emotional response and an antinomian insistence upon immediate experiences of communion with God, which took precedence over the churches' long-standing doctrinal and ecclesiastical traditions. Even worse, those who accepted revivalism attacked as unconverted Pharisees their pastors and neighbors who doubted the spiritual efficacy (or "graciousness") of the experiences, and the revivalists refused to recognize any less dramatic experiences than their own as truly Christian. A particularly horrible example occurred in New London, Connecticut, where some citizens gathered on the main street, built a bonfire, and threw into the flames "sundry goods and useful treatises, books of practical godliness, the works of able divines, and whilst said books were consuming in the flames, did shout, hollow and scream, &c." They defended these actions as "what they then judged in their consciences *Duty* and agreeable to the word of God."

By 1743, colonial clergymen and their parishioners began debating whether God or the devil ordained the Awakening. The division manifested itself at provincial and intra-provincial meetings of divines, such as the Massachusetts Ministerial Convention and the Presbyterian Synod of North America, and at the level of local churches as well. Neither supporters nor opponents of the revival were unanimous in their attitudes nor motivated in them by identical factors. Opponents (called Old Lights in New England and Old Sides in the middle colonies) fell broadly into two categories: traditionalist supporters of the pre-Awakening status quo and religious liberals influenced by eighteenth-century rationalism and skepticism. Supporters of the Awakening were greatly divided. Most simply felt the positive value of the revival and favored it without desiring or supporting any alterations in doctrine or ecclesiastical practices. A few of the most influential proponents of the revival, such as Gilbert Tennent and Jonathan Edwards, publicly attacked the same evils as its opponents but still thought the Awakening an act of God. Edwards and Tennent feared the extremist wing among the New Lights, who advanced a radical program of religious reformation which rejected existing churches and even traditional sacraments such as infant baptism. The radicals loudly criticized existing doctrine and practices within their local churches, especially in New England, and did not hesitate to break away from a church which would not reform. Much of the division and most of the local schisms were only partly attributable to the revival; they involved disagreements over more traditional issues, such as clerical authority and finances, endemic in America since its first settlement. Edwards himself lost his pastorate in Northampton over the issue of clerical authority.

The radical New Lights did not really get very far in breaking up the churches in settled regions of the colonies. But their pietistic emphasis on an immediate relationship with God, their objections to a classically educated "hireling Ministry" and ecclesiastical taxation, their zealous willingness to travel great distances and incur hardships to bring their message of Christ to the population – all these ideally suited backcountry areas where scattered population and poverty had made almost impossible the establishment of traditional religion. The radicals, many of whom rejected infant baptism as without scriptural ordination, soon discovered that they could not compete in settled areas with the traditional churches, but had the frontier virtually to themselves. Hundreds of revived pietists, convinced that their religious experiences were more vital than their lack of a university degree, moved into the backcountry areas of New England, the middle colonies, and especially the South, to bring religion to the people. The expansion of radical pietism onto the frontier knew no chronological limits and continued as a vital force during the American Revolution.

The Great Awakening and its aftermath still reverberated in North America as the colonies moved toward a confrontation with the mother country. Supporters of the revival always spoke of numbers converted and saved from sinful behavior, but these achievements – which in retrospect appear overstated at best – had less importance than other not so apparent consequences. The Great Awakening strengthened the long-standing American tendencies toward denominationalism and lay control, it provided the spiritual message required by American conditions, and it engendered debates and conflicts which paradoxically not only achieved the final separation of American churches from European control but helped reintegrate American Christianity into transatlantic developments. Most importantly, the Great Awakening conditioned Americans to the disputations which led to the American Revolution.

While both contemporaries and later historians have talked about great numbers converted during the revival, hard figures are impossible to acquire. Many may never have recorded their conversion by joining a church, and others quickly backslid. Records of church membership indicated that the revival meant no long-range net gain of communicants; it merely got a lot of people into churches in the early 1740s. But the revival did have a great appeal to the young male, and for the first time, members of minority groups like Indians and Negroes were admitted to some previously all-white churches. As for morality, its improvement was equally unmeasurable. The revival's emphasis upon moral living may have decreased the commission of "sinful" acts, but it also increased a sense of guilt about ones which were committed. Large numbers of Americans may suddenly have felt that premarital sexual intercourse, dancing, drinking, singing secular songs, and other amusements were dirty things even while they continued doing them. In the long run, the revival probably had no effect either on numbers or morality.

More concretely, the Awakening completely destroyed any religio-ideological consensus which may have existed in colonial America, and it fragmented existing denominations while creating new ones. The revival assured the prevalence in North America of denominational fragmentation dominated by strong overtones of Protestant pietism. The damage done to the unity of major religious denominations doomed the concept of a church establishment, already weakened by the prerevival growth of toleration. American pietism came to stress not simply toleration, but a "high wall of separation" between church and state. Equally important, the revival challenged established ministerial authority with an individualistic "my opinion is as good as anybody's" mentality. Learning and social standing, already debilitated as justifications for leadership by the American experience, were further damaged by an emphasis on a religious experience unrelated to education and position. The ministry further weakened its case by engaging in acrimonious controversy and name-calling over the revival. Among radical New Lights, the emphasis on the preeminence of the layman led to a doctrine close to the priesthood of all believers, certainly to an acceptance of any true believer as a qualified spiritual leader. The experience of conversion engendered by the revival did provide a sense of security for Americans in time of deep (if only temporary) emotional and psychological need, and the renewed emphasis on personal pietism provided a bulwark against continuing anxiety and alienation within the American experience, particularly on the expanding frontier.

In terms of the relationship of American religion with Europe, the Awakening led to two almost paradoxical developments. On the one hand, the revival exposed problems of organization and engendered struggles which made it almost impossible for any American denomination to be run from Europe. The churches had to settle the increased incidence of division and dispute with dispatch, and they could no longer allow themselves the luxury of consulting with European governing bodies. The obvious defensive need for an educated clergy to protect traditional religious values made it equally impossible to rely any longer on Old World educational facilities, and the leading denominations began to establish their own colleges in the colonies to train clergymen. But while American churches freed themselves from European political control, they discovered that colonial pietism was part of a great transatlantic movement. American intellectual figures like Jonathan Edwards and Gilbert Tennent found their writings circulated widely in Europe, and leaders of pietistic leanings – even the radical Baptists – established intellectual connections with their Old World counterparts. American religion rejoined Europe intellectually at the same time that it separated from it politically.

Most attempts to relate the Awakening with the American Revolution founder by trying to find correlations between sides in the two conflicts, or at least to discover an ideological continuity. The real point of the revival was not its status as America's first national experience – although it was certainly that – but as America's first mass movement. It introduced colonials to techniques and modes of thinking employed by both sides (or all sides) in the critical days of the 1760s and early 1770s. Both in strategy and in techniques – such as mass meetings, simplistic arguments, and intercolonial correspondence – the Awakening prepared the way for the Revolution. Americans became accustomed to polarization, sloganeering, and name-calling in the guise of ideology, and even to confrontation politics. The great debate over the meaning of the revival prefigured the great debate over the meaning of the British Empire, not in an ideological sense but rather in a structural one.

FOR FURTHER READING

Brydon, George M. *Virginia's Mother Church and the Political Conditions under which it Grew.* 2 vol. Richmond: Virginia Historical Society; Philadelphia: Church History Society, 1952.

Bumsted, J. M., ed. *The Great Awakening: The Beginnings of Evangelical Pietism in America.* Waltham: Ginn, 1970.

Heimert, Alan. *Religion and the American Mind: From the Great*

Awakening to the Revolution. Cambridge: Harvard University Press, 1966.

Miller, Perry. *The New England Mind: The Seventeenth Century.* Boston: Beacon Press, 1961.

Miller, Perry. *The New England Mind: From Colony to Province.* Boston: Beacon Press, 1961.

Morgan, Edmund S. *Visible Saints: The History of a Puritan Idea.* New York: New York University Press, 1963.

Tanis, James. *Dutch Calvinistic Pietism in the Middle Colonies: A Study in the Life and Theology of Theodorus Jacobus Frelinghuysen.* The Hague: Nijhoff Boekhandelan, 1967.

Trinterud, Leonard J. *The Forming of an American Tradition: A Re-Examination of Colonial Presbyterianism.* Philadelphia: Philadelphia Presbyterian B. D., 1949.

Walker, Williston. *The Creeds and Platforms of Congregationalism.* Boston: United Church, 1960.

Winslow, Ola. *Meetinghouse Hill 1630-1783.* New York: Macmillan Company, 1952.

1

The Cambridge Platform, 1648

SOURCE: *A Platform of Church Discipline Gathered out of the Word of God: And Agreed upon by the Elders: And Messengers of the Churches Assembled in the Synod at Cambridge in New England. To be presented to the Churches and Generall Court for their consideration and acceptance, in the Lord.* (Cambridge, 1649), 23-26.

CHAP: XV.
OF THE COMUNION OF CHURCHES ONE WITH ANOTHER.

Although Churches be distinct, & therfore may not be confounded one with another: & equall, & therfore have not dominion one over another: yet all the churches ought to preserve *Church-communion* one with another, because they are all united unto Christ, not only as a mysticall, but as a politicall head; whence is derived *a communion* suitable therunto.

The *communion* of Churches is exercised sundry wayes.

I   By way of mutuall *care* in taking thought for one anothers wellfare.

II   By way of *Consultation* one with another, when wee have occasion to require the judgment & counsell of other churches, touching any person, or cause wherwith they may be better acquainted than our selves. As the church of Antioch consulted with the Apostles, & Elders of the church at Ierusalem, about the question of circumcision of the gentiles, & about the false teachers that broached that doctrine. In which case, when any Church wanteth light or peace amongst themselves, it is a way of communication of churches (according to the word) to meet together by their Elders & other messengers in a synod, to consider & argue the points in doubt, or difference; & haveing found out the way of truth & peace, to commend the same by their letters & messengers to the churches, whom the same may concern. But if a Church be rent with divisions amongst themselves, or ly under any open scandal, & yet refuse to consult with other churches, for healing or removing of the same; it is matter of just offence both to the Lord Jesus, & to other churches, as bewraying too much want of mercy & faithfulness, not to seek to bind up the breaches & wounds of the church & brethren; & therfore the state of such a church calleth aloud upon other churches, to excertise a fuller act of brotherly communion, to witt, by way of *admonition*.

III   A third way then of communion of churches is by way of *admoni-*

tion, to witt, in case any publick offence be found in a church, which they
either discern not, or are slow in proceeding to use the meanes for the
removing & healing of. Paul had no authority over Peter, yet when he
saw Peter not walking with a right foot, he publickly rebuked him before
the church: though churches have no more authority one over another,
then one Apostle had over another; yet as one Apostle might admonish
another, so may one church admonish another, & yet without usurpation.
In which case, if the church that lyeth under offence, do not harken to
the church with doth admonish her, the church is to acquaint other
neighbour-churches with that offence, which the offending church still
lyeth under, together with their neglect of the brotherly admonition
given unto them; wherupon those other churches are to joyn in second-
ing the admonition formerly given: and if still the offending church
continue in obstinacy & impenitency, they may forbear communion with
them; & are to proceed to make use of the help of a Synod, or counsell
of neighbour-churches walking orderly (if a greater cannot conveniently
be had) for their conviction. If they hear not the Synod, the Synod having declared them to be obstinate, particular churches, approving &
accepting of the judgment of the Synod, are to declare the sentence of
non-communion respectively concerning them: & therupon out of a religious care to keep their own communion pure, they may justly withdraw
themselves from participation with them at the Lords table, & from such
other acts of holy communion, as the communion of churches doth other-
lyeth under publick offence; doe not consent to the offence of the church,
wise allow, & require. Nevertheless, if any members of such a church as
lyeth under publick offence; do not consent to the offence of the church,
but doe in due sort beare witness against it, they are still to be received
to wonted communion: for it is not equall, that the innocent should suffer
with the offensive. Yea furthermore; if such innocent members after
due wayting in the use of all good meanes for the healing of the offence
of their own church, shall at last (with the allowance of the counsel of
neighbour-churches) withdraw from the fellowship of their own church
& offer themselves to the fellowship of another; wee judge it lawfull for
the other church to receive them (being otherwise fitt) as if they had
been orderly dismissed to them from their own church.

   IV   A fourth way of communion of churches, is by way of *participation*: the members of one church occasionally comming unto another,
wee willingly admitt them to *partake* with us at the Lords table, it being
the seale of our communion not only with Christ, nor only with the
members of our own church, but also with all the churches of the saints:
in which regard, wee refuse not to baptize their children presented to us,
if either their own minister be absent, or such a fruite of holy fellowship
be desired with us. In like case such churches as are furnished with more
ministers than one, doe willingly afford one of their own ministers to
supply the place of an absent or sick minister of another church for a
needfull season.

   V   A fifth way of Church-communion is, by way of *recommendation*
when a member of one church hath occasion to reside in another church;
if but for a season, wee commend him to their watchfull ffellowship by
letters of recommendation: but if he be called to settle his abode there,

wee commit him according to his desire, to the ffellowship of their
covenant, by letters of dismission.

VI   A sixth way of Church-communion, is in case of *Need,* to minister
reliefe & succour one unto another: either of able members to furnish
them with officers; or of outward support to the necessityes of poorer
churches; as did the churches of the Gentiles contribute liberally to the
poor saints at Ierusalem.

3   When a company of beleivers purpose to gather into church fellowship, it is requisite for their safer proceeding, & the maintaining of the
communion of churches, that they signifie their intent unto the neighbour-churches, walking according unto the order of the Gospel, & desire
their presence, & help, & right hand of fellowship which they ought
readily to give unto them, when there is no just cause of excepting against
their proceedings.

4   Besides these severall wayes of communion, there is also a way of
propagation of churches; when a church shall grow too numerous, it is
a way, & fitt season, to propagate one Church out of an other, by sending
forth such of their members as are willing to remove, & to procure some
officers to them, as may enter with them into church-estate amongst
themselves: as Bees, when the hive is too full, issue forth by swarmes,
& are gathered into other hives, soe the Churches of Christ may doe the
same upon like necessity; & therin hold forth to them the right hand
of fellowship, both in their gathering into a church; & in the ordination
of their officers.

2

Nathaniel Ward on Toleration, 1647

SOURCE: Theodore de la Guard [Nathaniel Ward], *The Simple
Cobbler of Aggawam in America* . . ., 5th ed. (Boston, 1713),
3-13.

ON TOLERATION

[Those who] have given or taken any unfriendly reports of us *New
English,* should doe well to recollect themselves. We have been reputed
[to be] a Collovies [gathering of filth] of wild Opinionists, swarmed into
a remote wilderness to find elbow-room for our Phanatick Doctrines and

Practises: I trust our diligence past, and constant sedulity against such persons and courses, will plead better things for us. I dare take upon me, to be the Herauld of *New-England* so far, as to proclaim to the World, in the name of our Colony, that all Familists, Antinomians, Anabaptists, and other Enthusiasts shall have free liberty to keep away from us, and such as will come to be gone as fast they can, the sooner the better.

Secondly, I dare aver, that God doth no where in his word tolerate Christian States, to give Tolerations to such adversaries of his Truth, if they have power in their hands to suppress them.

Here is lately brought us an Extract of a *Magna Charta*, so called, compiled between the Sub planters of a *West-Indian* Island; whereof the first Article of constipulation, firmly provides free stable-room and litter for all kind of Consciences, be they never so dirty or jadish; making it actionable, yea, treasonable, to disturb any man in his Religion, or to discommend it, whatever it be. We are very sorry to see such professed Prophaneness in *English* Professors, as industriously to lay their Religious foundations on the ruine of true Religion; which thirdly binds every Conscience to *contend earnestly for the Truth: to preserve unity of Spirit, Faith and Ordinances, to be all like minded, of one accord; every man to take his Brother into his Christian care, to stand fast with one Spirit, with one mind, striving together for the faith of the Gospel;* and by no means to permit Heresies or Erronious Opinions: But God abhorring such loathsome beverages, hath in his righteous judgment blasted that enterprize, which might otherwise have prospered well, for ought I know; I presume their case is generally known ere this.

If the Devil might have his free option, I believe he would ask nothing else, but liberty to enfrancize all false Religions, and to embondage the true; nor should he need: It is much to be feared, that lax Tolerations upon State-pretences and planting necessities, will be the next subtle Strategem he will spread to diflate the Truth of God, and supplant the Peace of the Churches. Tolerations in things tolerable, exquisitely drawn out by the lines of the Scripture, and pencil of the Spirit, are the sacred favours of Truth, the due latitudes of Love, the fair Compartments of Christian fraternity: but irregular dispensations, dealt forth by the facilities of men, are the frontiers of error, the redoubts of Schisme, the perilous irricaments [wrath?] of carnal and spiritual enmity.

My heart hath naturally tested four things: The Standing of the Apocrypha in the Bible; Forainers dwelling in my Country, to crowd out Native Subjects into the corners of the Earth; Alchymized Coines; Tolerations of divers Religions, or of one Religion in segregant shapes; He that willingly assents to the last, if he examines his heart by day-light, his Conscience will tell him, he is either an Atheist, or an Heretick, or an Hypocrite, or at best a captive to some Lust: Poly-piety is the greatest impiety in the World. True Religion is *Ignis probitatis*, which doth *congregare homogenea & egregare heterogenea*. [True Religion is a fire of testing, which doth bring together what is compatible and separate what is not.]

Not to tolerate things meerly indifferent to weak Consciences, argues a Conscience too strong: pressed uniformity in these, causes much disunity: To tolerate more than indifferents, is not to deal indifferently with God: He that doth it, takes his Scepter out of his hand, and bids him stand by. Who hath to do to institute Religion but God. The power of all Religion and Ordinances, lies in their Purity: their Purity in their Simplicity: then are mixtures pernicious. I lived in a City, where a Papist Preached in one Church, a Lutheran in another, a Calvinist in a third; a Lutheran one part of the day, a Calvinist the other, in the same Pulpit: the Religion of that Place was but motly and meagre, their affections Leopard-like.

If the whole Creature should conspire to do the Creator a mischief, or offer him an insolency, it would be in nothing more, than in erecting untruths against his Truth, or by sophisticating his Truths with humane medleyes: the removing of some one iota in Scripture, may draw out all the life, and traverse all the Truth of the whole Bible: but to authorise an untruth, by a Toleration of State, is to build a Sconce against the walls of Heaven, to better God out of his Chair: To tell a practical lye, is a great Sin, but yet transient; but to set up a Theor[et]ical untruth, is to warrant every lye that lyes from its root to the top of every branch it hath, which are not few.

I would willingly hope that no Member of the Parliament hath skilfully ingratiated himself into the hearts of the House, that he might watch a time to Midwife out some ungracious Toleration for his own turn, and for the sake of that, some other, I would also hope that a word of general caution should not be particularly misapplied. I am the freer to suggest it, because I know not one many of that mind, my aim is general, and I desire may so be accepted. Yet good Gentlemen, look well about you, and remember how *Tiberias* pla'd the Fox with the Senate of *Rome*, and how *Fabius Maximus* cropt his ears for his cunning.

That State is wise, that will improve all pains and patience rather to compose, than tolerate differences in Religion. There is no divine Truth, but hath much Coelestial fire in it from the Spirit of Truth: nor no irreligious untruth without its propositions of antifire from the spirit of Error to contradict it: the zeal of the one, the virulency of the other, must necessarily kindle combustions. Fiery diseases seated in the Spirit, imbroil the whole frame of the body: others more external and cool, are less dangerous. They which divide in Religion, divide in God; they who divide in him, divide beyond *Genus Generalissimum*, where there is no reconciliation, without atonement; that is, without uniting in him, who is One, and in his Truth which is also one.

Wise are those men who will be perswaded rather to live within the pale of Truth, where they may be quiet, than in the purlieves, where they are sure to be hunted ever and anon, do Authority what it can. Every singular Opinion, hath a singular opinion of it self, and he that holds it a singular opinion of himself, and a simple opinion of all contrasentients: he that confutes them, must confute all three at once, or else he does nothing; which will not be done without more stir than the Peace of the State or Church can indure.

And prudent are those Christians, that will rather give what may be given, than hazard all by yielding nothing. To sell all Peace of Country, to buy some Peace of Conscience unseasonably, is more avarice than thrift, imprudence than patience: they deal not equally, that set any Truth of God at such a rate; but they deal wisely that will stay till the Market is fallen.

My Prognostics deceive me not a little, if once within three seven years, Peace prove not such a Penny-worth at most Marts in Christendom, that he that would not lay down his Money, his Lust, his Opinion, his Will, I had almost said the best flower of his Crown for it, while he might have had it; will tell his own heart, he plaid the very ill Husband.

Concerning Tolerations, I may further assert.

That Persecution of true Religion, and Toleration of false, are the *Jannes* and *Jambres* to the Kingdom of Christ, whereof the last is far the worst. *Augustines* Tongue had not owed his Mouth one Penny-rent though he had never spake word more in it, but his, *Nullum malum pagus libertate errandi.* [There is no evil worse (*peius* for *pagus*) than the freedom to err.]

Frederick Duke of *Saxon,* spake not one foot beyond the mark when he said. He had rather the Earth should swallow him up quick, than he should give a toleration to any Opinion against any Truth of God.

He that is willing to tolerate any Religion, or discrepant way of Religion, besides his own, unless it be in matters meerly indifferent, either doubts of his own, or is not sincere in it.

He that is willing to tolerate any unfound Opinion, that his own may also be tolerated, though never so sound, will for a need hand Gods Bible at the Devils girdle.

Every Toleration of false Religions, or Opinions hath as many Errors and Sins in it, as all the false Religions and Opinions it tolerates, and one found one more.

That State that will give Liberty of Conscience in matters of Religion, must give Liberty of Conscence and Conversation in their Moral Laws, or else Fiddle will be out of Tune, and some of the strings crack.

He that will rather make an irreligious quarrel with other Religions than try the Truth of his own by valuable Arguments, and peaceable sufferings; either his Religion, or himself is irreligious.

Experience will teach Churches and Christians, that it is far better to live in a State united, though a little Corrupt, than in a State, whereof some Part is incorrupt, and all the rest divided.

I am not altogether ignorant of the eight Rules given by Orthodox Divines about giving Tolerations, yet with their favour I dare affirm.

That there is no Rule given by God for any State to Give an affirmative Toleration to any false Religion, or Opinion whatsoever; they must connive in some Cases, but may not concede in any.

That the State of *England* (so far as my Intelligence serves) might in time have prevented with ease, and may yet without any great difficulty deny both Toleration, and irregular conivences *salva Republica.* [With proper regard for the Republic.]

That if the State of *England* shall either willingly Tolerate, or weakly connive at such Courses, the Church of that Kingdom will sooner become the Devils dancing-School, than Gods Temple: The Civil State a Bear-garden, than an Exchange: the whole Realm a Pais base[r] than an *England*. And what pity it is, that that Country which hath been the Staple of Truth to all Christendom, should now become the Aviary of Errors to the whole World, let every fearing heart judge.

I take Liberty of Conscience to be nothing but a freedom from Sin, and Error. *Conscientia in tantum libera, inquantum ab errore liberata.* [Conscience is free in so far as it is free from error.] And Liberty of Error nothing but a Prison for Conscience. Then small will be the kindness of a State to build such Prisons for their Subjects.

The Scripture saith, there is nothing makes free but Truth, and Truth Saith, there is no Truth but one: If the States of the World would make it their sum-operous Care to preserve this One Truth in its purity and Authority, it would ease you of all other Political cares. I am sure Satan makes it his grand, if not only task, to adulterate Truth; Falshood is his sole Scepter, whereby he first ruffles, and ever since ruined the World.

If Truth be but One, methinks all the Opinionists in *England* should not be all in that One Truth, Some of them I doubt are out. He that can extract an unity out of such a disparity, or contract such a disparity into an unity; had need be a better Artist, than ever was Drebell.

If two Centers (as we may suppose) be in one circle, and lines drawn from both to all the points of the Compass they will certainly cross one another, and probably cut through the Centers themselves.

There is talk of an universal Toleration, I would talk as loud as I could against it, did I know what more apt and reasonable Sacrifice *England* could offer to God for his late performing all his heavenly Truths than an universal Toleration of all hellish Errors, or how they shall make an universal Reformation, but by making Christ's Academy the Devils University, where any man may commence Heretick *per falsum*; [By a false doctrine] where he that is *Filius Diabolicus* [A son of the devil], or *simpliciter* [evil itself] . . . , may have his grace to go to Hell *cum Publico Privilegio* [by State Concession]; and carry as many after him as he can. . . .

3

The "Halfway Covenant," 1662

SOURCE: *Propositions Concerning the Subject of Baptism and Consociation of Churches, Collected and Confirmed out of the Word of God, by a Synod of Elders and Messengers of the Churches in Massachusets-Colony in New England. Assembled at Boston, according to Appointment of the Honoured General Court, In the Year 1662. . . .* (Cambridge, 1662), iv-xvi, 1.

THE PREFACE

TO THE

CHRISTIAN READER;

AND ESPECIALLY TO THE CHURCHES OF MASSACHUSETS-
COLONY IN NEW-ENGLAND.

That one end designed by God's All-disposing Providence, in leading so many of his poor people into this Wilderness, was to lead them unto a distinct discerning and practise of all the Wayes and Ordinances of his House according to Scripture-pattern, may seem an Observation not to be despised. That we are fit or able for so great a service, the sense of our own feebleness forbids us to think. But that we have large and great opportunity for it, none will deny. For, besides the useful Labours and Contemplations of many of the Lords Worthies in other places, and in former times, contributing to our Help, and shewing our Principles to be neither novell nor singular, the advantage of Experience and Practise, and the occasion thereby given for daily searching into the Rule, is considerable. And He that hath made the path of the just as a shining light is wont still to give unto them further light, as the progress of their path requires further practise, making his Word a Lanthorn to their feet, to shew them their way from step to step, though haply sometimes they may not see far before them. It is matter of humbling to us, that we have made no better improvement of our opportunities this way; but some Fruits God hath given, and is to be praised for.

In former years, and while sundry of the Lords eminent Servants, now at rest from their labours, were yet with us, *A Platform of Church-Discipline,* comprizing the brief summe thereof, especially in reference to the *Constitution of Churches* (which was our first work when we came into this Wilderness) was agreed upon by a Synod held at Cambridge, and published to the world: From which (as to the substance thereof) we yet see no cause to recede. Some few particulars referring to the *Continuation and Combination* of Churches, needed yet a more explicit stating and reducing unto practise. For though the Principles thereof were included in what is already published, yet that there hath been a defect in practise (especially since of late years there was more occasion for it) is too too apparent: For the rectifying whereof, a more particular Explication of the Doctrine also about these things, is now necessary.

In order hereunto, by the Care and Wisdome of our Honoured General Court, calling upon all the Churches of this Colony, to send their Elders and Messengers, this Synod was assembled, who after earnest Supplications for Divine Assistance, having consulted the holy Scriptures touching the Questions proposed to them, have proceeded to the following Issue; hoping that if it might seem meet to the Father of Lights to guide the Churches unto a right Understanding and Practice of his Will in these things also, the beauty of Christ's wayes and Spiritual Kingdome among us would be seen in some more compleatness then formerly. For that which was the prayer of Epaphras for the Colossians, ought to be both the prayer and labour of us all; viz. that we might stand perfect and compleat in all the will of God: And we trust it is our sincere desire, that his Will, all his Will, and nothing else but his Will, might be done among us. To the Law and to the Testimony we do wholly referre our selves, and if any thing in the following Conclusions be indeed found not to speak according thereunto, let it be rejected.

We are not ignorant that this our Labour will by divers be diversly censured; some will account us too strict in the Point of Baptism, and others too laxe and large: But let the Scriptures be Judge between us all. There are two things, the Honour whereof is in a special manner dear to God, and which He cannot endure to be wronged in; viz. His Holiness and His Grace. The Scripture is often putting us in minde how much the Lord loveth Holiness, and that in his House, and in the holy Ordinances thereof, and how he abhorreth the contrary, Mal. 2. 11. Psal. 93. 5. & 2. 6. Lev. 11. 44, 45. Ezek 22. 26. & 44. 7, 8. And hence neither dare we admit those unto the holy Table of the Lord, that are short of Scripture-qualifications for it; viz. Ability to examine themselves, and discern the Lords body; Nor yet receive or retain those in Church-estate, and own them as a part of the Lords holy People, that are visibly and notoriously unholy, wicked and prophane: such we are bidden to put away from among us, 1 Cor. 5. 13. and therefore ought not to continue among us. Neither may we administer Baptism to those whose parents are not under any Church-power or Government any where. To baptize such, would be to give the Title and Livery to those that will not bear the yoke of Christs Disciples, and to put the holy Name of God upon them, touching whom we can have no tolerable security that they will be educated in the wayes of Holiness, or in the knowledge and practise of Gods holy Will. Baptism, which is the Seal of Membership in the Church the Body of Christ, and an engaging Sign, importing us to be the devoted Subjects of Christ, and of all his holy

Government, is not to be made a common thing, nor to be given to those, between whom and the God-less licentious world there is no visible difference: This would be a provocation and dishonour to the Holy One of Israel.

On the other hand, we finde in Scripture, that the Lord is very tender of his Grace; that he delighteth to manifest and magnifie the Riches of it, and that he cannot endure any straitning or eclipsing thereof, which is both dishonourable unto God, and injurious unto men, Gal. 2 21. Eph. 2. 7. & 3. 2, 6, 8. Rom. 11. 1, 5. Acts 15. 10, 11. & 10. 15 & 20. 24, 26, 27. And in special he is large in the Grace of his Covenant which he maketh with his visible Church and People, and tender of having the same straitned. Hence when he takes any into Covenant with himself, he will not only be their God, but the God of their seed after them in their generations, Genes. 17, 7, 9. And although the apostate wicked parent (that rejecteth God and his Wayes) do cut off both himself and his Children after him, Exod. 20. 5. & 34. 7. Yet the Mercy and Grace of the Covenant is extended to the faithful and their seed unto a thousand generations, if the successive parents do but in the least degree shew themselves to be lovers of God, and keepers of his Covenant and Commandments, so as that the Lord will never reject them till they reject him, Exod 20. 6. Deut. 7. 9. Psal 105. 8, 9. Rom. 11. 16 - - 22. Hence we dare not (with the Antipædobaptist) exclude the Infant-children of the faithful from the Covenant, or from Membership in the visible Church, and consequently not from Baptism the Seal thereof. Neither dare we exclude the same children from Membership (or put them out of the Church) when they are grown up, while they so walk and act, as to keep their standing in the Covenant and doe not reject the same. God owns them still, and they doe in some measure own him: God rejects them not, and therefore neither may we; and consequently their children also are not to be rejected. Should we reject or exclude any of these, we should shorten and straiten the grace of God's Covenant, more then God himself doth, and be injurious to the Souls of men, by putting them from under those Dispensations of Grace, which are stated upon the visible Church, whereby the children of God's visible people are successively in their Generations to be trained up for the Kingdome of Heaven, (whither the Elect member shall still be brought in the way of such means) and wherein he hath given unto Officers and Churches a solemn charge to take care of, and train up such, as a part of his flock, to that end; saying to them, as sometimes to Peter, *If you love me, feed my lambs.* In obedience to which charge we hope it is, that we are willing and desirous (though with the inference of no small labour and burthen to our selves) to commend these Truths to the Churches of Christ; that all the Flock, even the Lambs thereof, being duly stated under Pastoral Power, we might after a faithfull discharge of our Duty to them, be able to give up our account another day with joy and not with grief.

How hard it is to finde and keep the right middle way of Truth in these things, is known to all that are ought acquainted with the Controversies there-about. As we have learned and believed, we have spoken; but not without remembrance that we are poor feeble frail men, and therefore desire to be conversant herein with much humility and fear before God and man. We are not ignorant of variety of judgements concerning this Subject; which notwithstanding, with all due reverence to Dissenters, after Religious search of the Scriptures, we have here offered what seems to us to have the fullest Evidence of Light from thence; if more may be added, and may be found contained in the Word of God, this shall be no prejudice thereunto. Hence also we are farre from desiring that there should be any rigorous imposition of these things (especially as to what is more narrow therein, and more controversal among godly men.) If the Honoured Court see meet so farre to adde their countenance and concurrence, as to commend a serious consideration hereof to the Churches, and to secure those that can with clearness of judgement practise accordingly, from disturbance, that in this case may be sufficient. To tolerate, or to desire a Toleration of damnable Heresies, or of Subverters of the Fundamentals of Faith or Order, were an irreligious inconsistency with the love of true Religion: But to bear one with another in lesser differences, about matters of a more difficult and controversal nature, and more remote from the Foundation, and wherein the godly-wise are not like-minded, is a Duty necessary to the peace and wel-fare of Religion, while we are in the state of infirmity. In such things let not him that practiseth despise him that forbeareth, and let not him that forbeareth judge him that practiseth, for God hath received him.

But as we do not thus speak from doubting of the Truth here delivered (Paul knows where the Truth lyes, and is perswaded of it, Rom. 14. 14. yet he can lovingly bear a Dissenter, and in like manner should we) So we do in the bowels of Christ Jesus commend the consideration of these things unto our Brethren in the several Churches. What is here offered is farre from being any declining from former Principles, it is rather a pursuance thereof; for it is all included in, or deducible from what we unanimously professed and owned in the fore-mentioned *Platform of Discipline,* many years since. There it is asserted, that Children are Church-members; That they have many priviledges which others (not Church-members) have not; and that they are under Discipline in the Church, chap. 12. sect. 7. and that will infer the right of their children, they continuing to walk orderly. And the other matter of Consociation, or exercise of *Communion of Churches,* is largely held forth Chap. 15. & 16.

It may be an Objection lying in the mindes of some, and which many may desire a fuller Answer unto; That these things, or some of them, are Innovations in our Church-wayes, and things which the Lord's Worthies in New-England, who are now with God, did never teach nor hold, and therefore why should we now, after so many years, fall upon new Opinions and Practises? Is not this a declining from our first Purity, and a blameable Alteration? To this: Although it were a sufficient Answer to say, That in matters of Religion, not so much what hath been held or practised, as what should be, and what the Word of God prescribes, ought to be our Enquiry and our Rule. The people in Nehemiah's time are commended for doing as they found written in the Law, though from the dayes of Joshua the son of Nun, unto that day, the children of Israel had not done so, Nehem. 8. 14, 17. See the like 2 Chron. 30. 5, 26. 2 Kings 23. 21, 22. they did not tye themselves to former use and custome, but to the Rule of Gods written Word, and so should we. It was Thyatira's praise, that their good works were more at the last then at the first, Rev. 2. 19. The Lord's humble and faithfull Servants are not wont to be forward to think themselves perfect in their attainments, but desirous rather to make a progress in the knowledge and practise of God's holy Will. If therefore the things here propounded concerning the children of Church-members, and the Consociation of Churches, be a part of the Will of God contained in the Scriptures, (as we hope the Discourse ensuing will shew them to be) that doth sufficiently bespeak their entertainment, although they had not formerly been held or heard of amongst us. Yet this must not be granted, the contrary being the Truth, viz. that the Points herein which may be most scrupled by some, are known to have been the judgement of the generality of the Elders of these Churches for many years, and of those that have been of most eminent esteem among us. As (besides what was before mentioned from the *Platform of Discipline*) may appear by the following Testimonies from sundry Eminent and Worthy Ministers of Christ in New-England, who are now with God.

First, Touching the children of Church-members.

Mr. Cotton hath this saying; The Covenant and Blessing of Abraham is that which we plead for, which the Apostle saith is come upon us Gentiles, Gal. 3. 14. which admitteth the faithful and their Infant-seed, not during their lives, in case their lives should grow up to Apostacy or open Scandal, but during their infancy, and so long after as they shall continue in a visible profession of the Covenant and Faith, and Religion of their fathers: otherwise, if the children of the faithful grow up to Apostacy, or any open Scandal, (as Ishmael and Esau did) as they were then, so such like now are to be cast out of the fellowship of the Covenant, and of the Seals thereof. *Grounds and Ends of Baptism of Children*, p. 106. *see also* p. 133, 134. *Again*, The seed of the Israelites, though many of them were not sincerely godly, yet whilest they held forth the publick profession of God's people, Deut. 26. 3 - - 11. and continued under the wing of the Covenant, and subjection to the Ordinances, they were still accounted an holy seed, Ezra 9. 2. and so their children were partakers of Circumcision. Yea further, though themselves were sometimes kept from the Lords Supper (the Passeover) for some or other uncleanness, yet that debarred not their children from Circumcision. Against this may it not seem vain to stand upon a difference between the Church of Israel and our Churches of the New-Testament — For the same Covenant which God made with the National Church of Israel and their seed, it is the very same for substance, and none other, which the Lord makes with any Congregational Church, and our seed. *Quæry 9th of Accommodation and Communion of Presbyt. and Congregat. Churches. And the same for substance with those Quæries, was delivered by him in 12. Propositions, as Mr. Tho: Allen witnesseth in Epist. to the Reader before Treat. of Covenant and those Quæries. Now in the 8th of those* Propositions *he hath these words:* The children of Church-members with us, though baptized in their infancy, yet when they come to age they are not received to the Lords Supper, nor admitted to fellowship of Voting in Admissions, Elections, Censures, till they come to profess their Faith and Repentance, and to lay hold of the Covenant of their parents before the Church; and yet their being not cast out of the Church, nor from the Covenant thereof, their children as well as themselves being within the Covenant, they may be partakers of the first Seal of the Covenant. *Lastly, speaking to that Objection,* That the Baptism of Infants overthrows and destroys the Body of Christ, the holy Temple of God; and that in time it will come to consist of natural and carnal Members, and the power of Government rest in the hands of the wicked. *He Answers,* That this puts a fear where no fear is, or a causless fear. *And in prosecution of his Answer he hath these words;* Let the Primitive Practise be restored to its purity, *(viz. that due care be taken of baptized members of the Church for their fitting for the Lords Table)* and then there will be no more fear of pestering Churches with a carnal generation of members baptized in their infancy, then of admitting a carnal company of hypocrites confessing their Faith and Repentance in the face of the Congregation. Either the Lord in the faithfulness of his Covenant will sanctifie the hearts of the baptized Infants to prepare them for his Table, or else he will discover their hypocrisie and profaneness in the presence of his Church before men and Angels, and so prevent the pollution of the Lords Table, and corruption of the Discipline of the Church by their partaking in them. *Grounds and Ends of Baptism, &c.* p. 161, 163. *See also Holiness of Church-members,* p. 41, 51, 56, 57, 63, 87. *Bloody Tenent washed,* p. 44, 78.

Mr. Hooker saith, Suppose a whole Congregation should consist of such who were children to Parents now deceased who were confederate, their children were true members according to the Rules of the Gospel, by the profession of their fathers Covenant, though they should not make any personal and vocal expression of their engagement as the fathers did. *Survey, part* 1. p. 48. *Again,* We maintain according to truth, that the believing parent covenants and confesseth for himself and his posterity, and this covenanting then and now is the same for the kinde of it. *Part 3.* p. 25. *See* p. 17, 18. & *part 1.* p. 69, 76, 77. *And in the Preface, setting down sundry things, wherein he consents with Mr. R. he expresseth this for one, that* Infants of visible Churches born of wicked parents, being members of the Church, ought to be baptized. In these *(saith he)* and several other particulars, we fully accord with Mr. R. *And Part 3.* p. 11. It is not then the Question, whether wicked members while they are tolerated sinfully in the Church they and their children may partake of the Priviledges? for this is beyond question, nor do I know, nor yet ever heard it denied by any of ours.

Mr. Philips, speaking of a people made partakers of Gods Covenant, and all the priviledges outwardly belonging thereto, *he saith,* Themselves and all that ever proceed from them, continue in the same state, parents and children successively, so long as the Lord continues the course of his Dispensation; nor can any alteration befall them, whereby this estate is dissolved, but some apparent act of God breaking them off from him. *Reply,* p. 126. *Again, speaking of that Holiness,* 1 Cor. 7. 14. *he saith,* I take it of fœderal holiness, whereby the children are with the believing parents taken by God to be his, and by him put under his covenant, and so they continue when men of years, though they never have any further grace wrought in them, nor have any other state upon them, then what they had when they were born. *Ibid.* p. 131. Again, a company become or are a Church, either by conversion and initial constitution, or by continuance of the same constituted Churches successively by propagation of members, who all are born in Church-state, and under the covenant of God, and belong unto the Church, and are a Church successively so long as God shall continue his begun dispensation, even as well & as fully as the first. *Ibid.* p. 145.

Mr. Shepard in Defence of the Nine Positions, p. 143. hath this expression, Concerning the Infants of Church-members, they are subject to Censures whensoever they offend the Church, as others are, though so long as they live innocently they need them not. *And in the year 1649, not three moneths before his Death, he wrote unto a friend a large Letter (yet extant under his own Hand) concerning the Membership of Children, wherein he proveth by sundry Arguments that they are Members, and answereth sundry Objections against it, and sheweth at large* what great good there is in children's Membership. *In which Discourses he asserteth,* That as they are Members in their infancy, so they continue Members when they are grown up, till for their wickedness they be cast out; and that they being Members, their seed successively are members also, until by Dissolution or Excommunication they be unchurched: That though they are Members, it follows not that they must come to the Lords Supper, but they must first appear able to examine themselves, and discern the Lords Body: That the children of godly parents, though they do not manifest faith in the Gospel, yet they are to be accounted of Gods Church, until they positively reject the Gospel, *Rom.* 11. That this Membership of children hath no tendency in it to pollute the Church, no more then in the Old Testament, but is a means rather of the contrary; And that there is as much danger (if not more) of the degenerating and apostatizing of Churches gathered of professing Believers, as of those that rise out of the seed of such.

Mr. Prudden in a Letter to a friend written in the year 1651. doth plainly express it to be his judgement, That the children of Church-members, are Members, and so have right to have their children baptized, though themselves be not yet admitted to the Lords Supper. *His words are these:*

Touching the desire of such Members children as desire to have their children baptized, it is a thing that I do not yet hear practised in any of our Churches. But for my own part, I am inclined to think, that it cannot justly be denied, because their next Parents (however not admitted to the Lords Supper) stand as compleat Members of the Church, within the Church-Covenant, and so acknowledged that they might have right to Baptism. Now they being in Covenant, and standing Members, their Children also are Members by virtue of their Parents Covenant and Membership, as well as they themselves were by virtue of their Parents Covenant and Membership; And they have not renounced that Covenant, nor are justly censured for breach of that Covenant, but do own it and profess it, and by virtue of it claim the priviledge of it to their Children. *Then he puts this his Argument into form thus:* Those Children who are within the Covenant of the C[h]urch, and so Members of it, Baptism cannot be denied unto. But the Children in question are within the Covenant of the Church, and so Members of it.

Therefore Baptism cannot be denied unto them. The Assumption is proved thus: The Children of such Parents as are within the Covenant of the Church, and so Members of the Church, are themselves within the Covenant of the Church, and so Members of it. But the Children in question are Children of such Parents as are in Covenant, and so Members of the Church. Therefore they are so themselves. The Proposition is clear, because the Parents Covenant for themselves, and for their Children, Deut. 29. 10,–16. Ezek. 16. 8, 13. And God accepts both, Gen. 17. 12, 13. the whole Nation is fœderally holy, Ezra 9. 2. they are expresly said to be in Covenant with their fathers, Deut. 29. not partly or partially in Covenant, Rom. 9. 3, 4. Acts 2. 39. and God styles himself their God as well as their fathers, Gen. 17. 7, 8, 9. and to have God to be our God, is to be in compleat Church-Covenant with him. The Assumption is evident, because else such their Parents had not had right to Baptism the Seal of the Covenant, but that they had right unto, and so received it; and the same right that they had, their Children have, who are included in their Covenant, as they were in their fathers — and are not less truely or less compleatly in Covenant.

Lastly, (to adde no more) Mr. Nath. Rogers, in a Letter to a Friend, bearing date 18. 11. 1652. hath these words:

To the Question concerning the Children of Church-members, I have nothing to oppose, and I wonder any should deny them to be Members. They are Members *in censu Ecclesiastico*; God so calls them, the Church is so to account of them: And when they are *adultæ ætatis*, though having done no personal act, yet are to be in Charity judged Members still, and till after due calling upon, they shall refuse or neglect to acknowledge and own the Covenent of their Parents, and profess their belief of, and subjection to the contents thereof — For Practise, I confess I account it our great default, that we have made no more real distinction between these and others, that they have been no more attended, as the lambs of the Flock of Christ: and whether it be not the cause of the corruption and woeful defection of our youth, *disquiri permittimus*.

So that it was the judgement of these Worthies in their time, that the children of Church-members are members of the Church as well as their parents, and do not cease to be members by becoming adult, but do still continue in the Church, untill in some way of God they be cast out; and that they are subject to Church-discipline, even as other members, and may have their children baptized before themselves be received to the Lords Supper; and yet that in this way there is no tendency to the corrupting of the Church by unworthy members, or of the Ordinances by unworthy partakers. And in the Synod held at Cambridge in the year 1648. that particular point of Baptizing the children of such as were admitted members in minority, but not yet in full communion, was inserted in some of the draughts that were prepared for that Assembly, and was then debated and confirmed by the like Arguments as we now use, and was generally consented to; though because some few dissented, and there was not the like urgency of occasion for present practise, it was not then put into the *Platform* that was after Printed. We need not mention the Meeting of Elders at Boston upon the Call of the Honoured Court in the year 1657. where in *Answer to XXI. Questions,* since Printed, this Point is particularly asserted. By all which it appeareth, that these are not things lately devised; or before unheard-of, nor can they justly be censured as Innovations or Declensions from the received Doctrine in New-England. It is true, that in the beginning of these Plantations, and the Infancy of these Churches, there was not so much said touching these things as there hath been since; and the reason is, Because then there was not the like occasion as since hath been: Few children of Church-members being then adult, at least few that were then married, and had children. Accordingly, when a Question was put about the priviledges of Members children, when come to years, these Churches then having been but of few years standing, our Answer was, That by reason of the Infancy of these Churches, we had then had no occasion to determine what to judge or practise in that matter. *Answer to the 5th. and 6th. of 32. Questions:* which may satisfie as to the Reason why in our first beginnings there was no more said touching these Questions. But afterwards, when there was more cause for it, many of the Elders in these Churches, both such as are now living, and sundry who are now deceased, did declare their judgements as aforesaid, and this many years ago.

Secondly, Touching Consociation of Churches, take these few Testimonies, in stead of many more that might be alledged.

Mr. Cotton, Keyes, p. 54, 55. It is a safe and wholsome and holy Ordinance of Christ, for particular Churches to joyn together in holy Covenant, or Communion & Consociation among themselves, to administer all their Church-affairs (which are of weighty, and difficult and common concernment) not without common consultation and consent of other Churches about them. *And how it is so, he there sheweth in all the particulars. See also* p. 24, 25, 47, 59.

Mr. Hooker, Survey, see *part* 4. p. 1, 2. & p. 45. *And in the Preface he professeth his consent with Mr. R.* That Consociation of Churches is not only lawful, but in some cases necessary. That when causes are difficult, the particular Churches want light and help they should crave the assistance of such a Consociation. That Churches so meeting have right to Counsel, Rebuke &c. as the case doth require. And in case any particular Church shall walk pertinaciously, either in the profession of Errour or sinful Practise, and will not hear their counsel, they may and should renounce the right hand of fellowship with them. *And after he sets down this of Consociation of Churches amongst other things, wherein he had leave to profess the joynt Judgement of all the Elders upon the River; of New-haven, Guilford, Milford, Stratford, Fairfield, and most of the Elders in the Bay. By which it is clear, that this point of Consociation of Churches is no new invention of these times, but was taught and professed in New-England many years agoe, for so it was we see in Mr. Hooker's time, and it is now above fifteen years since he departed this life.*

To these our own Ministers, we shall only adde a passage in the Apologetical Narration *of Dr. Goodwyn, Mr. Nye, Mr. Sidrach Simpson, Mr. Burroughes, and Mr. Bridge; wherein, besides much more to this purpose, touching the Remedy provided in the Congregational-way for mal-Administrations, or other miscarriages in Churches, p. 16-21. They set it down (in p. 21.) as their past and present Profession,* That it is the most to be abhorred Maxime that any Religion hath ever made profession of, and therefore of all other the most contradictory and dishonourable unto that of Christianity, that a single and particular Society of men, professing the Name of Christ, and pretending to be endowed with a Power from Christ, to judge them that are of the same Body and Society within themselves, should further arrogate unto themselves an exemption from giving account, or being censurable by any other, either Christian Magistrate above them, or Neighbour-Churches about them. *See also Mr. Burroughes Heart-Divis. pag* 43, 44.

Brethren, bear with us: Were it for our own Sakes, or Names, or Interests, we should not be sollicitous to beg Charity of you. With us it is a small thing to be judged of man's day. But it is for your sakes, for your children's sake, and for the Lord's sake, that we intreat for a charitable, candid, and considerate Acceptation of our labour herein. It is that the Congregations of the Lord might be established before Him in Truth and Peace, and that they might have one heart and one way in the fear of God, for the good of them and of their children after them. Do we herein seek our selves? our own advantage, ease or glory? Surely we feel the contrary! What is it we desire, but that we might do our utmost to carry your poor Children to Heaven; and that we might see these Churches bound up together in the Bonds of Truth and Peace? Forgive us this wrong. But should the Church-education of your children be by the want of your hearty concurrence, rendered either unfeizible or ineffectual; should they live as Lambs in a .arge place, for want of your agreement to own them of the Flock, we beseech you to consider how uncomfortable the account hereof would be another day: We pray with the Apostle, that you do no evil, not that we should appear approved, but that you should do that which is good and right, though we be rejected. For we can do nothing against the truth, but for the truth: and this also we wish, even your perfection, 2 Cor. 13. 7, 8, 9. However, we hope after-ages will bear witness, that we have been in some measure faithful to the Truth in these things, and to this part of Christs Kingdome also in our generation.

But we may not let pass this opportunity, without a word of Caution and Exhortation to the Youth of the Country, the children of our Churches, whose Interest we have here asserted. Be not you puffed up with Priviledges, but humbled rather, in the awful sense of the Engagement, Duty, and danger that doth attend them: It is an high favour to have a place in Bethel, in the house of God, and in the gate of Heaven; but it is a Dreadful place: God will be sanctified in all that come nigh him. A place nigh unto God (or among his people who are near to him, Ps. 148. 14.) is a place of great fear, Psa. 89. 7. Take heed therefore unto your selves, when owned as the people of the Lord your God, (Deut. 27, 9, 10.) lest there should be among you any root that beareth gall and wormwood. Take heed that you do not with a spirit of pride and haughtiness, or of vanity and slightness, either challenge or use any of your Priviledges. Think not to bear the Name of Christians, without bearing the Yoke of Christ. Remember, that all Relations to God and to his people, do come loaden with Duty; and all Gospel-duty must be done in humility. The wayes of the Lord are right, and the humble and serious shall walk in them, but proud Transgressors shall fall therein. Be not sons of Belial, that can bear no yoke: Learn subjection to Christs holy Government in all the parts and wayes thereof. Be subject to your godly Parents: Be subject to your spiritual Fathers and Pastors, and to all their Instructions, Admonitions and Exhortations: Be subject unto faithful Brethren, and to words of counsel and help from them: Ye younger, submit your selves unto the elder; and to that end, be clothed with humility. Lye under the Word and Will of Christ, as dispensed and conveyed to you by all his appointed Instruments in their respective places. Break not in upon the Lord's Table (or upon the Priviledges of full Communion) without due qualification, and orderly admission thereunto, lest you eat and drink your own damnation. Be ordered, and take not upon you to order the affairs of Gods Family; that is not the place of those who are yet but in the state of Initiation and Education in the Church of God. Carry it in all things with a spirit of humility, modesty, sobriety and fear, that our soules may not weep in secret for your pride, and that God may not resist & reject you as a generation of his wrath. Oh that the Lord would pour out a spirit of Humiliation & Repentance upon all the younger sort in the Country, (yea & upon elder too, for our neglects) from Dan to Beersheba! Oh that we might meet at Bochim, because so many Canaanites of unsubdued, yea growing corruptions are found among us! Let it not be said, that when the first & best generation in New-England were gathered to their fathers, there arose another generation after them that knew not the Lord. Behold, the Lord had a delight in your fathers to love them, and he hath chosen you their seed after them, to enjoy these Liberties & Opportunities, as it is this day: Circumcise therefore the fore-skin of your hearts, and be no more stiff-necked, but yield your selves to the Lord, and to the Order of His Sanctuary, to seek him, and wait on him in all his wayes with holy fear and trembling: for the Lord your God is gracious and merciful, and will not turn away his face from you, if you return unto him; if you seek him he will be found of you, but if you forsake him, he will cast you off for ever.

We shall conclude, when we have given the Reader a short account of the Work ensuing. The Propositions in Answer to the first Question, were (after much discussion and consideration from the Word of God) Voted and Concluded by the Assembly in the particular terms as they are here expressed. The Arguments then used for their Confirmation, being drawn up by some disputed thereunto, after they had been several times read and considered in the Assembly, were Voted and Consented to, as to the summe and substance thereof. The answer to the second Question is here given with great brevity, partly because so much is already said there-about in the foresaid *Platform of Discipline,* and partly by reason of great straits of time: But what is here presented was the joynt conclusion of the Synod. A Preface was desired by the Assembly to be prefixed by some appointed thereunto, which is here accordingly by them performed.

Now the God of truth & peace guide us & all his people in the wayes, & give us the fruits thereof; help us to feed his flock and his lambs, & to be fed by him as the sheep of his pasture, that when the chief-Shepherd shall appear, we may receive together a Crown of glory that fadeth not away, & may enter into the joy of our Lord, as those that have neither despised his little ones, nor denied to be our Brother's keeper: But having faithfully endeavoured to promote the continuation of his Kingdom, & Communion of his people, may Rest & Reign with all Saints .in the kingdom of his glory: Unto whom be glory in the Church by Christ Jesus throughout all ages world without end.

THE ANSWER
OF THE ELDERS AND OTHER
MESSENGERS
OF THE CHURCHES, ASSEMBLED AT BOSTON
IN THE YEAR 1662,
TO
THE QUESTIONS PROPOUNDED TO THEM BY ORDER OF THE
HONOURED GENERAL COURT.

Quest, 1.

Who are the Subjects of Baptism?

Answ:

The Answer may be given in the following propositions, briefly confirmed from the Scriptures.

1   They that according to Scripture, are Members of the Visible Church, are the subjects of Baptisme.

2   The Members of the Visible Church according to scripture, are Confederate visible Believers, in particular Churches, and their infant-seed, i. e. children in minority, whose next parents, one or both, are in Covenant.

3   The Infant-seed of confederate visible Believers, are members of the same Church with their parents, and when grown up, are personally under the watch, discipline and Government of that Church.

4   These Adult persons, are not therefore to be admitted to full Communion, meerly because they are and continue members, without such further qualifications, as the Word of God requireth therunto.

5   Church-members who were admitted in minority, understanding the Doctrine of Faith, and publickly professing their assent thereto; not scandalous in life, and solemnly owning the Covenant before the Church, wherin they give up themselves and their children to the Lord, and subject themselves to the Government of Christ in the Church, their children are to be Baptised.

6   Such Church-members, who either by death, or some other extraordinary Providence, have been inevitably hindred from publick acting as aforesaid, yet have given the Church cause, in judgment of charity, to look at them as so qualified, and such as had they been called thereunto, would have so acted, their children are to be Baptised.

7   The members of Orthodox Churches, being sound in the Faith, and not scandalous in life, and presenting due testimony thereof; these occasionally coming from one Church to another, may have their children Baptised in the church whither they come, by virtue of communion of churches: but if they remove their habitation, they ought orderly to covenant and subject themselves to the Government of Christ in the church where they settle their abode, and so their children to be Baptised. It being the churches duty to receive such unto communion, so farr as they are regularly fit for the same.

4

Relations with Europe: The Dutch Reformed Church in America and the Amsterdam Classis

SOURCE: Hugh Hastings, ed., *Ecclesiastical Records of the State of New York*, IV (Albany, 1902), 2366-2369.

CLASSIS OF AMSTERDAM.

Acts of the Deputies and their Correspondence.
The Classis of Amsterdam to Revs. Du Bois, Antonides, Boel and Vas, December 1st 1726. xxviii. 265.
To the Reverend Godly and Highly Learned Gentlemen, G. Du Bois, V. Antonides, H. Boel and P. Vas.

Reverend Sirs and Beloved Brethren:—

This letter serves as an accompaniment to the enclosed, which we request you to present to the Complainants at Raretans, being an answer to their letter to our Rev. Classis, written with your knowledge, and dated November 2, 1725. Hereby the Classis declares itself not to be able as yet, to answer the questions propounded in said letter, — so far as they respect the principal matter between the Complainants and Rev. Frilinghuysen — so long as she has not received the defence of Rev. Frilinghuysen, which has not yet arrived, because the Classis could not send off their letter to him before June last.

In the meantime we cannot help expressing our surprise at several things appearing in that letter. The first respects the shutting up of churches originally cared for by these very Complainants. The Rev.

Classis regards this as a very disorderly procedure, and not showing a spirit of gentleness. Without doubt, you will be doing well to rebuke those people for such conduct, and to warn them against all similar flagrant acts in the future; for such acts can produce nothing but offence, and contempt of our church government among other people, and would pave the way for the churches to lose their liberty.

Secondly, the Classis has not been able to refrain from observing how anxious the Complainants are, and that too with your knowledge and approval, to show their unwillingness to recognize the Rev. Classis under the title, and in the relation, of Competent Judge. On the other hand they simply address us as an advisory Assembly, and that, too, after they have, by shutting up these churches, taken the matter in their own hands. What reasons are hidden behind all this, we can hardly conjecture. Is it possible that, in case the decision of the Classis were not agreeable to them, they would still retain the liberty of not submitting to such decision, but would go before a secular tribunal, as the Preface of this Complaint indicates. But whatever the result may be, such expressions always seem to us to have the appearance of assuming independence; which is something not to be recognized by the Netherland churches.

It is said that Classis is not bound by its title, and — mark it well — by its position among churches under another (civil) power. But by such a style of argument the New York churches could be withdrawn altogether from the supervision and control of our Rev. Classis, and from under the control of all Synodical Assemblies, as well as from Classical, in this land, lest they should offend those other powers. But the authors of that letter do themselves furnish the solution of that difficulty, by saying, in conclusion, that the letters of privilege (the charters) granted by the New York government to the Dutch churches, order that the same shall regulate themselves according to the Synod of Dort. Now the entire Church-Order of that Synod is built up upon the foundation of the subordination of church members to Consistories: of these to Classes; and of these to the Synod, as you very well know.

And why indeed should the Classis not give a judicial decision, but only advice? And among other things, concerning these in particular: Whether the Rev. Frilinghuysen is to be tolerated as an orthodox minister in the Netherlands Church? and consequently, whether the accusations of the Complainants which are brought against him, who is a pastor belonging to this Classis and in union with the general body of the same, — whether their accusations are well-founded and legal, and that therefore the accusers and complainers are to be praised and justified? or whether the accusations are unfounded, and the accusers are to be rebuked, condemned and severely censured? Who can suppose in such a case that the Rev. Classis does not occupy the position of Competent Judge? and that their decision of the case should not be regarded by the accusers as something far higher than mere ecclesiastical advice? These accusers are members of Frilinghuysen's church. If the Classis is in such a matter only an adviser, who then is the judge?

We, indeed, know that the Classis has no power to carry out its decisions, and to enforce them in particular cases, against those subject to a foreign power. But this does not take away our right to pronounce a decisive judgement in a matter of such a nature, and to which both parties are bound to submit; and this, moreover, not as to an impartial and well-founded piece of advice; but as to an ecclesiastical decision, in consequence of subordination to Church-Order, which all are bound to recognize.

Heretofore, in another case, it was considered strange to you, that Classis gave no decisive judgement. That does not well harmonize with this present claim, endorsed with your names, and having your approval. We therefore judge it only fair that you reconsider your conduct, and inspire the writers of that letter with other opinions.

It also seems to us that the Classis was not exactly pleased with those hateful expressions which in that letter are hurled in her face — yet as if said by others — that she has nieces and nephews; and it is only of her grace that any of them are sent here. We do not think that the Classis was much disturbed by such language of evil-speaking persons, — who would also, when it came to the test, deny their utterances, as is generally the case with such people, — that she deems it necessary, for her defence, to transmit the extracts concerning the appointment of Frelinghuysen. You are also well aware that the sending of any one to the foreign field is not generally considered a particular mark of favor to them.

It grieves us to the soul to perceive the great divisions and grievous disputes which exist in the church of Raritans, and which are only too evident to us; on the one side, from the Complaint (against Frelinghuysen) ; and on the other, from the prolix and one-sided books of the Revs. Freeman and (Van) Zantwoord, which have been published in opposition to said Complaint, and also placed before us. To these writers also, we have given notice by letter, of our righteous sorrow and dissatisfaction, concerning these violent and spreading disputes, and the party-spirit excited thereby. We have exhorted them as well as yourselves to more pacific thoughts and sentiments.

May the Lord be merciful to his churches, and may he grant that peace may perpetually reign in our own. In closing, we commend you to God and the Word of his grace. We remain Rev. Sirs and Brethren,

Your affectionate and obedient Brethren in Christ,

John Hagelis, Ecc. Amst. Dep. ad res exteras. h. t. Praeses.

John Goesero, Clerk, p. t. and Ecc. Amst. Dep. ad res exteras.

Amsterdam,
    Dec. 1, 1726.

5

The Virginia Vestry of the Church of England And Its Work

SOURCE: C. G. Chamberlayne, ed., *The Vestry Book of Petsworth Parish Gloucester County, Virginia 1677-1793* (The Library Board, Richmond, Va., 1933), 242-248. Reprinted with permission from the Virginia State Library.

At A Vestory held for Petsworth Parish the 16th day of Febru 1736

Present

The Reverd Em¹ Jones   M^r. Francis Thornton C W
   Mr Aug^n Smith C W   M^r. Conq Wiat
   Mr John Royston   Mr Seth Thornton
   Maj^r John Washington   Cap^n. Sam¹ Buckner
   Cap^n Thomas Reade   Mr Thomas Booth
   Mr Thomas Green   Mr David Alexander

It is Agreed at this vestory that Mr William Ran Undertake & Build A Good & Substantial Gallery at the west End of the Church at Popler Spring for the Use of placing an Organ Winscoted painted hansom and Substantialy Well Built Workman like for the Use afors^d withall Convenient Speed & Upon the Due performance of the Said building it is agred by the Said Vestory that the Said Ran have forty pounds Corrant that is 20£ to be paid in hand and the Remainder to be paid by the Last day of March in the year 1738

At this Vestory Mr Bayley Seaton is Chosen Vestoryman in the Rome of Mr Gwyn Reade

It is Agreed At this Vestory with M^r Em¹ Jones that forasmuch that 2500^lb of Tobacco by a former Order hath been Leveyed and paid to the Said M^r Em¹ Jones for the Repairs on the Glieb & finding the Said Repairs not being Done It is Agreed that if they are not Done by the Laying the Next Parish Levey that then the Said Jones Refund the Said Tobacco or money at the Rate of Ten Per Centum

True Entry Test
WBrooking C V

At A Vestory held for Petsworth parish the 7th day of Ap[l] 1737

Present

M[r] John Royston	Cap Sam[l] Buckner
M[r] Aug[n] Smith C W	M[r] Tho Booth
M[r] Fra Thornton C W	
M[r] Seth Thornton	M[r] David Alexander

At this Vestory M[r] Augustin Smith Suing that he having Rec[d] of the Several Subscribers the mony Given for the purchase of An Organ the Said Subscriptions amounting to more mony then the Said Organ Cost. this present Vestory is of Oppinion that the Overplush of the Mony in the hands of M[r] Aug[n]. Smith Ought to be Apropriated towards the Suport and Maintanance of the Said Organ, and it is further Orderd And Agreed by the Gent[n]. of the Vestory hear present that if Any of the Overplush of the mony is demanded Back by Any of the Subscribers or any Sute of Law Commenced Against the Said Smith for the Same that the Said Aug[n]. Smith Shall Stand A Sute of Law for the Same and Emply An Attorney and that he be paid his Costs & Charges Out of the mony that Shall Remaine in his hands

True Entry Test
WBrooking C Ves

Memorandum

That the Gentl[n]. that Subscrib[d]. for the Organ hear present Unanimousely Agreed And Subscribed to An Instrument of Writing that the mony Given Towards the Organ that is Over & Above the purchase of the Said Organ Shall & Ought to Goe Towards the Support and bennifit of the Same As the Vestory Shall Think fitt to Order it

At A Vestory held for Petsworth Parish the 29th day of June 1737

Present

The Rev[d] Em[l] Jones	Cap Thomas Reade
M[r] John Royston	M[r] Conq[t] Wiat
M[r] Augustine Smith	M[r] Seth Thornton
Maj[r] Jn[o] Washington	M[r] Thomas Booth
M[r] Thomas Green	M[r] David Alexander
M[r] Francis Thornton	M[r] Baley Seaton

It is Ordered that M[r] Anthony Collins be Entertained An Organist for the Parish Church of Petsworth from the Eight day of April last and that he be paid as Shall be appointed at the laying the next parish Levey

It is Orderered that the Order of Vestory dated the Seventh day of April for M[r]. Augustin Smith to Stand a Trial at Law for the mony that Should be Demand[d]. back Given for the purchase of the Organ Be Reversed & of No Effect

At this Vestory M[r] Bayley Seaton was Sworn Vestory man for this Parish in the Rome of M[r] Gwyn Reade

Memorandom that Mr Augustin Smith Ch Warden Acquaint^d the Vestory that he Agreed with Mr James Dudley for the Keeping & Cure of Margret Thomas her Legg at the Uiseal Rate Per Annum from this date

True Entry Test
WBrooking

At A Vestory held for Petsworth Parish the 12th day of Oc^r. 1737

Present

the Revd Emanuel Jones	Mr Thos Green
Mr Augustin Smith C W	Mr Seth Thornton
Mr John Royston	Cap^n Saml Buckner
Major Jno Washington	Mr Thomas Booth
Mr Francis Thornton C W	Mr David Alexander
Mr Conq^t Wiat	

Petsworth Parish Dett^r in Tobacco

To the Revd Emanuel Jones his Sallery	16000
To Ditt^o. for Extrodinary Charge in Repairing the Glieb house	319
To Ditt^o. for Quitrents of the Glieb Land As Useial	054
To Mr Alexander Roane Cleark of the Church	1000
To James Booker Sextorn of Church	1000
To Wm Brooking Clark of the Vestory	600
To Cap John Claytons Acc^o for List of Tithables	020
To Mr Frances Thornton for 2 per Ct not Charged Last year	445
To D^o for 2 Leveys Ward & Allard Not to be found	056
To Jeremiah Darnel for Keeping Dorothy Goargy one year	800
To Wm Harington for Keeping Mary Mount one year	300
To James Dudley for Keeping Margret Thomas 3 mos & 14 days	233
To Mr Augustin Smiths Acc^o in Mony @ 18 per Ct is	196
To Cap^n Buckner & Mr Booth for bringunt Up the Organs	500
To Mr Francis Easters Acc^o	055
To Mr Augustin Smith for Comunion Wine the Year Ensuing	400
To Tobacco Levied for the Use of the Parish to be Sold for Cash	1395
	23373
To Cask & Sallery @ 10 per Ct Am^t to	2337
Paris Debt	25710
By Credit per 857 Tithabes @ 30 per pole	25710
Ballance Due is	00000
Carryed forward	
Brought forward	

At This Vestory Mr Augustin Smith Church warden is Appointed Collector for the parish this year and that he Collect of Every Titheable Person 30^{lb} of Tobacco to Discharg the Several Parish Credits

At This Vestory Mr Seth Thornton is apointed Church-warden in the Lower precint in the Rome of Mr Francis Thornton he being Discharge from the Said office

It is Ordered that Mr Anthony Collins be paid Ten pound Corrt mony by Mr Augustin Smith Out of the Mony Remaining in his hands it being for Six Months Servis as an Organist And Continue at the Same Rate per Annum he duly Officiating in the Said office & Oblidging himsel To Teach Som Other fit person in the Mistory of the Said Musick with all Convenient Speed he Can

It is Ordered And Agreed that Mr Augustin Smith have 7½ per C^t for Collecting the Mony Due for the purchasing the Organ And after the Making Up of the Said Account he has Made A present of the said per Ct to be Laid Out by the Vestory of this Parish Towards the Support and bennefit of the Said Organ or Organist

True Entry Test
WBrooking Cl Vestory

At A vestory held for Petsworth Parish ye 29th of June 1738

Present

the Rev^d Em^l. Jones	
Mr Augustine Smith C W	Mr Seth Thornton C W
Mr John Royston	Capⁿ Saml. Buckner
Maj^r Jno. Washington	Mr Thomas Booth
Mr Thos Green	Mr David Alexander

At this present vestory it is Ordered And Agreed with Mr Samuel Peacock that he Do with what Convenient Speed he Can hansomly paint the Aulter peace of Popler Spring Church in ye parsh afos^d as also the paint Coving Within the Church that has bent Spoilt by mens of the Leacage of the Roofe of the Church Angles As also to paint all the Cornish Doors Windors and Sashes and All Otherwork that Requirs painting And to find all the Oyles & Coulers Except the Leaf Gould that is to be made Use of for the Carving Work and Other work that is to be Done on the Said Aulterpeace. And for the Due performance of the Said Work Well & workmanlike to be Done and performed it is Agreed that the Said Saml Peacok or his Order is to have & Receive fifteen pounds Cor^t Mony by Vertue of this Order from the parish Afors^d.

At this Vestory Mr William Thornton Jn^r. is Chosen Vestory man in the Rome of Mr Fra Thornton De^d. for the Lower precints of this Parish

It is by this Vestory Agreed With M^r. Augustine Smith Gentⁿ Church warden that he Doe with all Convenient Speed he Can Send for 700 Leaves of Leafe Gould for ye Use of the Aulter peace and that he be

paid for it by The parish @ ye Rate of 5 per Cent from the prime Cost
in Corant Mony

Cary^d forward

It is Agreed With Cap^n. Samuel Buckner that he provide Six Barrels
of Tarr and Cause the Same to be made Use of In Tarring the Roofe of
Popler Spring Church as allso to find Shingles and put in And mend All
the places Where Any of the Old Ones is Decay^d or Gon and further it is
Agreed that if ther is more Tar then Six barils to be made Use of in
Well Tarring the Said Church to provid it & that ye Said Buckner is to
be allowed his Charge for the Same And in the Due performance of the
Said Work he is to be Allowed And paid Seven pounds Corant Mony

True Redgister Test
WBrooking C. Ves.

6

The Coming of The Great Awakening:
Josiah Cotton and the Perils of Life

SOURCE: Josiah Cotton, "Memoirs containing Some Account
of the Predecessors, Relations, Posterity & Alliances (with
some remarkable Occurrencies in the Life and Circumstances) of Josiah Cotton of Plymouth in New England,
Esq. . . ." (Boston, Manuscript in Massachusetts Historical
Society), 286-296. Reprinted with permission from the Massachusetts Historical Society.

Plym'o Dies Jovis Janu'y 30.1740/1

I have read of a certain Sect or sort of men that thought there were
two principles from whence all things proceed, the one the author of
good, the other of evil. But christianity informs us otherwise & better,
that God alone is the author of the evil that we suffer as well as of the
good that we enjoy, for shall we receive good at the hands of God, &
which we dont deserve, & not evil which we do? The evil of sin merits
the evil of punishment; & the Almighty as he is Judge & Gov'r of the
world is obliged in Justice to punish moral evil with penal. The diseases

of our bodies proceed from the distempers of our minds some of which diseases the nature & constitutions of men admits but one of the life of man. VIZ: the plague, smallpox & meazells, which last distemper came into our family about the middle of Janu'y last, our negro man Quominuh being first seized therewith, & then his son, a child about five years old, & then our youngest daughter, & eldest Granddaughter, all sick with it at the same time: and a great snow falling the 15th of January which lasted many weeks & rendered our case very difficult, having but little or no help but my wife & Sias but the author of our affliction carried us thro' it, tho the negro had a relapse, & was not well till about the beginning of march & what shall we render to the Lord for spairing our lives? That distemper run thro' the town very swiftly but proved favourable to a sinfull ill deserving people thro sovereign grace & mercy. Our Son Josiah belonged then to the Colledge, but was I think by a good providence detained at home, without whose help we had suffered much more than we did: & all the month of March was hindered by contrary winds from his return to Cambridge, so that he did not get there till the beginning of april, & then was fin'd or punish't 3 £ for absence; upon which occasion I wrote several letters to the President & the fellows, some passages whereof I shall transcribe: To the President I wrote, that he took a great deal of pains to obtain a passage walking near 40 times 4 miles a day in order thereunto, but Eolus not favouring him I wish Apollo may, & then add some news forreign to this affair, concerning a monstrous ly raised by an Indian to conceal some mischief he had done, a story ridiculous & incredible that Eight Spaniards had taken him & his house in the wood 4 miles from the salt water as if they sailed over the tops of the trees & landed safe a[t] Jo. Wainpums house howsoever it put this town into the utmost confusion upon the Lords day March the 30th but ended without blood. The story of 2 youngsters fooling & playing together viz: Eames & Morton, & the first runing a red hot Iron into the others throat & thereby killing him directly, was too true to make a jest of &c. I afterwards wrote a particular account of the occasion of my Sons tarrying so long at home to his Tutor Mr Joseph Mahen . . . & received an answer from him, with encouragement, that they would reconsider his fine, whereupon Josiah tarried at Cambridge till the last week in June at which time the Colledge broke up by reason of the throat distemper then prevailing in the town of which the Presidents Wife &c. died, & the Commencement was put off to the 27th of August, & the Schollars ordered to repair to the Colledge about that time, but considering that my Sons fine was not reconsidered, & he not sufficiently fitted up to go, I detained him to go, & on the 6th of Sept'r sent him to Narragansett to bring down Bille Dyre, which he happily accomplished on September 25 & blessed be God, who has thus answered our prayers & strenuous endeavours to rescue him from rudeness, ignorance & Quakerism. He tarried at our house till the 7th of Nov'r & then set sail for Boston, with his Uncle Sias, where they arrived the same day, & the poor fatherless & Motherless child was well received of his great Uncle. Sias tarried there & thereabouts till Dec'r 20th & then arrived home, I having left him at his liberty either to tarry or come away from the Colledge, which last he chose, & what the event will be God only knows. Oh that it may be the better, & not for the worse, & that we may now have direction from Heaven, what course to stear concerning him, & if this change of our designs may not prove ruinous to him. In my writing to the President &c. I hinted that reason & Justice were on my design, & that they ought to prevail in all societies, & refered to several instances wherein, those that had the powers relaxed the severity of penal laws, which would make sad work in the world if moderation were not used in the execution of them, & that no body ought to be punished purely as an example, only to deter others from taking too much, but that they were Gentlemen self sufficient & not obliged to copy of precedents. I wrote this because his Tutor promised to call at my house, but failed to be at the door &c. That civility, good manners, & all things else in law & Gospel had taken a different turn from what they had in the last century, and that I could not but consider they had not reconsidered the matter in Sept'r in as much as we ought to be as speedy in doing Justice as injustice &c. The reason of my labouring the matter so much was to prevent such proceedings in the future, supposing no appeal, or remedy but was as bad as the diseas, but all to no purpose, & so proceed to say we may sing of judgment as well as mercy, mercy in receiving our GrandChild & judgment perhaps in diverting the Education of our Son & in the loss of our Negro man, who strangly & unexpectedly left us on the 29th of Octob'r & after lurcking about the town 4 or 5 days went to Boston, altho pains have been taken to get him here, yet remains abroad, and may we not read our sin in our punishment? We have often deserted the service of our heavenly benefactor, & no wonder he permits our Servants to wonder if he permits our [ ] only in this but in other respects we may take notice of the divine goodness & severity. Our Son in law Dyre thro' the mismanagement of his owner & imployer one Cornet a Frenchman lost his whole Voyage to Hispaniola (which was near 9 mo) & had like to have lost his life with sickness, as several of his Company did, viz: young Thomas Howland & his Brother Joseph, one of Capt'n Benj'n Warrens Sons &c: Howsoever thro' divine Goodness Dyre at length returned as it were with the skin of his Teeth, & has since made a very quick & successful Voyage to Portugal — & our Son Theophilus has also made 2 good voyages to Jamaica this year. Oh that this sort of men were more gratefull to their gracious preserver from the danger of the Seas & enemies. The Spaniards have taken many of the English vessells this year, some perhaps that sailed from hence: and to reveng the injuries done upon us, a design has been formed in England of attacking (as tis said) the Havanna a very strong & rich City upon Cuba in the West Indies, for which purpose several Companies of voluntiers were listed in America, & in this Province 5 Companies, one of which was commanded by Maj'r John Winslow (Son of Col'o Winslow late Dec'd) formerly Clerk of our Court, who strangely and unaccountably left his farm, his family, his aged mother, & his business which was considerable, to ramble abroad in the world upon such a dangerious Enterprise &c. In my last years memoirs I mention the receipt of a letter from Cous'n Cotton of the Isle of Wight & since I returned an answer Dated March 25: 1740. . . . I inform him also of our danger by a French War

& the dangerous circumstances of our eclesiastical constitution for want
of a decisive power & I cant forbear informing him (upon giving occasion in his Letter from what he had heard concerning us) that we are
in this Countrey got into very ill methods of Living, the getting of a
mans living by the sweat of his face (according to the original Curse)
is too much out of fashion. The Sea Swallows up the land, too many
Sailers, & too few Husbandmen; we don't love to labour in bringing our
land too by which means & an extravagance of living beyond ourselves
we are forc'd to be beholden to other parts for provision. Ireland for
times for Butter, England for Cloathing &c which carries off our Silver
& leaves us nothing but Paper money, the difficulties & damage whereof
seem to be inextricable & insuperable. This year two several parcells
of men undertook & ventured to put out vast sums of paper money viz:
the Merchants at Boston 120 Thousand pounds to be repaid in silver
or Gold at the end of 15 years & the Countrey men in conjunction with
some at Boston to put out some Thousand pound reconed 60000 £ of the
old currant paper Bills to be paid in again in 20 years in the produce of
the countrey except Wooll & Fish upon which two schemes it was observed by one that the first will oppress the poor & the last the rich, the
first chiefly upon personal security, & the last upon land security, &
therefore called the land security as the first is called silver scheme
which has the favour & countenance of the Government but the land
scheme is exceedingly frowned upon in the first place before any of
their money came out a proclamation came forth to caution all from
taking any of their money, & after it did get out & many did & some did
not receive it, 2 proclamations more came forth from the Gov'r & Councill
threatning all Civil & military Officers with the displeasure of the Gov't
displacing if they incouraged the passing the land scheme money, in
pursuan whereof several worthy men have been dismist from their
Civil & military posts: & since that a threatning order to discourage
Tavern keepers from taking it, & directions to the Justices not to license
such as do, & what these things tend to, God end in God only knows,
Deus avertat omen, that it may not end in a Storm that will overwhelm
us all. I received order Jan'y 3d from the Gov'r & Councill to transmit
a list of all such persons names as had morgaged their estates or any
part thereof to the Society who have put forth notes of hand commonly
called manifactures Bills which List I sent to the Secretary & had prepared in a seperate letter the following animadversions but did not
send it viz; Sr. I am a little or rather not a little concerned at the aspect
of the Times. The Countrey seem to have their hearts much set upon
the Land scheme as that which will promot the manifactures of the
Countrey, & as their last shift & only asylum to deliver them from ex-
torting Rhode Islanders, designing hoarders & devouring usurers; &
Merchants among ourselves who require silver for their Notes of hand,
& take due care to prevent it out of the Countrey as fast as they can, &
may it not be justly feared that the strong efforts to prevent this extraordinary scheme will have a contrary effect to what may be intended, &
render the peccant humour more fervent & intense? *Nitimur in vetitium*
people have suckt in with their mothers milk, & when they see otherwise good & worthy men displac'd because they cant see just as others

do alas what will it come to? Thus far the Countrey talk, not considering
that the thinning of officers & Tavernskeepers may be of publick use.
For my own part I have been for many years an enemy to the multiply-
ing nay the very being of paper money, but as long as Rhode Island take
the liberty of pouring in such a floud upon us, & the Merchants make
what & when they please I can see no end to it, only some faint glimmer-
ing hopes that these excessive emissions will so Glutt us that we shall
have no future appetite to such a wretched medium or will otherwise
procure a total suppression of it. I shall finish this as I did my last.
Money, & the want of money will ruine me. There have been several
storms this year in Oct'r, Nov'r, Dec'r & this month, which have done
much damage to bridges Dams & Vessells: many wrecks &c, much &
many Snow & very hard & cold weather even to this day. . . . Our Bay
has been so filled with Ice that many have walked upon it from Plymouth
to Duxborough, that several vessells have not been able to reach the
shore for several weeks, & a Schooner partly loaden with Salt, belonging
to our town was Jan'y 4 driven out to Sea dragging her Anchors after,
& not yet heard of nobody being aboard to direct her Course, The Lord
wean us from fading & perishing Riches Amen. At our Dec'r Court
Mr. J. Spark was wholly dismist from being an Attorney for intemperance &c. Telix quem faciunt aliend pericula cautum
Let him that thinks he stands take heed lest he fall
Be not high minded but fear —
And oh that we may all fear him who is able to keep us from falling
[into Sin or mischeif] & to present us faultless before the presence of
his glory with exceeding Joy; To whom be praise & Glory now & forever Amen———

7

Jonathan Edwards On The Religious Affections And The Great Awakening

SOURCE: *The Works of President Edwards, in Eight Volumes* (London, 1817), IV, iii-vi.

PREFACE.

There is no question of greater importance to mankind, and that it more concerns every individual person to be well resolved in, than this: *What are the distinguishing qualifications of those that are in favour with God, and intitled to his eternal rewards?* Or, which comes to the same thing, *What is the nature of true religion? and wherein lie the distinguishing notes of that virtue which is acceptable in the sight of God?* But though it be of such importance, and though we have clear and abundant light in the word of God to direct us in this matter, yet there is no one point wherein professing Christians differ more one from another. It would be endless to reckon up the variety of opinions, in this point, that divide the Christian world; making manifest the truth of that declaration of our Saviour, *Strait is the gate, and narrow is the way, that leads to life, and few there be that find it.*

The consideration of these things has long engaged me to attend to this matter with the utmost diligence and care, and all the exactness of search and inquiry of which I have been capable. It is a subject on which my mind has been peculiarly intent, ever since I first entered on the study of divinity.—But as to the *success* of my inquiries, it must be left to the judgment of the reader of the following treatise.

I am sensible it is difficult to judge impartially of the subject of this discourse, in the midst of the dust and smoke of present controversy, about things of this nature. As it is more difficult to *write* impartially, so it is more difficult to *read* impartially.—Many will probably be hurt, to find so much that appertains to religious affection here condemned; and perhaps indignation and contempt will be excited in others, by finding so much justified and approved. And it may be, some will be ready to charge me with inconsistence with myself, in so much approving some things, and so much condemning others; as I have found that this has always been objected to me by some, ever since the beginning of our late controversies about religion. It is a difficult thing to be a hearty zealous friend of what has been *good* and glorious in the late extraordinary appearances, and to rejoice much in it; and, at the same time, to see the evil and pernicious tendency of what has been *bad,* and earnest-

ly to oppose that. Yet, I am *humbly* but *fully* persuaded, we shall never
be in the way of truth, a way acceptable to God, and tending to the
advancement of Christ's kingdom, till we do so. There is indeed something very mysterious in it, that so much good, and so much bad, should
be mixed together in the *church of God:* as it is a mysterious thing, and
what has puzzled and amazed many a good Christian, that there should
be that which is so divine and precious, as the saving grace of God,
dwelling in the same heart, with so much corruption, hypocrisy, and
iniquity, in *a particular saint.* Yet neither of these is more mysterious
than real. And neither of them is a new thing. It is no new thing, that
much false religion should prevail, at a time of great revival; and that,
at such a time, multitudes of hypocrites should spring up among true
saints. It was so in that great reformation, and revival of religion, in
Josiah's time; as appears by Jer. iii. 10. and iv. 3, 4. and also by the great
apostacy there was in the land, so soon after his reign. So it was in that
great out pouring of the Spirit upon the Jews, in the days of JOHN the
BAPTIST; as appears by the great apostacy of that people, so soon after
so general an awakening, and the temporary religious comforts and
joys of many; John v. 35. *Ye were willing for a season to rejoice in his*
light. So it was in those great commotions among the multitude, occasioned by the preaching of Jesus Christ. *Of the many that were then*
called, but few were chosen; of the multitude that were roused and
affected by his preaching — and at one time or other appeared mightily
engaged, full of admiration of Christ, and elevated with joy — but few
were true disciples, that stood the shock of trials, and endured to the
end. Many were like the *stony* or *thorny* ground; and but few, comparatively, like the *good* ground. Of the whole heap that was gathered, great
part was chaff, that the wind afterwards drove away; and the heap of
wheat that was left, was comparatively small; as appears abundantly
by the history of the New Testament. So it was in that great outpouring
of the Spirit in the apostles' days; as appears by Matth. xxiv. 10–13. Gal.
iii. 1. and iv. 11, 15. Phil. ii. 21. and iii. 18, 19.; the two epistles to the
Corinthians, and many other parts of the New Testament. And so it was
in the great *reformation* from Popery. — It appears plainly to have been
in the visible church of God, in times of great revivals as it is with the
fruit-trees in the spring; there are multitudes of blossoms, which appear
fair and beautiful, and there is a promising appearance of young fruits:
but many of them are of short continuance; they soon fall off, and never
come to maturity.

   It is not, however, to be supposed, that it will *always* be so; for, though
there never will, in this world, be an entire purity, either in particular
saints, by a perfect freedom from mixtures of corruption; or in the
church of God, without any mixture of hypocrites with saints — or counterfeit religion and false appearances of grace with true religion and real
holiness — yet, it is evident, there will come a time of much greater
purity in the church, than has been in ages past*. And one great reason
of it will be, that at that time, God will give much greater light to his

_____

   * This appears plain by these texts of scripture, Is. lii. 1. Ezek. xliv. 6, 7, 9.
Joel iii. 17. Zech. xiv. 21. Psal. lxix. 32, 35, 36. Is. xxxv. 8, 10. Chap. iv. 3, 4.
Ezek. xx. 38. Psal. xxxvii. 9, 10, 11, 29.

people, to distinguish between true religion and its counterfeits; Mal. iii. 3. *And he shall sit as a refiner and purifier of silver: and he shall purify the sons of Levi, and purge them as gold and silver, that they may offer to the Lord an offering in righteousness.* With ver. 18. which is a continuation of the prophecy of the same happy times, *Then shall ye return, and discern between the righteous and the wicked; between him that serveth God, and him that serveth him not.*

It is by the mixture of counterfeit religion with true, not discerned and distinguished, that the devil has had his greatest advantage against the cause and kingdom of Christ. It is plainly by this means, principally, that he has prevailed against all revivals of religion, since the first founding of the Christian church. By this he hurt the cause of Christianity, in and after the apostolic age, much more than by all the persecutions of both Jews and Heathens. The apostles, in all their epistles, shew themselves much more concerned at the former mischief, than the latter. By this, Satan prevailed against the reformation, begun by Luther, Zuinglius, &c. to put a stop to its progress, and bring it into disgrace, ten times more than by all the bloody and cruel persecutions of the church of Rome. By this, principally, has he prevailed against revivals of religion in our nation. By this he prevailed against New-England, to quench the love, and spoil the joy of her espousals, about a hundred years ago. And, I think, I have had opportunity enough to see plainly, that by this the devil has prevailed against the late great revival of religion in New-England, so happy and promising in its beginning. Here, most evidently, has been the main advantage Satan has had against us; by this he has foiled us. It is by this means that the daughter of Zion in this land now lies on the ground, in such piteous circumstances, with her garments rent, her face disfigured, her nakedness exposed, her limbs broken, and weltering in the blood of her own wounds, and in no wise able to arise; and, this, so quickly after her late great joys and hopes: Lam. i. 17, *Zion spreadeth forth her hands, and there is none to comfort her: the Lord hath commanded concerning Jacob, that his adversaries shall be round about him: Jerusalem is as a menstruous woman among them.* I have seen the devil prevail the same way, against two great revivals of religion in this country — Satan goes on with mankind as he began with them. He prevailed against our first parents, cast them out of paradise, and suddenly brought all their happiness and glory to an end, by appearing to be a friend to their happy state, and pretending to advance it to higher degrees. So the same cunning serpent that beguiled Eve through his subtilty, by perverting us from the simplicity that is in Christ, hath suddenly prevailed to deprive us of that fair prospect we had, a little while ago, of a kind of paradisiacal state of the church of God in New-England.

After religion has revived in the church of God, and enemies appear, people that are engaged to defend its cause are commonly most exposed, where they are least sensible of danger. While they are wholly intent upon the opposition that appears *openly* before them, in order to make head against that, and while they neglect carefully to look around, the devil comes behind them, and gives a fatal stab unseen; and he has opportunity to give a more home stroke, and to wound the deeper, because he strikes at his leisure, being obstructed by no resistance or guard.

And so it is likely ever to be in the church, whenever religion revives remarkably, till we have learned well to distinguish between true and false religion, between saving affections and experiences, and those manifold fair shews, and glistering appearances, by which they are counterfeited; the consequences of which, when they are not distinguished, are often inexpressibly dreadful. *By this means,* the devil gratifies himself, that multitudes should offer to God, under the notion of acceptable service, what is indeed above all things abominable to him. *By this means,* he deceives great multitudes about the state of their souls; making them think they are something, when they are nothing; and so eternally undoes them; and not only so, but establishes many in a strong confidence of their eminent holiness, who, in God's sight are some of the vilest hypocrites. *By this means,* he many ways damps religion in the hearts of the saints, obscures and deforms it by corrupt mixtures, causes their religious affections wofully to degenerate, and sometimes, for a considerable time, to be like the *manna* that bred worms and stank; and dreadfully ensnares and confounds the minds of others, brings them into great difficulties and temptations, and entangles them in a wilderness, out of which they can by no means extricate themselves. *By this means,* Satan mightily encourages the hearts of open enemies, strengthens their hands, fills them with weapons, and makes strong their fortresses; when at the same time, religion and the church of God lie exposed to them, as a city without walls. *By this means,* he brings it to pass, that men work wickedness under a notion of doing God service, and so sin without restraint, yea with earnest forwardness and zeal, and with all their might. *By this means,* he brings in even the friends of religion, insensibly, to do the work of enemies, by destroying religion in a far more effectual manner than open enemies can do, under a notion of advancing it. *By this means,* the devil scatters the flock of Christ, and sets them one against another with great heat of spirit, under a notion of zeal for God; and religion, by degrees, degenerates into vain jangling. During the strife, Satan leads both parties far out of the right way, driving each to great extremes, one on the right hand, and the other on the left, according as he finds they are most inclined, or most easily moved and swayed, till the right path in the middle is almost wholly neglected. In the midst of this confusion, the devil has great opportunity to advance his own interest, to make it strong in ways innumerable, to get the government of all into his own hands, and to work his own will. And by what is seen of the terrible consequences of this counterfeit, when not distinguished from true religion, God's people in general have their minds unsettled in religion, and know not where to set their foot, or what to think, and many are brought into doubts, whether there be any thing at all in religion; and heresy, infidelity and atheism greatly prevail.

Therefore, it greatly concerns us to use our utmost endeavours, clearly to discern, and have it well settled and established, wherein true religion does consist. Till this be done, it may be expected that great revivals of religion will be but of short continuance; till this be done, there is but little good to be expected of all our warm debates, in conversation and from the press, not knowing clearly and distinctly what we ought to contend for.

JAMES G. LYDON

English Mercantilism And North America

T HE CENTRALIZATION OF AUTHORITY by European monarchs in early modern times resulted in nation-states usually united by language similarities and limited by identifiable geographic boundaries. Formation of the nation state required the effective use of power, economic as well as military. Thus, coincident with the rise of European dynasties came a recognition of the importance of economic planning. Mercantilism was the economic system through which these nations mobilized their resources to support the power of their kings.

Concentrating upon national interests, the mercantilist strove to advance his country by fully developing its economy. Since these economic thinkers believed that world resources were static and limited, improvement of one nation necessarily took place at the expense of others, and wars would occur in the process. Thus the internal economy had to be organized to assure victory in those struggles.

Economic historians have argued at length over whether a coherent policy or expediency governed mercantilism. Certainly as early as the sixteenth century examples exist of the recognition of national economic policies. However, not until the full effects of the commercial revolution became obvious in the seventeenth century did mercantilists begin to think in terms of a fully-integrated economy. Even then, no state had the power to achieve a perfect control. Mercantilists of each nation were limited by the economic potentialities of their individual state. Historians, in examining mercantilism, have combined the varied approaches taken by European states and have erected that combination into a model system. Yet, even France, tightly organized under Louis XIV's famous minister, Jean Baptiste Colbert, never achieved the integrated economy he desired. A perfect mercantilist system was never attained. In fact, while the new bureaucracies of the nation-states exercised extraordinary authority, they never possessed enough power to bend all of a nation's economic forces to their wills.

Wealth is power. Since paper money only came into vogue during the eighteenth century, wealth to the mercantilist meant gold and silver — specie. Its accretion became the basic goal of various mercantile systems, for specie provided a nation with the sinews of war. To prevent drainage of gold and silver out of a country for the purchase of war materiel, nations sought an adequate internal supply. Enterprises which contributed to a nation's war potential (cannon foundries, powder manufactures, weapons producers, etc.) received legislative encouragement. Thus England avoided dependence upon foreign supplies and prevented the drainage of specie as well. Development of minerals essential for weapons production and of forests for ship timbers received similar encouragement and protection. Early mercantilist policies developed two interrelated programs simultaneously: one ensured a flow of specie into the nation, the other guaranteed the availability of the sinews of war.

As the economic philosophies of the mercantilists became more sophisticated, they advanced a variety of schemes for the retention of money within a nation. For example, sumptuary laws limited or forbade importation of certain goods, usually luxuries. Such laws had the additional advantage of encouraging the production of local substitutes, providing employment for workers, and advancing the internal economy.

In time economic theorists came to realize the importance of productivity at home. A growing population productively employed resulted in a larger exportation of finished goods and provided manpower in case of war. A large population also kept wages low and allowed exports to compete in world markets. Quality controls over those exports guaranteed the reputation and salability of a nation's goods. Since finished goods were more valuable than raw materials, a nation should import unfinished goods and process them for export, again expanding the internal economy.

In the sixteenth and early seventeenth centuries, as Europe's economy expanded rapidly, its rising population developed more expensive and even exotic tastes. Trade, which became a very important factor in economic growth, was spurred by the Spanish discovery of the treasures of Mexico and Peru. The wealth pouring out of American mines boggled European imaginations and played a major role in commercial expansion.

At first, most European states, jealous of Spain's newly found wealth, sought a share by seeking their own American mines or by seizing Spanish wealth through poorly cloaked piratic expeditions. But as the profits gained by the Dutch through trade came to rival Spain's American income, mercantilists more and more realized that treasure could be gained by other means. By the early seventeenth century, policies shifted to trade rather than piracy, and as the century progressed mercantilism reached full flower. Thomas Mun signalized this change in the title of his mercantilist tract: *England's Treasure by Forraign Trade*.

The increasing demand for non-European goods led to a rapid expansion overseas. Establishment of imperial control over lands in Asia, Africa, and America had as a basic aim the exploitation of those areas to answer the economic needs of Europe. Mercantilists now sought not only to gain bullion, but also to dominate or monopolize trading areas. They erected complicated systems to assure control by the state of its own trade and plantations to the advantage of its merchants at home. They set up special councils to oversee the colonies and enacted laws closing overseas territories to foreign trade.

The exchange of European goods for those of Asia had from early medieval times involved luxury products such as spices, porcelains, and silks rather than bulky commodities. Europeans did not settle overseas in large numbers. Instead, they established mercantile factories or trading centers occupied by a factor with his assistants and guards. In some cases, the number of merchants trading to one area created an enclave of Europeans in a city. For example, Italian merchants controlled certain cities in the Near East and in the Black Sea area. The Portuguese followed the same practice when they expanded into Africa and later into Asia, and other European nationals adopted the same system. Local factories gathered in the foreign goods, while fleets came out with European produce and carried home the exotic merchandise.

When Europeans expanded into America, however, they faced a

totally different problem. The indigenous population did not produce finished goods or spices in demand in Europe. Only in the fur trade could the Europeans apply the factor method. The Spanish first faced the problem. The Indians had gathered only limited amounts of bullion, and thus the Spaniards had to send to America fairly large numbers of people who could overawe and control the Indian population and force it to produce the desired gold and silver. (Of course, the christianization and civilization of the primitive Indian society provided an added motive, and Europeans justified exploitation of the natives on the basis of this religious and cultural transferral.) Even then, Spain with its limited population sent only tens of thousands into the Americas.

The Spanish and Portuguese in America employed a largely exploitative pattern of expansion. Though their American empires contained fairly large native populations, the demand for European goods remained modest. On the other hand, their American territories produced very valuable commodities, and they made every effort to exclude foreigners. To ensure that American specie was not diverted from Seville or Lisbon, the Spaniards and Portuguese centered all trade in selected ports in Europe and America and prohibited the export of specie from the Iberian states under penalty of death. There emerged an elaborate system of controls aimed at keeping foreigners out of the Indies, thereby retaining its treasure for Spain and Portugal.

By the early seventeenth century, however, the internal economies of Spain and Portugal failed to develop enough to satisfy the demand for finished goods within their empires. This led to heavy drainage of specie to northern Europe to purchase products for internal consumption and for export to the colonies, and northern merchants came to dominate in the Iberian ports which controlled the Indies trade.

The early seventeenth-century settlements by northern Europeans utilized the same system as the Iberians, with the same objective in mind of discovering and exploiting silver and gold deposits. The French and Dutch approach to settlement in North America followed very similar patterns and employed the factory type of settlement. They emphasized the fur trade and only utilized immigration to support or protect that primary economic goal. Actually, the initial settlements made by the English in Virginia and Newfoundland were based upon the same kind of thinking. However, the small Indian population of the areas claimed by the northern Europeans and developments of the seventeenth and eighteenth centuries changed this early pattern of exploitation.

The increasing affluence of the European society in the seventeenth and especially in the eighteenth centuries created a demand for raw materials, including foodstuffs and other agricultural products from overseas. A steadily advancing technology saw shipbuilders emphasize cargo capacity which facilitated the relatively cheap transfer of bulk products over long distances. In consequence, where imperial expansion had previously centered upon areas producing extremely expensive products in relation to their bulk, now colonies with totally different potentialities became important. As the attractions of certain colonial areas changed, so too did the attitudes of the mercantilist thinkers.

Mercantilists emphasized the development of a nation's internal economy by creating opportunities for employment at home. If exports of finished goods stimulated imports of money, then the greater the production and exportation, the more efficient the mercantilist program. Immigration abroad reduced the work force at home and raised the cost of labor, making goods exported less competitive in price. Immigration to overseas colonies might also create competition with the mother country. Some English interests strongly opposed settlement in Newfoundland because a shore-based fishery would compete with vessels coming out from home. In the same way, English authorities discouraged the immigration abroad of technicians since technical innovations affected productivity and competitiveness and must be jealously guarded. As new colonies began to produce goods which European markets demanded and which could not be produced at home, mercantilists viewed immigration more liberally.

Certain kinds of colonies were thought to contribute to the wellbeing of the mother country while others did not. The most desirable colonies sent home goods marketable in other European states and exportation of those products through the mother country created an accretion of specie. Exclusive production of such goods gave an even greater advantage. Competition for overseas empire in the seventeenth and eighteenth centuries rose largely from the race to gain control of such producing areas and to monopolize such goods. Maximum profits from colonial settlements could be realized only when production, transportation, and distribution of their goods rested in the merchants of the mother country.

The development of the English mercantile system as applied to its North American colonies will clarify the goals of the mercantilists, their methods, and their changing views.

The applications of early mercantilist theory in England became apparent by the late 1400s, and they began to become some-what sophisticated by the later sixteenth century. The tide of English immigration to North America and the Caribbean after 1600, though created mainly by religious and political ferment at home, marked England's entrance upon its imperial era. Its first colonies in the Caribbean, North America, and Newfoundland were created to gain "treasure," a foothold in the fur trade, or the fisheries. None of these required the settlement of a large English population overseas. Puritan migration after 1625 created such alarm that laws limited immigration in the late 1630s.

Profits from growing tobacco for export to Europe helped en-courage migration, and as a result changed the mercantile rela-tionship between England and its colonies. Tobacco was the first American agricultural product grown in bulk for transportation to Europe. Over time, an increasing number of other American products found markets there, including sugar, coffee, rice, cereals, iron, and wood products. Over the next century and a half, American goods transformed the traditional ocean-trade patterns, caused an enormous expansion of European merchant marines, and, most important, necessitated the employment of large seden-tary populations in the overseas territories of these nations. Codfish had always been caught, dried, and carried to Europe by fishermen sailing from European ports. Sugar had been shipped from America to Europe, but only in small quantities. After 1640 Europeans settled in America produced a steadily increasing vol-ume of these and other goods for European consumption.

The salability of American staples from agriculture, sea, or forest, produced by a population settled overseas, marked a dis-tinct change from earlier colonial exploitation. This economic revolution forced changes in the views of English mercantilists toward colonies and immigration. They had to consider problems of integrating and controlling large populations overseas, as well as the goods they produced and their external trade. Staples, rather than treasure in gold, furs, or fish, became the goal of the mercantilists.

Even the Puritans, escaping to religious freedom, had been re-affirmed in their flight by the knowledge that the New World offered solid economic promise. The success of tobacco in Virginia and Barbados and the possibility of a shore-based fishery encour-aged colonies elsewhere. The first settlements, established under corporate structures, had presumed a factory-type of exploitation, but they soon gave way to proprietary grants which emphasized landholding by immigrants. Agricultural production was their purpose. The first of these, the Baltimore grant in 1632, set a pattern followed through the remainder of the century. Some colonies began in the hope that they might produce goods which England lacked and which it had to import from foreign sources. Silk, wine, olives, and countless other products fitted this pattern. Colonies launched upon these expectations soon faltered, but in time they discovered other bulk crops which could form the staples for their economies. Immigrants poured into North America in the eighteenth century, some as religious refugees and others by force, but they came or were brought essentially because of the economic potentialities of England's empire.

The value of American products and the steadily increasing competition for both markets and the sources of these goods required a much more elaborate mercantilist system. An ever more powerful nation was needed to control, direct, and protect the expanding overseas empire. How did English mercantilists react to this changing situation? What kind of program did they develop for applying their concepts within the empire?

Though James I abhorred tobacco and wrote a tract against it, he could not deny the economic fact of the European demand for it. One of the earliest mercantilist laws affecting the colonies aimed at controlling the tobacco trade in the interest of England and its merchants. All tobacco was to be routed through England, paying customs there before its export to Europe. Baltimore's charter for Maryland a few years later contained the same strictures, since tobacco was expected to be that colony's staple crop. The English quickly insisted on restriction of colonial trade and control over colonial produce. American tobacco was to be an English monopoly. Its production was forbidden in England and foreign tobacco was heavily taxed. Concessions in the English market worked to the colonials' advantage even if English control over tobacco distribution did not. Enactment of this law, however, did not guarantee its acceptance and enforcement in Virginia and Barbados (or in rural England where tobacco cultivation continued). The gap between legislation and enforcement remained a major weakness of the English mercantile system throughout its whole existence.

The confused period preceding the English civil war of the 1640s prevented the government from executing its regulations concerning tobacco at home or abroad. Flagrant Dutch involvement with the tobacco trade by 1650 demanded a reaction in London, as did their general trade competition. The Lowlanders were by this date at the peak of their commercial power. Since mercantilists believed resources to be static, expansion of English economic strength necessarily created tensions with the Dutch. Tobacco smuggling and dominance of the fur trade by the Dutch through New Amsterdam contributed to the growing demand for war against them. Between 1652 and 1675 the English fought the Dutch three times in order to reduce their economic power.

The Dutch had expanded on the basis of a near monopoly of the carrying trade of all of Europe. From very early times English laws periodically confined the nation's trade to English vessels. As mercantilist thought and theory gained more and more adherents, the government established this as a basic principle with the Navigation Acts of 1650 and 1651. These laws closed the colonies to all foreign trade; provided that all imports from the colonies be carried in vessels owned, commanded, and manned by Englishmen; and required that goods entering England must arrive in English vessels or those of the country of the goods' origin. The latter provision England aimed directly against the Dutch as middlemen. Thus, the English laid down the basic principle of restricting imperial trade to the advantage of English merchants and shipowners.

Charles II, upon his restoration to the throne in 1660, reissued and somewhat amplified these laws. Despite repeated attempts to close loopholes in the Navigation Acts, an inefficient customs system led to lax enforcement of the regulations down to the 1690s. By that time, improvements in bureaucratic methods and a growing use of statistical trade information demonstrated the system's ineffectiveness. In 1696, England again revamped the trade laws, making improvements in administration and policy-making procedures. Imperial trade and the colonies, previously the responsibility of one or more committees chosen from among the king's councillors, now became centralized in a committee, commonly referred to as the Board of Trade. This body had an advisory role on trade and colonial affairs, but its working members were knowledgeable men, well paid for their efforts, and their reports and suggestions very often became the basis for final decisions. Throughout the Board's history, mercantilist theories dominated its translation of ideas into action. Its vitality depended on its membership and especially on its leadership. When poorly led, as during the secretaryship of the Duke of Newcastle, its efficiency was sharply reduced. Its era of greatest influence lasted from 1696 through 1724.

The Board of Trade, as initiator and overseer of mercantilist policy, naturally dealt with shipping and commerce in addition to the colonies. Even before the reorganization of 1696, the government had established principles which aimed at a monopolization of American staples and of the American market for finished goods from Europe.

An addition to the Navigation Acts in 1663 required that goods produced in Europe pass through England before shipment to America, and that only English vessels carry them. Certain "specified" articles could be directly imported from Europe to America: to aid the fisheries, salt could go direct to Newfoundland and New England; wine from Madeira and the Azores, as well as provisions, horses, and servants from Ireland and Scotland, could also enter directly. By 1660 the relatively large English population overseas had begun to produce staples, other than tobacco, of value to the mercantilists. These "enumerated" articles, including sugar, cotton, indigo, and dyewoods, could only be exported through England. Shippers posted bonds on their exportation and had to submit proof within a year of their delivery at a port in England, Ireland, or Wales. With the passage of time, the list lengthened as new products proved advantageous to the mother country's trade. The system became increasingly more restrictive.

Following the precept that the mother country should produce finished products, the government sought to limit competition in manufacturing when American-produced goods began to appear. Thus it forbade the exportation of woolen goods, hats, and finished iron products from the colonies. The Wool Act (1699) affected Ireland more than the American colonies, the Hat Act (1732) had little impact, but the Iron Act (1750) worked to the disadvantage of the North American settlers. Interests in England facing competition initiated such laws, but their protests did not always result in restrictive legislation. When shipbuilders complained about American competition in the 1720s, no protective statutes were passed. However, protests against North American trade with the foreign West Indies in the early 1730s led Parliament to issue the Molasses Act. Depressed markets for sugar and other British island goods led to the placing of prohibitive duties on goods from the foreign West Indies.

The mercantilists obviously had to develop a system which provided maximum profits to the mother country while also encouraging colonial growth. The whole program depended upon the demand in England and in Europe for American goods. To the mercantilists, the most advantageous colony was that which produced the most valuable goods.

Colonies producing plantation goods most readily satisfied Eng-

lish mercantilist interests. Tobacco, rice, and sugar found a good
market in Europe. Those settlements north of Maryland competed
within the system rather than contributed to its wealth. With the
exception of furs, the northern colonies competed directly with the
English in the West Indies and southern European trades. Colonial exportation of cereals and flour to those areas rose steadily
through the eighteenth century and in the late 1730s roused a
reaction at home. Again, no protective legislation followed the
criticism of this competition. In fact, Britain's rising population
gradually became dependent upon American grain and flour. By
the early 1770s, American production of these staples had become
an advantage to the empire, since the American supplies prevented
a drainage of money to purchase them from foreign sources. On
the other hand, the competition offered by shore-based fisheries to
the English fishing interests caused continuous complaints. North
American fish cargoes reached the southern European market
earlier than English shipments from Newfoundland and supplied
about a third of that area's demand for salt fish. Any depression
of the Newfoundland fishery brought about demands for restrictions on the Americans.

English shipbuilding also suffered from the competition of the
northern colonies. But again, the cheapness of American-built
vessels guaranteed a continual supply of shipping at costs which
lowered freight charges throughout the empire. Perhaps one-third
of the vessels in service when the Revolution began were American
built.

On balance, lack of limitations on the American fisheries, grain
production, and even shipbuilding worked to the advantage of
English commercial expansion. They provided very important
credits to cover the balance of payments deficit constantly faced
by the colonists in their trade with the mother country. The permissiveness of English mercantilists in these instances indicates
their realization of the problem faced by the colonials.

The forced transferral of valuable plantation staples through
England guaranteed important profits to merchants in London,
Bristol, and other British ports. British shippers dominated the
transport of some of these goods, and thus returns from freight
charges centered in the home area. England's traders also profited
by commissions on sales of colonial produce in the metropolis and
on the buying and shipping of goods to American clients. The
tobacco trade was notorious for the numerous charges exacted,
with English agents often profiting to a much greater degree than

the tobacco growers. Fees for shipping, insurance, warehousing, bonding, and inspection, when added to the commissions and the government's duties, meant that plantation goods perfectly fitted mercantilist principles.

Some products in demand could not be produced competitively by the colonials. Therefore, the government provided incentives for their production in order to avoid drainage of money from the empire by their purchase elsewhere. Dependence on foreign sources for some of these products, especially naval stores, could be dangerous in time of war. Thus, adhering to the system's policies, England paid bounties for colonial production of each ton of pitch, tar, rosin, turpentine, and hemp, and for masts, spars, and bowsprits. Although they encouraged the northern colonies through subsidies to concentrate upon these important products, Scandinavian sources still delivered them more cheaply to English and European markets. Bounties paid upon indigo, an extremely valuable dyestuff, resulted in a fairly large output from South Carolina and Georgia, but similar efforts failed to establish wine and silk as staples.

Almost all of these American products were produced, not by a handful of factors and their aides located in an enclave as in Asia, but by Europeans who migrated to America to exploit it. This transferral of manpower was a new phenomenon for mercantilists, who found it at odds with their program for development at home. Much earlier, during the sixteenth century, Spain had partially answered its colonial labor needs by importing blacks from Africa. Within the plantation economies slave power could be employed to grow sugar, rice, tobacco, and other crops. The French, English, and Dutch also accepted slavery as the best source of labor for plantation work. The large-scale, lucrative, and heinous slave trade provided laborers and employed a large number of ships and crewmen. Even this, one of the greatest forced migrations in history, did not fully satisfy colonial needs for labor. Some crops and products required free laborers rather than slave workers. The amazing expansion of Pennsylvania resulted from the availability of manpower to increase the production of cereals, meat, and forest products.

England's mercantile thinkers were much more liberal in their views on immigration than were the French and Spanish. England welcomed foreign settlers despite language and religious differences. Germans, French, Dutch, and Swiss entered from Europe in numbers which were matched by Scottish and Irish immigrants.

They expanded the population of colonial America so rapidly that, combined with its normal growth, it doubled almost every twenty years through the eighteenth century. Migrations from England also occurred and, in addition, the Crown transported about 50,000 convicts to America during the colonial period. Except for the West Indian colonies which employed slaves, other non-English colonies did not require such a large labor supply, since they did not produce agricultural products in volume. The demand for labor in British North America resulted in the first large-scale migration of Europeans overseas.

Although mercantilists emphasized the exportation of goods to Europe, the program of exploitation also had another side. In order to ensure that the colonials would contribute to the growth of the home economy, they were confined, wherever possible, to the consumption of English goods. With the exception of the few "specified" articles which could directly enter from southern Europe, all other imports had to come by way of England. Tariffs limited consumption to English finished goods and, where non-English products entered, merchants in the mother country gained a middleman's profit. With rapid population growth, the American market became more and more important to English exporters.

Since England discouraged colonial manufacturing, the Americans exchanged raw materials for finished goods and often depended upon England for the most inconsequential items. The exchange of unfinished for manufactured products generally created a major problem through currency imbalance. If long continued, the staple producing area found its money drained away and its economy stagnant. The drainage of money to England was, of course, a primary goal of the mercantilists. This practice, as early as 1639, led to a major depression in Massachusetts Bay. As the colonial population rose, the increase in imports created a wider gap in the balance of payments, even though exports also increased. The application of a mercantilist system to a large population, which viewed itself as economically equal to the mother country, was seriously compromised if exploitation led to stagnation of the colonial economy.

Letterbooks of colonial merchants testified to their constant struggle to reduce debts they owed to English creditors. Colonials dealt with the payments problem in a number of ways. Since they always lacked specie, they used commodities in place of money. Usually a colony's staple became the basis for figuring debts and credits. Virginia and Maryland so employed tobacco, exchanging it at a fixed rate in comparison to hard money. However, this sophisticated barter system presented obvious difficulties of movement and storage and of the real value of a fluctuating staple commodity. This led to two price scales, since specie payment always possessed the advantage over commodity payment.

In line with its purpose of drawing hard money to England, the government forbade the importation of English coinage into America, but permitted foreign coin and bullion. However, the government prohibited the minting of coinage in America, and the Privy Council disallowed colonial laws which hindered the flow of coins homeward.

One important innovation developed by Americans to answer the scarcity of specie was the use of paper money as a medium of exchange. Backed by credit, the paper was to be exchanged at a later date for specie. First issued by Massachusetts in 1690, paper money was employed universally in the colonies after 1730. Inflation weakened its effectiveness as assemblies varied in their willingness to levy taxes to redeem it, thus creating a crazy-quilt of currency values throughout the continent. Again, a dual system appeared, with goods bringing one price in hard money and another in paper. The English government, dedicated to hard-money principles, opposed paper money as inflationary and vetoed other schemes to alleviate the scarcity of specie. In 1751, the government called for an end to paper money issues except in wartime and insisted on the gradual withdrawal of those in circulation.

The balance-of-payments problem forced the widespread use of credit, not only within the colonies, but throughout the English economy. Long-term credit and barter exchange enabled the colonials to continue in business. To a considerable degree, the willingness of English merchants to extend long-term credit allowed the North American economy to expand. Nine-months credit had been customary in the early period, but by the close of the colonial era credit was commonly extended for twelve months. Despite constant scrambling to meet their debts, American merchants usually managed to pay on time, partly by shipping goods home and partly by developing flourishing trades with the English and foreign West Indies, Newfoundland, and southern Europe (fostered by special exceptions in the Crown's policies) which provided credits which could be transferred to England. Building ships on order for English buyers also produced usable credits. They also paid portions of the debt by direct remission of specie, some of which came from the flow of immigrants, many of whom brought hard money with them. Even then, in periods of depressed trade, when credit tightened and overseas returns shrank, specie drained rapidly from the colonies and deep deflation occurred. All in all, the continuing expansion of the colonial economy suggests that the balance-of-payments problem did not limit growth to the extent maintained by some earlier historians.

Did the English mercantile system work efficiently? Obviously England's increasing affluence in the seventeenth and eighteenth centuries suggested that it did. Possessing relatively limited advantages, England quickly became the banking and commercial leader of Europe and laid the economic basis for its own great industrial expansion after 1800. England's wealth and power was in no small part the result of its successful exploitation of its overseas empire. Certainly its mercantile system might have been more tightly controlled and organized, but for a number of reasons tighter regulations were not imposed. In some cases, the government was permissive by choice, as with the nonenforcement of the Molasses Act and special exceptions for the southern European trades. England apparently viewed a permissive policy as more profitable in the long run than an unduly limiting one. As it was, the merchant community fretted against what it considered as an excess of restrictions – an excess of "red tape."

On the other hand, though many loopholes had been closed by 1696, the trade laws were commonly evaded. In a governmental organization based upon appointment by influence rather than by merit, the bureaucracy that handled customs collection was neither totally honest nor totally dedicated. Colonial customs officers laxly enforced the regulations and very often were corruptible as well. Absenteeism was common with an underpaid substitute replacing the regular appointee. Even royal governors engaged in peccadilloes arising out of a casual attitude toward trade regulations. When criticizing the morality of public servants, historians often assume the existence of an absolute code of behaviour. However, bureaucrats, then as now, were scarcely more honest elsewhere in the empire than they were in North America. If smuggling prevailed more in the colonies than elsewhere – a debatable point – then geography alone may have been the reason. Any honest examination of mercantilism indicates that illegal trading represented a chronic problem for the Spanish, French, Portuguese, and Dutch, as well as for the English.

Maintenance of an empire was expensive, and by 1750 the English had established one that reached into all parts of the world.

The costs of naval and military protection, the large diplomatic corps overseas, and the steadily increasing administrative bureaucracy, all placed a heavy burden on the English taxpayer. Yet the expenses were amply repaid. London was the entrepot of the western world, and its merchants, bankers, tradesmen, seamen, and dock workers prospered as the wealth of goods poured in from overseas. As a result of England's permissive mercantilist system, its American colonies prospered as well. Problems existed, but the system nonetheless operated very efficiently.

English mercantilism definitely evolved through expediency. No economic program can be considered immutable, and any attempt to develop one applicable to all empires of that era would have failed because of the variety of problems faced by each nation expanding outside Europe. Certain general principles were universally applicable — especially concerning the internal economy, trade monopolies, and the imperial balance of payments — but it was an era of constant change. Between 1600 and 1750, a great commercial revolution occurred. Europe's tastes and appetites were revolutionized with the appearance of confectioneries, new beverages, new clothes and furs, new dyes, new furnishings, and even tobacco. These new products reflected the kaleidoscopic changes effecting trade patterns. The English established and maintained a workable balance between their interests and those of their North American colonies, but policy makers had to accept change and innovation as they struggled to apply the general principles of mercantilism. England's rapid economic growth certainly proved the balance and innovativeness of its policies.

Between 1750 and 1763, the British Empire underwent further extraordinary expansion, and the French and Indian War severely tested its administrative organization. The world-wide struggle against the French and Spanish added new burdens and magnified unsolved problems. In the immediate postwar period, pressed by the war debt and by sharply increased costs for imperial protection and administration, the government took stock of its position. It decided to shift some of these costs to the colonials and to improve the method of revenue collection. The extent of illegal trade with the enemy during the past war and the flagrant lack of colonial cooperation had aroused the government's anger.

Thus the government moved to centralize authority and began a new and more restrictive approach to mercantilism. The Proclamation of 1763 halted westward expansion in order to permit development of a coherent program for future colonies across the

mountains. The American Revenue Act of 1764 initiated a badly
needed reform of the imperial customs service. England gave more
care to the collection of revenues and to the seizure and punishment of smugglers at home as well as abroad by ending absenteeism among customs officials and by increasing the number of
patrolling vessels. Parliament rewrote the Molasses Act of 1733
with lower and more reasonable rates. However, England laid
heavier duties on wine from the Western Islands and on other
goods, added hides, skins, potash, and logwood to the list of "enumerated" products, forbade colonial exports of iron and lumber
to European ports, and in general reduced the latitude which had
existed under the former's permissive system. Colonials, who had
always complained of the "red tape" involved in the trade controls,
had operated outside the strict letter of the law because of a relaxed attitude on the part of the customs officers. Now all voyages,
coastal as well as overseas, required bonds, search and seizure
procedures were broadly interpreted under the writs of assistance,
and expanded Vice-Admiralty court powers allowed more effective
control of illegal trade. At the same time, laws left long in abey-
ance, such as the White Pine Act protecting mast trees for the
Royal Navy, began to be literally and rigorously enforced. The
government moved also to end once and for all the inflationary
paper money issues with the Currency Act of 1764, which forbade
all further issues of paper money and threatened heavy penalties
for any governor who acquiesced in such issuance.

This legislation sharply diverged from the old mercantile system; it raised a storm of protest in America. Customs revenues
rose abruptly under the tariffs and more efficient enforcement, and
the number of condemnations for smuggling increased markedly.
Laws, honored in the breach for decades, were now so rigidly enforced that they caught up even honest merchants and seamen,
who complained bitterly against customs racketeering. The change
in policy came so abruptly that few colonials had any appreciation
of or sympathy with its aims. The government seemed intent upon
making the colonials totally subservient economically, thus making
even more difficult the bridging of the steadily increasing payments gap.

This initial legislation was extended and revised over the next
few years with an attendant integration and coordination of the
empire. In the colonials' eyes, it ended their economic equality
within the empire by destroying the traditional balance of interests. They fought these changes in a number of ways: by petition,
by harassment of customs officials, by riot, by nonimportation of

English manufactures, and finally by revolution. Shortly the real issue centered upon how much authority the mother country possessed over its colonies. Here again, the uniqueness of the heavily populated North American settlements became extremely important.

To the government, colonials were Englishmen temporarily settled in another place. As long as the number of colonials was limited and the society in which they had settled temporarily differed significantly from that at home, they tended to be more English than those in England and fiercely cherished their heritage. But when they immigrated in very large numbers, faced no threat from an alien society, and established their own replica of England in America, they did not long to return to their own country. Changed over the years by the environment and by the infusion of a large non-English population, their society and their outlook differed. Then, the conquest of Canada removed the last major threat to their well-being.

Colonials had traditionally enjoyed the same rights as Englishmen in the mother country. The contrast between the permissive program of earlier days and the new, "oppressive" system now appeared to threaten their equality as Englishmen. Certainly some actions of the government flew in the face of English constitutional precedents. Policy makers in London failed to recognize that the agriculturally-based American colonies differed markedly from the factory-type of colony. To the English, intent upon fiscal problems and efficiency and coordination, concessions indicated weakness. The colonial economy could support the proposed taxes. Protests represented treason. Despite the crushing impact of the nonimportation agreements, the English insisted upon Parliament's absolute supremacy. Failing to realize that the New World colonials had become Americans, the government insisted upon enforcing the new mercantilism and thus reaped a whirlwind.

FOR FURTHER READING

Andrews, C. M. *The Colonial Period of American History* 4 vol. New Haven: Yale University Press, 1934-1938.

Beer, G. L. *The Old Colonial System 1660-1754.* New York: Macmillan Company, 1912.

Cole, C. W. *Colbert and a Century of French Mercantilism* 2 vol. New York: Columbia University Press, 1939.

Haring, C. H. *The Spanish Empire in America.* New York: Oxford University Press, 1947.

Harper, L. A. *The English Navigation Laws.* New York: Columbia University Press, 1939.

Harper, L. A. "Mercantilism and the American Revolution," *The Era of the American Revolution* ed. by R. B. Morris. New York: Columbia University Press, 1939.

Hecksher, Eli. *Mercantilism* 2 vol. London: George Allen & Unwin Ltd., 1935.

Nettels, Curtis. "British Mercantilism and the Economic Development of the Thirteen Colonies." *Journal of Economic History* 12 (1952): 105-114.

Wilson, Charles. "Mercantilism: Some Vicissitudes of an Idea." *Economic History Review* 2nd Series, 10: 181-188, 1957.

1

An Elizabethan Sumptuary Law

Controls over the consumption of foreign goods were an obvious means of limiting the outflow of bullion. A secondary advantage of sumptuary laws was the encouragement of employment at home.

SOURCE: *Statutes, 5 Elizabeth I, c. 7.*

AN ACT AVOIDING DIVERS FOREIGN WARES MADE BY HANDICRAFTSMEN BEYOND THE SEAS

Whereas heretofore the artificers of this realm of England (as well within the city of London as within other cities, towns, and boroughs of the same realm) that is to wit, girdlers, cutlers, saddlers, glovers, point-makers, and such like handicraftsmen, have been in the said faculties greatly wrought, and greatly set on work, as well for the sustentation of themselves, their wives and families, as for a good education of a great part of the youth of this realm in good art and laudable exercise, besides the manifold benefits, that by means or by reason of their knowledges, inventions, and continual travel, daily and universally came to the whole estate of the commonwealth of this said realm:

II.   Yet notwithstanding so now it is, that by reason of the abundance of foreign wares brought into this realm from the parts of beyond the seas, the said artificers are not only less occupied, and thereby utterly impoverished, the youth not trained in the said sciences and exercises, and thereby the said faculties, and the exquisite knowledges thereof, like in short time within this realm to decay; but also divers cities and towns within this realm of England much thereby impaired, the whole realm greatly endamaged, and other countries notably enriched, and the people thereof well set on work, to their commodities and livings, in the arts and sciences aforesaid, and to the great discouragement of skilful workmen of this realm, being in very deed nothing inferior to any stranger in the faculties aforesaid.

III.   For reformation whereof, be it enacted by our sovereign lady the Queen's Highness, and by the Lords Spiritual and Temporal, and the Commons of this present parliament assembled and by the authority of the same, that no person or persons whatsoever, from or after the feast of the Nativity of St. John Baptist now next ensuing, shall bring or cause to be brought into this realm of England from the parts of beyond the seas, any girdles, harness for girdles, rapiers, daggers, knives, hilts, pummels, lockets, chapes, dagger-blades, handles, scabbards, and sheaths for knives, saddles, horse-harness, stirrups, bits, gloves, points, leather-laces or pins, being ready made or wrought in any parts of beyond the seas, to be sold, bartered or exchanged within this realm of England or Wales; upon pain to forfeit all such wares so to be brought contrary to the true meaning of this act, in whose hands soever they or any of them shall be found, or the very value thereof. This act to continue and endure to the end of the next parliament.

2

Mercantilist Concepts of the Mid-Seventeenth Century

Thomas Mun's *England's Treasure by forraign trade* was one of many early mercantilist tracts that found a wide audience in the seventeenth century. The economic management he favored contributed directly to English expansionist sentiment in this era. Here he discusses means of encouraging exports and indirectly "Shipping, Trade, Treasure, and the King's Customes."

SOURCE: Thomas Mun, *England's Treasure by forraign trade* (London: B. Blackwell, 1933), 9-12.

The revenue or stock of a Kingdom by which it is provided of forraign wares is either *Natural* or *Artificial*. The Natural wealth is so much only as can be spared from our own use and necessities to be exported unto strangers. The Artificial consists in our manufactures and industrious trading with forraign commodities, concerning which I will set down such particulars as may serve for the cause we have in hand.

1. First, although this Realm be already exceeding rich by nature, yet might it be much encreased by laying the waste grounds (which are infinite) into such employments as should no way hinder the present revenues of other manured lands, but hereby to supply our selves and prevent the importations of Hemp, Flax, Cordage, Tobacco, and divers other things which now we fetch from strangers to our great impoverishing.

2. We may likewise diminish our importations, if we would soberly

refrain from excessive consumption of forraign wares in our diet and rayment, with such often change of fashions as is used, so much the more to encrease the waste and charge; which vices at this present are more notorious amongst us than in former ages. Yet might they easily be amended by enforcing the observation of such good laws as are strictly practised in other Countries against the said excesses; where likewise by commanding their own manufactures to be used, they prevent the coming in of others, without prohibition, or offence to strangers in their mutual commerce.

3. In our exportations we must not only regard our own superfluities, but also we must consider our neighbours necessities, that so upon the wares which they cannot want, nor yet be furnished thereof elsewhere, we may (besides the vent of the Materials) gain so much of manufacture as we can, and also endeavour to sell them dear, so far forth as the high price cause not a less vent in the quantity. But the superfluity of our commodities which strangers use, and may also have the same from other Nations, or may abate their vent by the use of some such like wares from other places, and with little inconvenience; we must in this case strive to sell as cheap as possible we can, rather than to lose the utterance of such wares. - - - - For when Cloth is dear, other Nations doe presently practice clothing, and we know they want neither art nor materials to this performance. But when by cheapness we drive them from this employment, and so in time obtain our dear price again, then do they also use their former remedy. So that by these alterations we learn, that it is in vain to expect a greater revenue of our wares than their condition will afford, but rather it concerns us to apply our endeavours to the times with care and diligence to help our selves the best we may, by making our cloth and other manufactures without deceit, which will encrease their estimation and use.

4. The value of our exportations likewise may be much advanced when we perform it ourselves in our own Ships, for then we get only not the price of our wares as they are worth here, but also the Merchants gains, the charges of ensurance, and fraight to carry them beyond the seas. As for example, if the *Italian* Merchants should come hither in their own shipping to fetch our Corn, our red Herrings or the like, in this case the Kingdom should have ordinarily but 25. s. for a quarter of Wheat, and 20. s. for a barrel of red herrings, whereas if we carry these wares ourselves into *Italy* upon the said rates, it is likely that wee shall obtain fifty shillings for the first, and forty shillings for the last, which is a great difference in the utterance or vent of the Kingdoms stock. And although it is true that the commerce ought to be free to strangers to bring in and carry out at their pleasure, yet nevertheless in many places the exportation of victuals and munition are either prohibited, or at least limited to be done onely by the people and Shipping of those places where they abound.

5. The frugal expending likewise of our own natural wealth might advance much yearly to be exported unto strangers; and if in our rayment we will be prodigal, yet let this be done with our own materials and manufactures, as Cloth, Lace, Imbroderies, Cutworks, and the like, where the excess of the rich may be the employment of the poor, whose

labours notwithstanding of this kind, would be more profitable for the Commonwealth, if they were done to the use of Strangers.

6. The Fishing in his Majesties seas of *England, Scotland* and *Ireland* is our natural wealth, and would cost nothing but labour, which the *Dutch* bestow willingly, and thereby draw yearly a very great profit to themselves by serving many places of Christendom with our Fish, for which they return and supply their wants both of forraign Wares and Mony, besides the multitudes of Mariners and Shipping, which hereby are maintain'd, whereof a long discourse might be made to shew the particular manage of this important business. Our Fishing plantation likewise in *New-England, Virginia, Groenland,* the *Summer Islands* and the *New-found-land,* are of the like nature, affording much wealth and employments to maintain a great number of poor, and to encrease our decaying trade.

7. A Staple or Magazin for forraign Corn, Indico, Spices, Raw-silks, Cotton wool or any other commodity whatsoever, to be imported will encrease Shipping, Trade, Treasure, and the Kings customes, by exporting them again where need shall require, which course of Trading, hath been the chief means to raise *Venice, Genoa,* the *low-Countreys,* with some others; and for such a purpose *England* stands most commodiously, wanting nothing to this performance but our own diligence and endeavour.

3

The Navigation Act of 1660

The Navigation Acts laid down the basic principles by which the government encouraged the English carrying trade. Closing off the colonial and coastal trades from foreign shipping, and thus competition, they guaranteed that colonial staples would come direct to England and assured English dominance of the market for finished products in the overseas empire.

SOURCE: *Statutes, 12 Charles II, c. 18.*

AN ACT FOR THE ENCOURAGING AND INCREASING OF SHIPPING AND NAVIGATION

For the increase of shipping and encouragement of the navigation of this nation, wherein, under the good providence and protection of God, the wealth, safety and strength of this kingdom is so much concerned; be it enacted by the King's most excellent majesty, and by the lords and commons in this present parliament assembled, and by the authority thereof, That from and after the first day of December, [1660], and from thenceforward, no goods or commodities whatsoever shall be imported into or exported out of any lands, islands, plantations or territories to his Majesty belonging or in his possession, or which may hereafter belong unto or be in the possession of his Majesty, his heirs and successors, in *Asia, Africa* or *America,* in any other ship or ships, vessel or vessels whatsoever, but in such ships or vessels as do truly and without fraud belong only to the people of *England* or *Ireland,* dominion of *Wales* or town of *Berwick* upon *Tweed,* or are of the built of and belonging to any of the said lands, islands, plantations or territories, as the proprietors and right owners thereof, and whereof the master and three fourths of the mariners at least are *English*; under the penalty of the forfeiture and loss of all the goods and commodities which shall be imported into or exported out of any of the aforesaid places in any other ship or vessel, as also of the ship or vessel. . . .

II. And be it enacted, That no alien or person not born within the allegiance of our sovereign lord the King, his heirs and successors, or naturalized, or made a free denizen, shall from and after the first day of February 1661, exercise the trade or occupation of a merchant or factor in any the said places; upon pain of the forfeiture and loss of all his goods and chattels, . . . and all governors of the said lands, islands etc., are hereby strictly required and commanded, — by his Majesty, — shall before their entrance into their government take a solemn oath, to do their utmost, that every the afore-mentioned clauses, and all the matters and things therein contained, shall be punctually and *bona fide* observed according to the true intent and meaning thereof. . . .

III. And it is further enacted . . . , That no goods or commodities whatsoever, of the growth, production or manufacture of *Africa, Asia* or *America* or of any part thereof, or which are described or laid down in the usual maps or cards of those places, be imported into *England, Ireland* or *Wales*, islands of *Guernsey* and *Jersey*, or town of *Berwick* upon *Tweed*, in any other ship or ships, vessel or vessels whatsoever, but in such as do truly and without fraud belong only to the people of *England* or *Ireland*, dominion of *Wales*, or town of *Berwick* upon *Tweed* or of the lands, islands, plantations or territories in *Asia, Africa* or *America*, to his Majesty belonging, as the proprietors and right owners thereof, and whereof the master, and three fourths at least of the mariners are *English*; under the penalty of the forfeiture of all such goods and commodities, and of the ship or vessel in which they were imported. . . .

IV. And it is further enacted . . ., That no goods or commodities that are of foreign growth, production or manufacture, and which are to be brought into *England, Ireland, Wales,* the islands of *Guernsey* and *Jersey*, or town of *Berwick* upon *Tweed*, in *English*-built shipping or other shipping belonging to some of the aforesaid places, and navigated by *English* mariners, as aforesaid, shall be shipped or brought from any other place or places, country or countries, but only from those of the said growth, production or manufacture, or from those ports where the said goods and commodities can only, or are, or usually have been, first shipped for transportation, and from none other places or countries; under the penalty of the forfeiture of all such of the aforesaid goods as shall be imported from any other place or country contrary to the true intent and meaning hereof, as also of the ship in which they were imported, . . .

V. And it is further enacted . . ., That any sort of ling, stock-fish pilchard, or any other kind of dried or salted fish, usually fished for and caught by the people of *England, Ireland, Wales*, or town of *Berwick* upon *Tweed;* or any sort of codfish or herring, or any oil or blubber made or that shall be made of any kind of fish whatsoever, or any whale-fins or whale-bones, which shall be imported into *England, Ireland, Wales*, or town of *Berwick* upon *Tweed*, not having been caught in vessels truly and properly belonging thereunto as proprietors and right owners thereof, and the said fish cured saved and dried, and the oil and blubber aforesaid (which shall be accounted and pay as oil) not made by the people thereof, and shall be imported into *England, Ireland* or *Wales*, or town of *Berwick* upon *Tweed*, shall pay double aliens custom.

VI. And be it further enacted, . . . That from henceforth it shall not be lawful to any person or persons whatsoever, to load or cause to be loaden and carried in . . . vessel or vessels whatsoever, whereof any stranger or strangers-born (unless such as shall be denizens or naturalized) be owners, part-owners or master, and whereof three fourths of the mariners at least shall not be *English,* any fish, victual, wares, goods, commodities or things, of what kind or nature soever the same shall be, from one port or creek of *England, Ireland, Wales,* islands of *Guernsey* or *Jersey,* or town of *Berwick* upon *Tweed,* to another port or creek of the same, or of any of them; under penalty for every one that shall offend contrary to the true meaning of this branch of this present act, to forfeit all such goods shall be loaden and carried in any such ship or vessel, together with the ship or vessel, . . .

XVIII. And it is further enacted . . . That from and after the first day of April, [1661], no sugars, tobacco, cotton-wool, indicoes, ginger, fustick, or other dying wood, of the growth, production or manufacture of any *English* plantations in *America, Asia* or *Africa,* shall be shipped, carried, conveyed or transported from any of the said *English* plantations to any land . . . other than to such other *English* plantations as do belong to his Majesty. . . .

4

Encouragement for the Initiation of a Naval Stores Industry

The strength of the Royal Navy as the first line of imperial defense depended upon the availability of naval stores. The preamble to this act of Queen Anne's reign perfectly expresses what mercantilists viewed as the proper role of the colonies.

SOURCE: *Statutes, 3 & 4 Anne, c. 10.*

AN ACT FOR ENCOURAGING THE IMPORTATION OF NAVAL STORES FROM HER MAJESTY'S PLANTATIONS IN AMERICA

Whereas the Royal Navy, and the Navigation of England, wherein, under God, the Wealth, Safety and Strength of this Kingdom is so much concerned, depends on the due Supply of Stores necessary for the same, which being now brought in mostly from foreign Parts, in foreign shipping, at exorbitant and arbitrary Rates, to the great Prejudice and Discouragement of the Trade and Navigation of this Kingdom, may be

provided in a more certain and beneficial Manner from Her Majesty's
own Dominions: And whereas Her Majesty's Colonies and Plantations
in America were at first settled, and are still maintained and protected,
at a great Expence of the Treasure of this Kingdom, with a Design to
render them as useful as may be to England, and the Labour and Industry of the People there, profitable to themselves: And in Regard the said
Colonies and Plantations, by the vàst Tracts of Land therein, Lying
near the Sea, and upon navigable Rivers, may commodiously afford great
Quantities of all Sorts of Naval Stores, if due encouragement be given
for carrying on so great and advantageous an Undertaking, which will
likewise tend, not only to further Imployment and Increase of English
Shipping and Seamen, but also to the enlarging, in a great Measure, the
Trade and Vent of Woollen and other Manufactures and Commodities
of this Kingdom, and of other Her Majesty's Dominions, in exchange
for such Naval Stores, which are now purchased from foreign Countries
with Money or Bullion: and for enabling Her Majesty's Subjects, in the
said Colonies and Plantations, to continue to make due and sufficient
Returns in the Course of their Trade; Be it therefore enacted, . . .

5

Sir Joshua Gee, an Eighteenth — Century Mercantilist, 1729

Mercantilist writer and advisor to the Board of Trade, Sir
Joshua Gee praised the English system but found weaknesses
in it as well. He recognized that the plantation trades were
most lucrative but also saw that other sectors of the empire
contributed significantly to its wealth.

SOURCE: Joshua Gee, *The Trade and Navigation of Great
Britain Considered* (London, 1760, sixth edition), 113, 114-
115.

I shall therefore humbly recommend it to such gentlemen as are the
guardians of the trade of the nation, that our own interest is not mistaken for that of the planters; for every restraint and difficulty put upon
our trade with them, makes them have recourse to their own products
which they manufacture; a thing of great consequence to us, and ought

to be guarded against: for if they are supplied with their own manufactures, one great part of the advantages we should otherwise receive, is cut off; and therefore, as it is elsewhere observed, if care is taken to find them employment, and turn their industry another way, now in their infancy, it may be done with a very little trouble; and it is to be hoped, the regulations proposed in this discourse would entirely effect it. . . .

We have a great many young men who are bred to the sea, and have friends to support them; if they cannot get employment at home, they go to New-England, and the northern colonies, with a cargo of goods, which they there sell at a very great profit, and with the produce build a ship, and purchase a loading of lumber, and sail for Portugal or the Streights, etc. and after disposing of their cargoes there, frequently ply from port to port in the Mediterranean, till they have cleared so much money as will in a good part pay for the first cost of the cargo carried out by them, and then perhaps sell their ships, come home, take up another cargo from their employers, and so go back and build another ship; by this means multitudes of seamen are brought up, and upon a war the nation better provided with a greater number of sailors than hath been heretofore known, here the master becomes merchant also, and many of them gain by this lumber trade great estates, and a vast treasure is thereby yearly brought into the kingdom, in a way new and unknown to our forefathers; for indeed it is gaining the timber trade, (heretofore carried on by the Danes and Swedes) our plantations being nearer the markets of Portugal and Spain than they are, those advantages have made some people think, that tho' we esteem New-England and the northern colonies of small advantage to us; yet if things were truly stated, they are as profitable as most other of our plantations.

6

Sir John Barnard's Speech Against the Molasses Act, 1733

In this parliamentary debate, Barnard opposed monopolistic policies, emphasizing the problem overseas as one of enforcement. His ideas suggest recognition of the need to maintain a balance of interests in the empire; no one sector to be grossly favored over another.

SOURCE: William Cobbett, *Parliamentary History of England* (London, 1811), VIII (1722-1733), 1198.

That as the trade then stood between our northern colonies and the French sugar islands, it appeared, that our colonies bought molasses of them at a very low price, and distilled them into rum, by which they provided themselves at a small charge with the rum that was necessary for them in their trade with the Indians, and in their fishing trade; they had, it was true, most of the materials for making this rum from the French; but then the manufacture was all their own, and thereby a great many of our subjects in that part of the world were employed and maintained: That by laying such an high duty on French molasses, we should lay them under a necessity of manufacturing it themselves; so that our subjects would lose all that employment, and instead of buying molasses in their natural dress from the French, as they did formerly, they would be obliged to purchase the same molasses manufactured into rum, whereby the French sugar islands would take of them at least three times the money they took formerly: That as molasses was a bulky commodity, it would not be easy to run them into any of our northern colonies, so that the French would be laid under an absolutely [sic] necessity of manufacturing them into rum, and when manufactured into rum, it would be easy to carry that rum, and sell it in a smuggling way to our fishing vessels at sea, and even to run it into every one of our colonies on the continent of America: That the sea coasts belonging to us in that part of the world were of such a vast extent, and so many little harbors and creeks to be every where met with, the roads so little frequented, and the towns so open, that it would be impossible to prevent the running of French rum on shore, or the conveying it from one town to another after it is landed. No, not even if we should send thither the whole army of Excise officers which we have here at home; the sending of them thither, might indeed, add a good deal to our happiness in this country, but all of them together could be of no service for such a purpose in that country: That as to the laying a duty both on foreign rum and molasses, he would not be altogether against it, but then it ought to be only a small duty, for the sake of giving an advantage to our own sugar colonies in that respect, not such an high duty as was in a manner equal to a prohibition; for that was really granting a monopoly to our sugar islands, with respect to a commodity that is absolutely necessary for our northern colonies, both in their fishing trade and in trade with the native Indians; and as the French were our rivals likewise in both those trades, we were about giving them a certain advantage as to these trades, and that without doing them any harm as to their sugar-trade; for if they sold sugar and rum cheaper than our colonies did, they would have vend enough for all they could make; they would have a stolen market for it in the British dominions, and an open market in all other parts of the world.

7

Proclamation Concerning Seizures of Smugglers, 1763

Proper enforcement of the customs laws and collection of royal revenues became of great importance in the years immediately following the French and Indian War, because of the financial crisis faced by the empire.

SOURCE: *Pennsylvania Gazette,* October 6, 1763.

COURT AT ST. JAMES'S   JUNE 1, 1763.   PRESENT,

The King's Most Excellent MAJESTY in Council, Whereas by an Act made in the last Session of Parliament, entitled, "An Act for further Improvement of His Majesty's Revenue of Customs; and for the Encouragement of Officers making Seizures; and for the Prevention of the clandestine Running of Goods into any Part of His Majesty's Dominions," it is, amongst other Things, enacted, That for the more effectual Prevention of the infamous Practice of Smuggling, and for the better Encouragement of the Officers and Seamen of all such Ships and Vessels of War belonging to His Majesty, His Heirs, and Successors, who may be employed in preventing the clandestine Running of Goods on the

Coasts of Great-Britain and Ireland, and of the other Dominions and Colonies belonging to the Crown of Great-Britain, one Moiety of the Nett Produce arising by the Sale of Smuggling Vessels, and prohibited Goods, which shall be seized after the first Day of May, 1763, and condemned and sold according to Law (the Charges whereof being first deducted) shall be vested in the said Officers and Seamen; and His Majesty is thereby empowered to cause the same to be divided amongst the said Officers and Seamen, in such Proportions, and in such Manner, as His Majesty, His Heirs, and Successors, shall think fit to order and direct, ...

8

A Newspaper Commentary on the New Customs Controls, 1763

This selection with comment by an American newspaper editor offers an idea of the American viewpoint on English mercantilism, stressing the full use of natural advantages, without restraints.

SOURCE: *Pennsylvania Gazette,* October 27, 1763.

New York. October 20.

"We hear that His Majesty's Ships are so stationed as to keep up a Chain of Communications from one End to the other of the British Dominions in America and to keep continually cruising, so as effectually to crush the Contraband Trade."

[As all Parts of His Majesty's Dominions are equally entitled to his paternal Care, and we have Reason to think Him disposed to dispense The Blessings of a just and wise Government impartially to all His Subjects, considering them as one People, however remote their Situation from His Presence; As the Welfare, the Strength, and Security of the whole, consists in the equitable Distribution of Advantages to all Parts of the Government; and as we are characteristically a trading Nation; there can be no Doubt but that, upon a proper Representation to His Majesty and His Ministry, we shall have every just Cause of Complaint removed, and be allowed all the Advantages in Trade that we could reasonably ask; — and what can we desire more?

It is greatly to be wished that some System of Trade might be discovered, that it would be equally the Interest of all parts of the British
Dominions to adhere to; — and this seems to me to be not impracticable;
for why should we not be beneficial to each other in our trading, as well
as our social Capacities? In Society, we find our Wants and Necessities
are mutually supplied by the Superfluities of each other. — As the British
Dominions are so extensive, so different in Climate, Produce, and Manufactures, surely the Business of every Part might be so appropriated,
that each might have the full Use of their natural Advantages, without
Restraint. Prohibitions upon Trade shew a Defect in Government, and
plainly call for an Amendment; and if, instead of acting contrary to the
Laws in being, every one would exert himself to have them amended, and
made just and equitable; we might, probably, in a little Time, obtain such
a System of trading Laws, that none would have an Inclination to violate them.]

9

Excerpts from the American Revenue Act

The decision of the government to enforce the Navigation
System rigorously as a part of the "new" mercantilism is
evident in the precision of the wording of this act. Shortly
"honest traders" were complaining against the new rigid
regulation of all trade.

SOURCE: *Pennsylvania Gazette,* June 12, 1764.

British vessels with any British American goods, or foreign melasses
or syrups, discovered near the British American coasts, not producing a
certificate as required by law; or not producing one of the port of
arrival, shall be forfeited.

The bond for non-enumerated goods shall be in force for one year after
the voyage; when, if no fraud appear, it shall be given up.

Coffee, and other enumerated goods of the British American plantations, shall be imported under like securities and penalties, as those in
acts 12 and 25 Car. II.

Bond and security shall be given before lading any iron or lumber of
the British American plantations, conditioned to land the same, if for
Europe, in Great-Britain; and to produce a certificate thereof within 18
months; and if for any of the British American plantations, within 6

months; and if for any other place in America, Africa, or Asia, within 12 months. Where the goods perish, or are taken, the bond shall be discharged.

No goods shall be shipped in one British colony to be carried to another, without a sufferance, and taking out a proper cocket; which shall be produced at the port of discharge; on forfeiture of the goods. The goods shall also be forfeited, if they do not agree with the cocket. A vessel discovered near the coast shall be stopt; and the goods, for which no cocket is produced, shall be seized.

No vessel shall be cleared out for any of the British colonies in America, unless the whole cargo be shipped in this kingdom; and where any European vessel is discovered near such coasts, the goods for which no such cocket is produced, shall be seized; salt, Madeira wines, &c. horses, provisions, or linens from Ireland, excepted. The penalty on counterfeiting, &c. any affidavit, or certificate, shall be 500 £.

Foreign vessels found at anchor, or hovering on the coasts of any of the British American dominions, and not departing, unless distressed, within 48 hours after notice, shall be forfeited, together with the goods except French fishing vessels off Newfoundland.

British vessels found standing into, or coming out from the isles of St. Pierre and Miquelon, or hovering, &c. on the coasts, or with goods on board from thence, &c. shall be forfeited, together with the goods; and the master, &c. shall forfeit also treble value.

Concealed goods found on board, after report made by the master, and not comprised in his report, shall be forfeited; and the master, being privy to the fraud, shall forfeit treble the value.

If customed goods be either laden on board, or landed, before the duties are paid, or prohibited goods be imported into, or exported out of, and of the British colonies in America, the persons concerned therein shall forfeit treble the value; together with the boats, carriages, and cattle employed. An officer receiving any bribe, &c. conniving at a false entry; making a collusive seizure; or being guilty of other frauds in his office; shall forfeit 500 £, and be disabled from serving the King in any office. And persons giving, or promising any bribe, &c. to such officer, in order to betray his trust, shall forfeit 50 £.

10

Excerpt from a Letter of
Benjamin Marshall, Merchant

This Philadelphia merchant's letter demonstrates American reaction to the laws of the 1760s as well as the difficulty of meeting debt commitments.

SOURCE: "Extracts from the Letter-Book of Benjamin Marshall, 1763-1766" in *The Pennsylvania Magazine of History and Biography*, XX (1896), 208.

Philada Octr 22d 1764.

. . . Bills are very scarce here, I had a deall of trouble to persuade Reese Meredith to draw it . . . as Reese is a man of great credit I thought it might be depended on. . . . Cash Monstrous scarce (I believe we must learn to Barter) as the Men of War are here so strict that nothing can escape them . . . and so many new Acts of Parlimt lately made seems as if America would be much distressed the dreadfull Lumbr Acts if continued will I fear be of great disadvantage & help to Ruin us however I hope that on proper remonstrances the rigour will in some measure be abated or the Edge taken off. . . .

To Dr. James Tapscott.

11

The Currency Act, 1764

The government's negative view on paper money ran directly counter to the wishes of the colonials, who saw it as invaluable since it provided a medium of exchange on the local level.

SOURCE: *Pennsylvania Gazette,* July 12, 1763.

An ACT to prevent PAPER BILLS OF CREDIT, hereafter to be issued in any of His Majesty's Colonies or Plantations in America, from being declared to be a legal Tender in Payment of Money; and to prevent the legal Tender of such Bills as are now subsisting, from being prolonged beyond the Periods limited for calling in and sinking the same.

Whereas great Quantities of Paper Bills of Credit have been created and issued in His Majesty's Colonies or Plantations in America, by virtue of Acts, Orders, Resolutions, or Votes of Assembly, making and declaring such Bills of Credit to be legal Tender in Payments of Money: And whereas such Bills of Credit have greatly depreciated in their Value, by Means whereof Debts have been discharged with a much less Value than was contracted for, to the great Discouragement and Prejudice of the Trade and Commerce of His Majesty's Subjects, by occasioning Confusion in Dealings, and lessening Credit in the said Colonies or Plantations: For Remedy whereof, May it please Your most Excellent Majesty, that it may be enacted, and be it enacted by the King's most Excellent Majesty, by and with the Advice and Consent of the Lords Spiritual and Temporal, and Commons, in this present Parliament assembled, and by the Authority of the same, That from and after the First Day of September, [1764], no Act, Order, Resolution, or Vote of Assembly, in any of His Majesty's Colonies or Plantations in America, shall be made, for creating or issuing any Paper Bills, or Bills of Credit of any Kind or Denomination whatsoever, declaring such Paper Bills, or Bills of Credit, to be legal Tender in Payment of any Bargains, Contracts, Debts, Dues or Demands whatsoever; and every Clause or Provision which shall hereafter be inserted in any Act, Order, Resolution, or Vote of Assembly, contrary to this Act, shall be null and void.

And whereas the great Quantities of Paper Bills, or Bills of Credit, which are now actually in Circulation and Currency in several Colonies or Plantations in America, emitted in Pursuance of Acts of Assembly, declaring such Bills a legal Tender, make it highly expedient that the Conditions and Terms, upon which such Bills have been emitted, should not be varied or prolonged, so as to continue the legal Tender thereof beyond the Terms respectively fixed by such Acts for calling in and discharging such Bills; be it therefore enacted by the Authority aforesaid, That every Act, Order, Resolution, or Vote of Assembly, in any of the said Colonies or Plantations, which shall be made to prolong the legal Tender of any Paper Bills, or Bills of Credit, which are now subsisting and current in any of the said Colonies or Plantations in America, beyond the Times fixed for the calling in, sinking, and discharging of such Paper Bills, or Bills of Credit, shall be null and void.

And be it further enacted by the Authority aforesaid, That if any Governor or Commander in Chief for the time being, in all or any of the said Colonies or Plantations, shall, from and after the said First Day of September, 1764, give his Assent to any Act or Order of Assembly, contrary to the true Intent and Meaning of this Act, every such Governor or Commander in Chief shall, for every such Offence, forfeit and pay the Sum of One Thousand Pounds, and shall be immediately dismissed from his Government, and for ever after rendered incapable of any Public Office or Place of Trust.

12

Petition against the American
Stamp Act, 1766

Their trade badly injured by the first nonimportation
agreements, British merchants interceded on behalf of the
colonists, calling for the repeal of the Stamp Act. Self-interest was of course here expressed as well as imperial interest.

SOURCE: William Cobbett, *The Parliamentary History of
England from the Earliest Period to the Year 1803* (London:
T. C. Hansard, 1813), XVI (1765-1771), 134.

A PETITION OF THE MERCHANTS OF LONDON,
TRADING TO NORTH AMERICA.

That the petitioners have been long concerned in carrying on the trade
between this country and the British colonies on the continent of North
America; and that they have annually exported very large quantities of
British manufactures, . . . besides other articles imported from abroad,
chiefly purchased with our manufactures and with the produce of our
colonies; by all which, many thousand manufacturers, seamen, and
labourers, have been employed to the very great and increasing benefit
of this nation; and that, in return for these exports, the petitioners have
received from the colonies, rice, indico, tobacco, naval stores, oil, whale
fins, furs, and lately pot-ash, . . . besides remittances by bills of exchange
and bullion, obtained by the colonists in payment for articles of their
produce, not required for the British market, . . . and that, from the
nature of this trade, consisting of British manufactures exported, and
of the import of raw materials from America, many of them used in our
manufactures, and all of them tending to lessen our dependence on neigh-
boring states, it must be deemed of the highest importance in the commercial system of this nation; and that this commerce, so beneficial to
the state, and so necessary to the support of multitudes, now lies under
such difficulties and discouragement, that nothing less than its utter
ruin is apprehended, without the immediate interposition of parliament;
and that, in consequence of the trade between the colonies and the mother
country, as established and as permitted for many years, and of the

experience which the petitioners have had of the readiness of the Americans to make their just remittances to the utmost of their real ability, they have been induced to make and venture such large exportations of British manufactures, as to leave the colonies indebted to the merchants of Great Britain in the sum of several millions sterling; and at this time the colonists, when pressed for payment, appeal to past experience, in proof of their willingness; but declare it is not in their power, at present, to make good their engagements, alledging, that the taxes and restrictions laid upon them, and the extension of the jurisdiction of vice admiralty courts . . . have so far interrupted the usual and former most fruitful branches of their commerce, restrained the sale of their produce, thrown the state of the several provinces into confusion, and brought on so great a number of actual bankruptcies, that the former opportunities and means of remittances and payments are utterly lost and taken from them, and that the petitioners are, by these unhappy events, reduced to the necessity of applying to the House, in order to secure themselves and their families from impending ruin. . . .

ROY N. LOKKEN

The Progress of Science
in Early America

AMERICA AND MODERN SCIENCE grew up together. While Vasco da Gama, Bartolomeo Diaz, Christopher Columbus, and Fernando Magellan actively engaged in overseas discovery and exploration, scientific thought in Europe began its gradual emergence from the Aristotelian tradition of medieval scholasticism to tradition-free scientific investigation. The publication in 1543 of Nicholas Copernicus's *De Revolutionibus Orbium Caelestium* revolutionized traditional conceptions of the universe and set in motion significant discoveries in every field of physical science.

Europe's commercial expansion required developments in the practical sciences, and there were important advances in navigation and cartography by the fifteenth and sixteenth centuries. Explorations of the New World helped develop the life sciences, as Europeans studied the variety of plant and animal life and its medical and commercial value. Stimulated by observation of natural phenomena, scientific and technological changes necessarily accompanied commercial expansion and overseas exploration. Moreover, the progress of theoretical science changed conceptions of the natural universe, and eventually of the relations between man and his physical environment, man and God, and man and society.

The relationship between science and commerce in the late sixteenth century revealed itself in the activities of Thomas Hariot
(1560-1621), an English scientist who participated in Sir Walter
Raleigh's first colonizing venture at Roanoke Island in 1585. A
prominent mathematician, astronomer, and surveyor, Hariot
studied the flora and fauna of Virginia for their commercial value,
and published in 1588 a report of "marchantable commodities"
native to Virginia.

Captain John Smith (1580-1631), best known as an adventurer,
seaman, and administrator in Jamestown Colony, also studied
American plant and animal life with an eye to their commercial
value for England. Books II and IV of Smith's *The Generall His-
torie of Virginia, New England, and the Summer Isles* (1624)
discussed natural history and its possible commercial utilization.
Book IV contained a description of the exploitable natural resources of New England. In his *Advertisements for the unexperi-
enced Planters of New England* (1631), Smith advised the Puritan founders of Massachusetts Bay Colony that exploitation of
that region's natural resources would enrich the English kingdom.
Fox, beaver, marten, and other animals offered opportunities
for a lucrative trade in furs. However, the rich fishing grounds off
the New England coast impressed Smith the most. He thought that
development in New England of a fishing fleet and of salt works
for the preservation of fish would be as profitable as the Spanish
American gold mines.

Commerce, fisheries, shipbuilding, and the carrying trade were
to characterize the New England economy by the end of the seventeenth century, but the initial thrust of Puritan colonization in
New England was religious. For Puritans who sought to complete
the Protestant Reformation on American soil, theology was the
most important of all intellectual disciplines and held the key to
all knowledge. University-educated Puritan leaders, however, did
not regard their theological views as incompatible with natural
science. In the Puritan world-view science harmonized with religion and served a religious purpose. Scientific thought supported
and reinforced Christian (i.e., Puritan) assumptions about God,
the universe, and man. Harvard College, founded by the Puritans
in 1636 to prepare young men for the ministry, offered courses
during the 1640s in arithmetic, geometry, physics, astronomy,
and botany. Harvard, as time went by, became a center of scientific learning which testified to the receptivity of the New England
mind to the Scientific Revolution then taking place in Europe.

Educated New England Puritans looked upon natural phenomena as evidence of divine providence; scientific observations therefore offered a means of discovering God's purposes in the world. Puritans knew of the new European scientific discoveries and accepted them, but always with the reservation of God's sovereignty and His sometimes miraculous intervention in the natural universe to warn men of the consequences of sin. Divine miracles were always possible in the physical cosmos, and astronomical phenomena, such as comets, were studied in terms of their theological implications. Toward the late seventeenth century New England Puritan intellectuals, strongly influenced by scientific thought in Europe, believed that God operates within natural laws that are a part of His creation. God still intervenes, but without violating His own ordinances. Hence, a Puritan, such as Samuel Danforth (1626-1674), could interpret comets both as natural phenomena explainable in terms of physical causes and attributes and as divine portents of impending disaster.

Aside from their providential interpretation of natural phenomena, seventeenth-century New England Puritans accepted, or at least tolerated, scientific ideas more readily than did ecclesiastical authorities in Europe. Many New England Puritans accepted the Copernican system, which had the earth rotating about the sun rather than retaining its traditional, honored position at the center of the Ptolemaic universe. The struggle between modern science and Catholic and Protestant churches and clergymen in Europe was not duplicated on American soil. In 1633 the Inquisition condemned Galileo Galilei for his acceptance of Copernicus's heliocentricism; New England almanacs after 1659 propagated the new astronomy, to which Galileo made significant contributions. Not all Puritan clergymen approved of the Copernican system, but none prohibited it. By 1659, to be sure, opposition in Europe to the new astronomy was declining. Nevertheless, the intellectual climate in America from the beginning favored the Scientific Revolution.

During the course of the seventeenth century a mechanistic conception of the universe, expressed in geometrico-mathematical language, developed in the works of René Descartes (1569-1650), Galileo Galilei (1564-1642), and Pierre Gassendi (1592-1655), and culminated in the *Principia Mathematica* of Sir Isaac Newton (1642-1727), first published in 1687. Newton's *magnum opus* interpreted the physical universe as a great machine, or clockwork, which functioned in accordance with mathematically described natural laws. Newton's work marked the culmination of the Scientific Revolution which had begun with Copernicus in 1543, and it dominated scientific thought during the eighteenth century in both Europe and America. Moreover, it exerted a profound influence on almost every area of eighteenth-century knowledge and thought.

Colonial intellectuals favorably received Newton's cosmology from the beginning. Indeed, Newton based his *Principia* in some small part on observations of the comet of 1680 by Thomas Brattle (1658-1713) in Massachusetts. Brattle's observations of a comet moving in an elliptical orbit around the sun helped Newton in his mathematical formulation of the law of gravitation — essential to his cosmological scheme. Mathematics is the most logical, the most rational of intellectual disciplines, and Newton's cosmology based on mathematical principles enthroned Reason as the mistress of the eighteenth-century universe. The very neatness and orderliness of Newton's rational cosmos appealed to the colonial mind, as indeed it appealed to the European mind.

A rational cosmos appealed to Cotton Mather (1663-1728), a powerful orthodox New England Puritan divine. Newtonian cosmology figures largely in Mather's *The Christian Philosopher,* a compendium of scientific knowledge published in 1721, although Newton was only one of many authorities cited in that work. *The Christian Philosopher,* however, contained no evidence that Mather had a working knowledge of Newton's mathematics; indeed evidence suggests that although Mather enthusiastically received the new science he did not fully understand it. What appealed to Mather was the harmonious, orderly, and rational nature of God's creation in Newton's cosmology. Mather articulately represented a transitional period in colonial thought; he looked forward, in some respects, to the approaching Enlightenment and, at the same time, backward to the revealed religion of John Winthrop's Bible Commonwealth, not to mention an older belief in magic and demonology. For Mather, Newton's science was another revelation of the glories of God. Mather accepted Newton's law of gravitation with all its mechanistic implications, but he did so without sacrificing any of his theological preconceptions. Newton had left unanswered the question: what causes gravitation? What causes the moon, held in orbit by the earth's gravitational pull, to rotate about the earth? What causes the planets, held in their orbits by solar gravity, to move about the sun? English scientists such as Edmund Halley provided Mather with the answer; the cause of gravitation would have to be determined religiously because science provided no answer. God was the Prime Mover.

The trend, however, was toward the secularization of science. Increasingly God receded into the background. In Cotton Mather's *The Christian Philosopher*, scientific discussion was accompanied by repeated expressions of religious piety. Such expressions seldom appeared, if at all, in the scientific writings of eighteenth-century colonial intellectuals. God might still be the Prime Mover, but that was not a subject for scientific discussion. Scientists only concerned themselves with events in the natural universe, and sought natural causes of natural phenomena. They could still believe that scientific observations revealed the wonders of God's creation, but they made little of that in their writings. James Logan (1674-1751), a devout, although independent, Philadelphia Quaker, did not mention God in his published work on the refraction of light and optics. Cadwallader Colden (1688-1776), in his unsuccessful attempt to find the cause of gravitation, denied God's role as Prime Mover and denied His relevance to the problem. Science had long been regarded as a branch of philosophy, and the eighteenth century still referred to physical science as natural philosophy, but philosophy as a study of abstract principles and the nature and being of God was becoming a separate intellectual discipline. Scientists, although they still sometimes speculated on philosophical implications of scientific discoveries, tended increasingly to avoid strictly philosophical questions.

Newtonian cosmology and the secularization of science significantly determined the character of scientific activity in eighteenth-century Anglo-America. Also significant in stimulating scientific work in the English colonies was the organization of the Royal Society of London in 1662. The institutionalization of the sciences and the periodical publication by the Royal Society of the *Philosophical Transactions* encouraged colonial intellectuals to contribute to the expanding frontiers of modern science, and some of them were elected Fellows of the Royal Society. The first colonist accorded the honor of appending the letters F.R.S. to his name was John Winthrop, Jr. (1606-1676), son of the founding father of Massachusetts Bay Colony and for a time governor of Connecticut. By 1783 thirty-three American Fellows had been elected, among them Cotton Mather, Professor John Winthrop (1714-1779) of Harvard, Dr. John Mitchell (1690?-1768) of Virginia, and Benjamin Franklin. Moreover, many more colonial correspondents to the Royal Society of London were not elected members, and their contributions to the *Philosophical Transactions* included observations of such natural phenomena as earthquakes, lightning and thunderstorms, atmospheric refraction, fruit trees, rattlesnakes, and comets. The Royal Society actively promoted scientific observation and experimentation in the colonies, and assisted colonial scientists with money, books, and scientific instruments when necessary.

The English colonies had few professional scientists, and they were either college professors or physicians. In 1727 Thomas Hollis (1659-1731), a London merchant, established an endowed chair at Harvard in mathematics and natural philosophy. Isaac Greenwood (1702-1745) assumed the Hollis chair in 1728, but made no important original contribution to science; he did promote the study of mathematics and Newtonian science in his teaching. After his death in 1745, John Winthrop succeeded in the Hollis chair, which he held until 1779, and he acquired an international reputation as a productive scholar. During the course of the eighteenth century other colonial colleges — Yale, College of New Jersey, King's College, College of Philadelphia, College of Rhode Island, and the College of William and Mary — installed science curricula and professorships. Thomas Clap (1703-1767), Rector of Yale College, promoted Newtonian science at that school. His reports to the Royal Society of London on his observations of comets, however, revealed him as having less stature as a scientist than Winthrop. More comparable to Winthrop was Dr. William Small, science professor at William and Mary between 1758 and 1764. Small aroused enthusiasm for the sciences during his tenure, but his contributions to scientific knowledge came after he returned to England in 1764.

Among the physicians were Cadwallader Colden and Dr. Alexander Garden (1730-1791), both Scotsmen who had studied medicine at the University of Edinburgh before migrating to America. Although primarily interested in pharmacopoeia, botany, and medicine, some of the physicians — Colden and Dr. John Mitchell, for example — tried to make contributions in other fields of science, such as mathematics, physics, and chemistry, in which they were amateurs.

The amateur in the colonies played an important role in the scientific activities of the eighteenth century despite increasing professionalism in European science. The late seventeenth-century New England scientific community, although few in numbers, consisted mostly of amateurs. The middle and southern colonies for the most part got off to a later start; settlers in those areas first had to conquer the wilderness, build farms and towns, create political institutions and a viable social order, and develop a thriving economy. By the 1730s, however, the problems of colony-building had been pretty well worked out, and men acquired sufficient leisure time and affluence to undertake scientific research. For such amateurs as James Logan, Benjamin Franklin, and Cadwallader Colden, scientific observation and experimentation were an "amusement," a recreation that put their leisure time to productive use.

The principal scientific communities were in the urban centers of Philadelphia, New York, Boston, Williamsburg, and Charleston, where merchants, lawyers, physicians, clergymen, and public officials actively participated in science in the last four and one-half decades before Independence. Transatlantic commerce provided a means of communication between scientific intellectuals, both amateur and professional, of the New and Old Worlds. Moreover, intercolonial trade, improved roads, and a dependable intercolonial postal service facilitated correspondence between scientists of different colonies.

Colonial amateurs and physicians were important figures in an international natural history circle — an informal group of naturalists in Europe and America who exchanged ideas, data, and botanical specimens. The eighteenth century was not only the age of Newton, but the age of botany. Interest in natural history had been stimulated very early in the European explorations of the Americas by the discovery of new species of plant and animal life. The story actually began with Gonzalo Fernandez de Oviedo y Valdes (1478-1557) who, as overseer of the mines at Hispaniola, wrote a *Natural History of the West Indies* (1526) for the King of Spain, and it continued through both Hispano-American and Anglo-American history. In the late sixteenth and early seventeenth centuries the English studied plant and animal life of North America for their commercial value. By the eighteenth century, however, the emphasis had shifted to the expansion of scientific knowledge and the classification of species of plant life. Carolus Linnaeus (1707-1778), the Swedish botanist, developed a system of classifying plant life, and colonial naturalists supplied him with data and specimens which helped him to complete his work. Linnaeus's *Systema naturae* appeared in 1735, and it was further developed after that year.

The international natural history circle actually began before Linnaeus. James Petiver (1663-1718), an English apothecary, promoted natural history collecting throughout the world in the early 1700s. Petiver came into contact with scientific intellectuals in Anglo-America through William Byrd of Westover, to whom he had been introduced by English botanists, and he also had correspondents in the Carolinas, among them John Lawson (d. 1711). The international natural history circle began with Petiver and his group, and it expanded after his death. Better known than Petiver as central figures in the circle were Peter Collinson (1694-1768), a Quaker merchant of London and a great collector of botanical specimens during the period, and John Frederick Gronovius (1690-1760), the Dutch botanist and collector. Both Collinson and Gronovius maintained an active communication with colonial scientists, and through that circle Linnaeus acquired plant specimens and information necessary to complete his work.

The international natural history circle — with participants in Germany, Italy, France, Sweden, and Holland, as well as in England and its colonies — gave powerful stimulus to the advancement of science in the eighteenth century. Such cooperation not only transcended political boundaries, but brought American scientists into closer relationship with those in Europe. Most colonial correspondents, such as Dr. Alexander Garden and Cadwallader Colden, were collectors of plant species, many of which did not exist in Europe. Collecting necessarily preceded classification, and American collectors sent seeds, dried specimens, and descriptions of plant life to Collinson, Gronovius, and sometimes directly to Linnaeus.

The most important collectors, however, were not physicians. John Bartram (1699-1777), a small farmer and a Pennsylvania Quaker, had had a meager boyhood education. Ambitious to learn the new botany, he attracted the attention of the wealthy Philadelphia merchant, James Logan, who was in touch with, although not a direct participant in, the natural history circle, and who loaned Bartram books on botany and taught him the Linnaean system of classification. He also brought Bartram into contact with Linnaeus and with Peter Collinson. A man of limited means, Bartram obtained financial assistance from English gentlemen-farmers and the king and, for a time, from the Pennsylvania government so that he could devote full time to collecting; both Collinson and Benjamin Franklin aided him in procuring such financing. Bartram traveled extensively along the Atlantic coast, primarily in the South, collecting specimens and writing observations not only of plant life but of all wild life and natural phenomena. When his son William (1739-1823) grew up, father and son traveled together, and after the father died in 1777 William continued the work.

Collinson brought John Bartram into contact with other Anglo-American naturalists, among them John Clayton of Virginia (1694-1773). Clayton, a well-to-do planter, also contributed to the natural history circle by collecting and sending dried specimens to European botanists, and by describing North American plant life. Gronovius published the results of Clayton's labors in 1739, 1743, and 1762 as the *Flora Virginica*.

Colonial naturalists did not limit themselves entirely to collecting. Some experimented. In a 1716 letter to James Petiver, Cotton Mather reported experiments in plant hybridization undertaken near Boston and later described them in his *The Christian Philosopher*. However, James Logan performed perhaps the most famous botanical experiment in the British colonies. Logan experimented with Indian corn (or maize) to determine the process of plant reproduction, and he proved the role of wind pollination in the sexual generation of maize, and, by implication, of all plant life. The idea that wind-blown semen fertilizes the female ova in plants had been suggested earlier by Marcello Malpighi (1628-1694), an Italian botanist and anatomist, by Nehemiah Grew (1641-1721), an English botanist, and by Rudolph Jacob Camerarius (1665-1721), a German botanist, but Logan described the process in detail. Logan's report of his experiment was published in the *Philosophical Transactions* of the Royal Society in 1735. Gronovius published his longer account in Latin in 1739. By mid-century it was cited as an authority in botanical literature in both Anglo-America and Europe.

The correspondents in the natural history circle also contributed to the advancement of other sciences. Collinson, primarily an amateur botanist, was interested in all the sciences, and promoted scientific work outside the scope of natural history. Through his gifts of books and apparatus in 1746 and 1747, he encouraged Benjamin Franklin to undertake electrical experiments. European interest in electricity went back to William Gilbert (1540-1603) whose book, *De Magnete* (1600), introduced the subject, but electrical science really began with Francis Hauksbee (d. about 1713) who demonstrated in 1709 the relationship between light and electricity. Others contributed to the science, notably Charles Francois

de Cisternay du Fay (1698-1739), a French chemist, Sir William
Watson (1715-1787), an English physician and naturalist whose
electrical experiments greatly influenced Franklin, and Jean
Theophile Desaguliers (1683-1744), Curator of the Royal Society
of London. Lectures on electrical science became popular in
Europe, and that popularity spread to Anglo-America in the
1740s. Professor John Winthrop at Harvard lectured on the subject in 1746. Colonial amateurs in New England and New York
experimented with electricity at the same time that Franklin
began his own work.

Franklin approached the study of electricity through his reading of Newton's *Optics* (1704) and the contemporary works of
European electrical scientists, especially Watson. Franklin's experiments were in harmony with scientific thought in Europe.
Du Fay, in his experiments, had concluded that there were two
kinds of electricity — vitreous electricity produced by rubbing
glass with silk and resinous electricity produced by rubbing resin
with wool and fur. Franklin confirmed du Fay's finding that unlike
kinds of electricity attract each other and that like kinds repel
each other, and he renamed the two kinds of electricity positive
and negative. Franklin applied this theory to explain the Leiden
jar that had been invented independently in 1745 by Pieter van
Musschenbroek in Leiden and E. G. von Kleist in Pomerania, and
he went on to invent an electrical battery. Franklin's most important discovery was the identity of lightning and electricity; his
published reports of his experiments, including the kite experiment, and his invention of the lightning rod made him the most
notable American scientist of his time. However, Franklin could
find no practical use for electricity; the lightning rod only protected buildings from fires caused by lightning, and his electrical
battery was little more than an amusing toy. Franklin's major
contribution, in his electrical experiments, was in basic science.

Colonial science reached the peak of achievement in the mid-
eighteenth century, not only in Franklin's electrical experiments
but in astronomy. Astronomy had attracted colonial scientists,
both amateur and professional, ever since the seventeenth century,
partly because of the Copernican theory and the significant discoveries of Galileo, Johan Kepler, Edmund Halley, and other European astronomers, partly because of the Newtonian cosmology,
and partly because of the practical considerations involved for
navigation and surveying. Anglo-American scientists, for the most
part, focused on problems of positional astronomy, solar eclipses,

comets, motions of the moon, and the determination of the longitude and latitude of places on the earth's surface. Determining motions of the moon, an important concept in the eighteenth century, involved the navigational problem of determining longitude at sea.

The determination of longitude had puzzled European astronomers as early as Galileo. Charles II had erected the Greenwich Observatory to find a practicable solution. Newton suggested that a table of the moon's motions would provide a sort of astronomical clock useful in accurately determining longitude at sea. Subsequently John Flamsteed (1646-1742), England's first Astronomer Royal, and Edmund Halley (1656-1742) who succeeded him in 1719, worked on lunar theory. Halley compiled a set of lunar tables in 1719 which, although printed at that time, were not publicly available until 1749. James Logan, who obtained Halley's tables from a London bookseller, checked them against his own observations of the moon's motions and prepared a critical analysis of Halley's work in Latin. Although Logan's "Calculus motus lunae ex his tabulis halleianis" was never published (the manuscript is in the Library Company of Philadelphia), it greatly enriched Halley's tables.

The invention of the octant, or Hadley's quadrant, contributed to the solution of this problem of positional astronomy. This quadrant with reflecting specula was invented several months apart in 1730 by John Hadley (1682-1744), a professional astronomer in England, and Thomas Godfrey (1704-1749), a common glazier in Philadelphia whose scientific interest had attracted James Logan's attention. Godfrey and Hadley, who did not know each other, had worked independently, and the question of priority of invention was for a time controversial. The British government rewarded both for their services to navigation, but the instrument was known by Hadley's name. Hadley's quadrant, or octant, eventually became the present-day sextant.

Eighteenth-century English and Anglo-American astronomers concerned themselves not only with determining longitude, but also with measuring the size of the solar system. The solution of this problem involved finding the accurate value of the solar parallax (i.e., a measure of the distance between the earth and the sun determined by triangulation). The astronomer could not observe the sun, because of its brightness, against the background of stars so as to determine its parallax. Therefore its parallax had to be determined indirectly through observations of other celestial bodies, preferably a planet in transit between sun and earth. Observations at different points on the earth's surface of the apparent position of the planet gave the angle or the parallax. Knowledge of the angle and of the distance between the points of observation provided a triangle, and by simple geometry one could determine the distance from earth to sun. Of course, the number of variable factors involved made the problem complex. Therefore, observations at various points would yield a variety of measurements and allow determination of the average value of the solar parallax.

During the seventeenth century, French astronomers had arrived at a wide variety of estimates of the solar parallax. In 1676 Edmund Halley, then twenty years old, sailed to the island of St. Helena to observe the position of stars in the Southern Hemisphere. There he also observed the transit of Mercury, but such a brief transit did not allow the observer time enough to make reasonable calculations. However, the experience gave Halley the idea that observations of the transit of Venus might prove very useful, since that transit lasted several hours, as against a few minutes taken by the Mercury transit. In 1716 Halley published an explanation of his theory in the *Philosophical Transactions,* and it aroused widespread discussion on both sides of the ocean. However, no transit of Venus would occur until 1761; another would take place in 1769, and then not again for 105 years. Halley knew that he would not live to make observations in 1761, but he urged astronomers to make advance preparations for the benefit of those who would use the 1761 and 1769 transits of Venus in estimating the solar parallax.

In 1761 European astronomers observed the transit of Venus at various points in South Africa, Siberia, and the East Indies, but their calculations of the solar parallax were inconclusive. The transit could not be observed in most of North America, but Professor John Winthrop of Harvard voyaged to Newfoundland where he viewed the phenomenon, and he provided the learned world with the only recorded American observations of the 1761 transit of Venus. In his *Relation of a Voyage from Boston to Newfoundland, for the Observation of the Transit of Venus,* Winthrop expressed confidence that better observations in 1769 would accurately determine not only the solar parallax, but the quantity of matter in the earth and the longitude of places on the earth's surface. Moreover, he believed that such observations would also validate the Copernican theory, the solar system's size, variations in the sun's magnitude, and the velocity of light in space. Such expressions of confidence, however, proved somewhat premature.

Colonial American astronomers, amateurs and professionals alike, evinced great enthusiasm for observing the 1769 transit of Venus. Accounts of the observations made in all the British North American colonies and other parts of the world were published in the *Philosophical Transactions*. The imperial crisis and the rising spirit of American patriotism may partially explain the eagerness of colonial scientists to prove their ability in competition with their English and European colleagues. Local organizations and some colonial assemblies cooperated in financing and procuring the necessary equipment for the observations. However, most amateur astronomers proved their incompetence by their carelessness in calculating the latitude of the point of observation and the distance between points of observation and in clocking exactly to the second the time of transit. Professor Winthrop wrote the best American account, but other valuable ones were prepared by David Rittenhouse (1732-1796), a Philadelphia clock-maker and self-taught amateur astronomer, and Rev. William Smith (1727-1803), Provost of the College of Philadelphia. Comparison of American observations with European ones revealed a myriad of different values of the solar parallax. The calculations of Rittenhouse and Smith at Norriton near Philadelphia, when compared with those made at Greenwich Observatory, resulted in a mean value of 8.805", and that yielded a distance of about 94 million miles, close to the internationally accepted figure today. The experience of 1769 proved the necessity of international cooperation among scientists in observations of this type, as Smith acknowledged in his report.

On the eve of the War of Independence, science in colonial America appeared to be coming of age and it started to become institutionalized. The first intercolonial scientific society – the American Philosophical Society – had appeared in 1743, but inadequate support and patronage led to its early demise. The imperial crises after 1765 resulted in the appearance of several scientific organizations with a utilitarian emphasis. Nonconsumption as a method of opposing the Sugar, Stamp, and Townshend acts necessarily involved the promotion of colonial manufacturing. The disruption of imperial trade relations required agricultural improvements to maintain the most important sector of the colonial economy at a reasonably prosperous level. In 1764, the Society for the Promotion of Arts, Agriculture, and Economy, in the Province of New York (New York Society of Arts) was organized; in 1766, the American Society held at Philadelphia for Promoting and Propagating Useful Knowledge was founded.

Such societies, of course, followed scientific trends in Europe, which were as much characterized by Sir Francis Bacon's emphasis on practical applications to benefit society as by the quest for scientific truth. The model for American societies was the Society Established at London for the Encouragement of Arts, Manufactures, and Commerce (London Society of Arts), which awarded premiums for new inventions, improved techniques, and production of certain commodities. Some Americans, including Benjamin Franklin, were members of the London Society of Arts, and it awarded premiums to Americans for contributions to applied science and agriculture. The New York Society cooperated with its London counterpart, but the New York Society's promotion of the manufacture of linen cloth, clearly at variance with English interests, indicated the patriotic motivations of applied science in Anglo-America. The New York Society of Arts was most successful during the Stamp and Townshend acts crises, but did not survive.

In 1767 the revived American Philosophical Society merged with the American Society as the American Philosophical Society, held at Philadelphia, for Promoting Useful Knowledge, a name adopted in January 1769. This society combined theoretical and applied science, but increasingly emphasized useful knowledge. Its first *Transactions,* published as an appendix to the *American Magazine or General Repository,* reflected the emphasis on useful knowledge, especially in agriculture. In 1771 the society published a quarto volume of *Transactions,* divided into four sections. One section devoted to American observations of the 1769 transit of Venus provided the most complete account of American observations. The other three sections emphasized the utilitarian aspects of agriculture, medicine, and inventions. No other volume of the *Transactions* was published until 1786.

Applied science in eighteenth-century thought included technology, and colonial societies of useful knowledge promoted technological progress. Colonists utilized technologies of European origin. European farmers and artisans settling in the colonies brought with them their skills, and sometimes their tools, although different environmental conditions often required improvisation and modification of European techniques. For example, an immediate problem in American farming during the colonial period was felling timber to clear the land. The European axe was too heavy and awkward, and colonial craftsmen developed an axe with a better balanced handle and a thinner, sharper, and broader blade — the broadaxe. Colonial craftsmen also developed improved mattocks and plows to cope with agricultural conditions for which Old World farm tools were not suited. In most cases, however, American farmers made their own tools, roughly and crudely. In other aspects of agricultural technology colonial farmers often modified European farming methods to suit American conditions. England's intensive farming techniques were not practicable in the colonies where the abundance of land led to extensive farming. Regardless of improvisation and innovation in agricultural technology, American farming on the eve of the Revolution badly needed improvement. Scientific farming, then in development in England, did not exist in the colonies, but societies of useful knowledge and the author of *American Husbandry* (1775) urged the colonists to adopt scientific farming and improved agricultural technology.

The colonial American economy on the eve of the Revolution also needed improvements in industrial technology. Skilled craftsmen in colonial towns had brought manufacturing technologies from Europe, and, working in shop and home, they made shoes, rope, furniture, clocks, and other goods in limited quantity for local markets. The English mercantilistic system imposed severe restrictions on colonial manufacturing, for the mother country viewed the colonies primarily as a source of raw materials and agricultural products which should not compete with English industry in the world market. But the English government encouraged some colonial manufacturing, especially the production of naval stores and shipbuilding. Unfortunately the story of the transfer of European technologies to Anglo-America has never been fully told, but shipbuilding technology was derived from England with some modifications and with one Anglo-American invention — the schooner. The commercial emphasis in the colonial economy and the involvement of New Englanders in the carrying trade as early as the seventeenth century, led to a well-developed shipbuilding industry by 1775, particularly in the New England and middle colonies.

Iron manufacturing also developed rapidly, especially in Pennsylvania, in mid-eighteenth century — so rapidly that iron manufacturers in England, fearful of American competition, persuaded Parliament to pass the Iron Act of 1750, which limited colonial

iron manufacturing to the production of bar iron. The law, however, was not effectively enforced, and the manufacture of iron
axes, shovels, guns, and other tools continued unabated in the
eighteenth-century colonies. Americans derived their iron manufacturing technology from England with some local modifications.
Blast furnaces in Pennsylvania were modeled upon those in England, but larger in size. By 1775 iron manufacturing in America
appeared to have a good future, and with further improvements
would become of central importance in future American industrial development.

Americans faced a more serious problem on the eve of the Revolution in the inadequacy of colonial textile technology. Americans
had a textile technology after the early seventeenth century, but
it was derivative and undeveloped. When they imported English
textile technology, they used the simple tools of cloth manufacture
— spinning wheels, hand cards, brushes, combs, and looms — in
their homes. Their widespread manufacture of homespun provided a primitive clothing in comparison to the better quality
cloth then manufactured in English shops. The wearing of homespun after 1765 became a symbol of American patriotism, but
Americans knew that they needed improvements in textile technology so that they could manufacture woolen and linen goods for
an expanding market. Although encouraged by societies of useful
knowledge before 1775, such improvements did not come until well
after independence.

Inland transportation technology also needed improvement.
The rivers were the highways of North America, and river-craft
appeared early in colonial history. The flatboat, invented about
1750 by Jacob Yoder, a German settler, served as the principal
means of inland water cargo transportation at the time of the
Revolution, although Indian canoes and rafts were also used. The
application of steam power technology, being developed in England by Thomas Newcomen and James Watt, to inland water
transportation after the war would solve a major American
problem.

Basic science did not contribute much to technology during the
colonial period. Settlers in the British colonies brought with them
European techniques and tools and modified them, when necessary, to suit peculiarly American environmental conditions. Invention resulted from trial and error rather than scientific theory.
To be sure, Benjamin Franklin's lightning rod and Pennsylvania
fireplace were based on theoretical science, but most colonial in-

ventors did not have Franklin's scientific knowledge. On the eve of the Revolution, colonial societies of useful knowledge actively urged placing technology on a scientific basis.

In mid-eighteenth century, medicine was recognized as a science, and colonial physicians and surgeons, trained in European universities, sought to raise the standards of medical practice and to establish medical schools in America. They recognized the need to regulate medical practice by law, and to reduce the number of untrained practitioners of the medical arts. In 1765 and 1766 professional physicians and surgeons, imbued with the patriotic ardor of the time, organized medical societies in Boston, Philadelphia, and New Jersey to regulate the medical profession and to exclude unqualified practitioners and mountebanks. Generally, such medical societies failed, because they could not get charters from colonial legislatures nor could they get public support. Colonial laymen, failing to understand the difference between a trained medical scientist and a quack, opposed any attempt by the medical profession to establish its own standards and fee schedules. Of the prewar medical societies, only the Medical Society of New Jersey had any success. Although long unchartered, it established rules for its members and to that extent regulated New Jersey's medical profession. Its attempt to establish a fee schedule failed, however, because of public hostility.

In their efforts to place Anglo-American medicine on a scientific basis, colonial physicians and surgeons had greater success in establishing medical schools and hospitals. Successful medical schools were created in Philadelphia in 1766 and in New York in 1767. Philadelphia, a logical place for medical education, already had a fine hospital and a good medical library. Construction of a hospital in New York facilitated development of a medical school there. By 1773 Virginia had a mental hospital.

By 1775, when the colonies were on the verge of war with Britain, colonial intellectual leaders sanguinely viewed the future of science, technology, and the arts in America. Europe seemed to them corrupted by monarchical tyranny and aristocratic luxury, and such a decadent environment seemed unlikely to encourage the sciences. American scientist-patriots acknowledged their indebtedness to past cooperation with European scientists, and they had no quarrel with scientists in England. However, they thought that the American environment would be more conducive to scientific progress as long as Americans avoided the evils that corrupted Europe. Further cooperation with European scientists, as

David Rittenhouse believed, would only result in the decline of science in America. The corrupting influence of luxury, imported from Europe, already plagued colonial urban society. With luxury appeared what Dr. Benjamin Rush (1745-1813) called "British diseases" – nervous fever, consumption, and hypochondriac disorders. The exclusion of such contaminating European influences appeared essential to American progress.

American scientist-patriots had no doubt about such progress. Rittenhouse prophesied astronomical discoveries in America that would not be possible in Europe. Other prophets of American glory stressed improvements in transportation and agriculture. Local movements developed to promote manufacturing technology, although some patriots, such as Dr. Rush, opposed the development of industrialism as possibly corrupting. But even Dr. Rush became almost speechless as he contemplated the American future. The men of the American Revolution were as committed to the pursuit of science in the new nation as they were to republican political institutions.

The War of Independence temporarily interrupted scientific activities. It disrupted city life, as the British and Americans alternately occupied urban areas. Armies often converted colleges into army hospitals. The war split scientific societies into loyalist and patriot factions. Men of learning for a time concentrated on military and governmental affairs, and scientific activity became war-oriented – military medicine, munitions manufacture, and military engineering.

The trend toward cultural nationalism, which had been evident between the Stamp Act crisis and the fighting at Lexington, became more pronounced after 1783. But optimistic prophecies of the flowering of science and technology in a free republic had been premature. The new nation did not have adequate college programs and facilities for science education, Americans were deficient in mathematics, the foundation of modern physical science, and their libraries, museums, and philosophical societies were inferior to those in Europe. Organizational work continued. The American Academy of Arts and Sciences was organized in Boston in 1780, and more local societies appeared to encourage technological development and agricultural improvement. Scientific achievement, however, fell below American expectations.

The most important developments in the sciences and technology continued to take place in Europe, and Americans would still learn much from the Old World. Americans emphasized "useful knowledge" and thereby retarded the progress of basic science; they separated basic science and technology in their minds and thereby also retarded technology's progress. A century would elapse after Benjamin Franklin's electrical experiments before another American, Josiah Willard Gibbs, would make a significant contribution to basic science. During that century Americans would make important contributions in natural history, especially after the Louisiana Purchase in 1803, and would engage in considerable astronomical activity. In the long run, however, American scientific progress would depend on increased private patronage, government aid, improvement of collegiate science faculties and curricula, and the stimulus of scientific discoveries in Europe. Nevertheless, the men of the American Revolution had expressed their faith that science would flourish in the new nation. The future would justify their faith.

FOR FURTHER READING

For a solid understanding of the history of early American science and technology the student should acquaint himself with background developments in Europe. The following list begins with several readable and important books on the history of science which should be available in any college library. Following them is a list of recommended books on the history of early American science and technology. Those books which are available in paperback are indicated by the letters "pb."

Crombie, A. C. *Medieval and Early Modern Science,* 2 vols. Garden City, N. Y.: Doubleday, 1959. pb

Dijksterhuis, E. J. *The Mechanization of the World Picture,* translated from the Dutch by C. Dijkshoorn. New York: Oxford University Press, 1961. pb

Hall, A. R. *The Scientific Revolution, 1500-1800: The Formation of the Modern Scientific Attitude.* Boston: Beacon Press, 1954. pb

————. *From Galileo to Newton. (The Rise of Modern Science.)* New York: Harper, 1962.

Singer, Charles, and others. *History of Technology,* 5 vols. Oxford: Clarendon Press, 1954 —.

Bell, Whitfield J. *Early American Science: Needs and Opportunities for Study.* Williamsburg, Va.: Institute of Early American History and Culture, 1955.

Berkeley, Edmund and Dorothy Smith Berkeley. *John Clayton: Pioneer of American Botany.* Chapel Hill: University of North Carolina, 1963.

Cohen, I. Bernard. *Benjamin Franklin's Experiments.* Cambridge: Harvard University Press, 1941.

————. *Some Early Tools of American Science.* Cambridge: Harvard University Press, 1950.

————. *Franklin and Newton*. Philadelphia: American Philosophical Society, 1956.

Hindle, Brooke. *The Pursuit of Science in Revolutionary America, 1735-1789*. Chapel Hill: The University of North Carolina Press; for the Institute of Early American History and Culture, 1956. pb

————. *Technology in Early America: Needs and Opportunities for Study*. Chapel Hill: Published for the Institute of Early American History and Culture at Williamsburg, Va. by the University of North Carolina Press, 1966.

Hornberger, Theodore. *Scientific Thought in the American Colleges, 1638-1800*. Austin, Texas: University of Texas Press, 1945.

Oliver, John W. *History of American Technology*. New York: Ronald Press, 1956.

Stearns, Raymond P. *Science in the British Colonies in America*. Urbana: University of Illinois Press, 1970.

1

Of Gravity

SOURCE: Cotton Mather, *The Christian Philosopher: A Collection of the Best Discoveries in Nature, with Religious Improvements* (Gainesville, Fla.: Scholars' Facsimiles & Reprints, 1968).

To our Globe there is one Property so exceedingly and so generally subservient, that a very great Notice is due to it; that is, GRAVITY, or the Tendency of Bodies to the *Center*.

A most noble Contrivance (as Mr. *Derham* observes) to keep the several Globes of the Universe from shattering to pieces, as they would else evidently do in a little Time, thro their swift Rotation round their own *Axes*. Our *Globe* in particular, which revolves at the rate of above a thousand Miles an Hour, would, by the centrifugal Force of that Motion, be soon dissipated, and spirtled into the circumambient Space, were it not kept well together by this wondrous Contrivance of the Creator, *Gravity*, or the *Power of Attraction*. By this Power also all the Parts of the *Globe* are kept in their proper Place and Order; all Bodies gravitating thereto do unite themselves with, and preserve the Bulk of them entire; and the fleeting Waters are kept in their constant AEquipoise, remaining in the *Place which God has founded for them, a Bound which He hath set, that they may not pass, that they turn not again to cover the Earth.* It is by the virtue of this glorious Contrivance of the *great God, who formed all Things,* that the Observation of the Psalmist is perpetually fulfilled: *Thou rulest the raging of the Sea; when the Waves thereof arise, thou stillest them.*

Very various have been the Sentiments of the Curious, what *Cause*

NOTE: Some source materials have been reprinted in book form, for example the facsimile reprint of Cotton Mather's *The Christian Philosopher*. The author, however, has relied considerably on the Readex Microprint Series which contains all books printed in America before 1800 and listed in Charles Evans, *American Bibliography*. Because of space limitations, it is not possible to reprint all documents used in the preparation of the foregoing essay, but the student is referred to the following books: Thomas Hariot, *A Brief and True Report of the New Found Land of Virginia: A Facsimile Edition of the 1588 Quarto, with an Introduction by the Late Randolph G. Adams* (New York: The History Book Club, Inc., 1951); *John and William Bartram's America,* edited by Helen Gere Cruickshank (The Natural History Library, Anchor Books, Garden City, N. Y.: Doubleday & Co., Inc., 1961 pb); and the author's forthcoming "The Scientific Papers of James Logan," *Transactions* of the American Philosophical Society.

there should be assign'd for this great and catholick Affection of Matter, the *Vis Centripeta:* I shall wave them all, and *bury* them in the *Place of Silence,* with the *Materia Striata of Descartes,* which our *Keil* has very sufficiently brought to *nothing*; and perhaps the *Fluid* of Dr. *Hook* must go the same way. 'Tis enough to me what that incomparable Mathematician, Dr. *Halley,* has declar'd upon it: That, after all, *Gravity* is an Effect insolvable by any *philosophical Hypothesis*; it must be religiously resolv'd into the *immediate Will* of our most wise CREATOR, who, by appointing this *Law,* throughout the material World, keeps all Bodies in their proper Places and Stations, which without it would soon fall to pieces, and be utterly destroy'd.

All Bodies descend still towards a Point, which either is, or lies near to, the *Center* of the *Globe.* Should our Almighty GOD change that *Center* but the two thousandth part of the *Radius* of our Globe, the Tops of our highest Mountains would be soon laid under Water.

In all Places equi-distant from the *Center* of our Globe, the Force of Gravity is nearly equal.

Indeed, as it has been proved by Sir *Isaac Newton,* the *Equatorial* Parts are something higher than the *Polar* Parts; the difference between the Earth's *Diameter* and *Axis* being about thirty-four *English* Miles.

Gravity does equally affect all *Bodies.* The *absolute Gravity* of all is the same. Abstracting from the resistance of the Medium, the most *compact* and the most *diffuse,* the *greatest* and the *smallest,* would descend an equal Space in an equal Time. In an exhausted Receiver a *Feather* will descend as fast as a *Pound of Lead.* But this resistance of the *Medium* has produc'd a *comparative Gravity.* And upon the difference of *Specifick Gravity* in many Bodies, the Observations of our Philosophers have been very curious.

According to the exquisite *Halley* and *Huygens,* the *Descent of heavy Bodies* is after the rate of about *sixteen Foot* in *one Second* of Time.

Nevertheless this Power *increases* as you descend to, *decreases* as you ascend from the *Center* of the Globe, and that in proportion to the Squares of the Distances therefrom reciprocally; so as, for instance, at a double distance to have but a quarter of the Force. A *Ton* Weight on the Surface of the Earth, raised Heaven-wards unto the height of one Semidiameter of the Earth from hence, would weight but one quarter of a *Ton.* At three Semidiameters from the Surface of the Earth, it would be as easy for a Man to carry a *Ton,* as here to carry little more than an hundred Pounds. At the distance of the *Moon,* which suppose to be sixty Semidiameters of the Earth, 3600 Pounds weigh but *one Pound*; and the Fall of Bodies is but sixteen Foot in a whole Minute.

I remember I have somewhere met with such a devout Improvement of this Observation: "The further you fly towards *Heaven,* the more (if I may use the *Falconers* Word) you must *lessen.* There is great reason why it should be so. *Defamations* particularly will be Things by which you must be *lessen'd:* you must meet with *heavy* Things; *Defamations* are in a singular manner such; they are not easy to *carry*; 'tis not easy to carry it well under them; some of them are a *Ton* Weight. But, *my Friend,* if you were as near *Heaven* as you ought to be, you would make *light* of them; you would bear them wonderfully!"

The *acute Borelli* has demonstrated that there is no such thing as *positive Levity*, and that *Levity* is only a lesser degree of *Gravity*. But how useful is this, not only to divers Tribes of *Animals*, but also to the raising up of the many *Vapours*, which are to be convey'd about the World? The Evaporations, which, according to Mr. *Sedileau*'s Observations, and others, are the fewest in the Winter, and greatest in the Summer, the most of all in windy Weather, and considerably exceed what falls in *Rain*, many being tumbled about and spent by the Winds, and many falling down in Dews.

The ingenious *Halley* has yet a suspicion that there may be some certain Matter, which may have a *Conatus* directly contrary to that of *Gravity*; as in *Vegetation* the Sprouts directly tend against the *Perpendicular*.

Dr. *Gregory* demonstrates, that the antient Astronomers were not ignorant of the heavenly Bodies *gravitating* towards one another, and being preserv'd in their Orbits by the Force of Gravity.

Mr. *Keil* shews, that the Force of *Gravity* to the *centrifugal Force*, in a Body placed at the Equator of our Globe, is as 289 to 1; so that by the *centrifugal Force* arising from the Earth's Rotation, any Body placed in the Equator loses a 289th part of the Weight it would have if the Globe were at rest. And since there is no *centrifugal Force* at the *Poles*, a Body there weighs 289 Pounds, which at the Equator would weigh but 288. On our Globe the decrease of *Gravity*, in going from the Poles towards the *Equator*, is always *as the Square of the Cosine of the Latitude.* — *Quod facit Natura* (to use *Tully's* Words) *per omnem Mundum, omnia Mente & Ratione conficiens.*

Mr. *Samuel Clark* observes, 'Tis now evident that the most universal Principle of *Gravitation*, the Spring of almost all the great and regular inanimate Motions in the World, answering not at all to the *Surfaces* of Bodies, by which alone they can act one upon another, but entirely to their *Solid Content*; cannot possibly be the result of any *Motion* originally impressed on *Matter*, but must of necessity be caused by something which penetrates the very Substance of all Bodies, and continually *puts forth in them a Force* or *Power* entirely different from that by which *Matter* acts on *Matter*. This (he adds) is *an evident Demonstration, not only of the World's being made originally by a supreme intelligent Cause, but moreover that it depends every moment on some Superior Being, for the Preservation of its Frame, and that all the great Motions in it are caused by some immaterial Power, not having originally impressed a certain Quantity of Motion upon Matter, but perpetually and actually exerting itself every Moment in every Part of the World: which preserving and governing Power gives a very noble Idea of* PROVIDENCE.

Dr. *Cheyne* demonstrates, That *Gravity*, or the *Attraction* of Bodies towards one another, cannot be mechanically accounted for. The *Planets* themselves cannot continue their Motions in their Orbs without it. It is not a Result from the *Nature of Matter*, because the Efficacy of *Matter* is communicated by *immediate Contact*, and it can by no means act at a distance. Whereas this Power of *Gravitation* acts at all Distances, without any *Medium* or Instrument for the Conveyance of it, and passes as far as the Limits of the Universe. *Matter* is indeed entirely *passive*, and can't either *tend* or *draw*, with regard unto other Bodies, no more than it can *move itself*. And what is essential to *Matter* cannot be intended or be remitted; but *Gravity* increases or diminishes reciprocally, as the Squares of the Distances are increased or diminished. 'Tis plain this universal Force of *Gravitation* is the Effect of the *Divine Power* and *Virtue*, by which the Operations of all *material Agents* are preserved. They that press for a *mechanical Account* of *Gravity*, advance a Notion of a *subtile Fluid*, unto the Motion whereof they would ascribe it. But then still those Parts of Matter must be destitute of *Gravity*, which were very unlikely! And this *Hypothesis* would still remove us but one Step further from *immechanical Principles*; for the Cause of the Motion of your *Subtile Fluid*, this, *Gentlemen*, you must own to be *immechanical*. Since you must admit a *first Cause*, you had as good be sensible of it in this place. 'Tis *He* who does immediately impress on *Matter* this Property. There never was yet afforded unto the World (as my Doctor observes) a *System of Natural Philosophy* which did not require *Postulates*, that are not *mechanically* to be accounted for. The fewest any one pretends to, are, *the Existence of Matter*, and *the Impression of rectilinear Motions*, and *the Preservation of the Faculties of natural Agents*. No Man has pretended to fetch from the Principles of *Mechanism* an Account for these. The *Impression of an attractive Faculty upon Matter*, is no harder a *Postulate* than the rest. It is a *Matter of Fact*, that *Matter* is in possession of this Quality. And it can be referred unto nothing, but the Influence of that Glorious ONE, who is the *first Cause* of all Things.

"Behold, a continual Opportunity for a considerate and religious Man, to have a *Sense* of a Glorious GOD awaken'd in him! And what is a *Walk with God*, but that *Sense* kept alive in every Step of our *Walk*? I am continually entertain'd with *weighty Body*, or *Matter* tending to the *Center of Gravity*; I feel it in *my own*. The *Cause* of this *Tendency*, 'tis the Glorious GOD, *Great GOD, Thou givest this Matter such a Tendency, and thou keepest it in its Operation*. There is no other Cause but the *Will* and *Work* of the Glorious GOD. I am now effectually convinc'd of that antient Confession, and must with Affection make it, *He is not far from every one of us*. When I see any thing moving or settling that way that its *heavy Nature* carries it, I may very justly think, and I would often form the Thought, *it is the Glorious GOD, who now carries this Matter such a way!* When *Matter* sinks *downward*, my Spirit shall even *therefore* mount *upward*, in acknowledgment of the God who orders it. I will no longer complain, *Behold, I go forward, but He is not there, and backward, but I cannot perceive Him; on the Left-hand, where He doth work, but I cannot behold Him; He hideth himself on the Right-hand, that I cannot see Him*. No, I am now taught where to meet with Him, even at *every turn. He knows the way that I take*. I cannot stir *forward* or *backward*, but I *perceive* Him in the *Weight* of every *Matter*; on the *Left-hand* and on the *Right* I see Him *at work*. My *way* shall be to improve this as a *weighty* Argument for the Being of a God. I will argue from it, *Behold, there is a God, whom I ought for ever to love, and serve, and glorify*. Yea, and if I am *tempted* to the doing of any wicked thing, I may reflect, that it cannot be done without some Action, wherein the

Weight of Matter operates. But then I may carry on the Reflection, *How near am I to that Glorious GOD, whose Commands I am going to violate! Matter keeps his Laws; but, O my Soul, wilt thou break 'em! How shall I do this Wickedness, and therein deny the God, who not only is above, but also is most sensibly now exerting His Power in the very Matter, upon which I make my criminal Misapplications!"*

Before we go any further, it appears high time to introduce an Assertion or two of that excellent Philosopher Dr. *Cheyne*, in his *Philosophical Principles of natural Religion*. He asserts, and with Demonstration, (for truly without *that* he asserts nothing!) that there is no such thing as an *universal Soul*, animating the vast System of the World, according to *Plato*; nor any *Substantial Forms*, according to *Aristotle*; nor any omniscient *radical Heat*, according to *Hippocrates*; nor any *plastick Virtue*, according to *Scaliger*; nor any *hylarchick Principle*, according to *More*. These are mere *allegorical* Terms, coined on purpose to conceal the Ignorance of the Authors, and keep up their Credit with the credulous Part of Mankind. These *unintelligible Beings* are derogatory from the Wisdom and Power of the Great GOD, who can easily *govern* the Machine He could *create*, by more direct Methods than employing such subservient *Divinities*; and indeed these Beings will not serve the Design for which we invent them, unless we endow them with Faculties above the Dignity of *Secondary Agents*. It is now plain from the most *evident Principles*, that the Great GOD not only has the *Springs* of this immense *Machine*, and all the several Parts of it, in his own Hand, and is the *first Mover;* but that without His *continual Influence* the whole Movement would soon fall to pieces. Yet besides this, He has reserved to Himself the power of *dispensing* with these *Laws*, whenever He pleases.

My Doctor has made it evident, That it is not essential to *Matter* to be either in *Rest* or in *Motion:* But tho there is in *Matter* a *Vis inertiæ*, by which all Bodies resist, to the utmost of their power, any *Change* of their State, whether of *Rest* or *Motion*; yet this *Vis* is not essential to *Matter*, but a *positive Faculty* implanted therein by the Author of Nature. It is therefore evident that the Preservation of a *Body* in *Rest* or in *Motion* (after the first Instant) absolutely depends on the Almighty GOD, as the Cause. No part of *Matter* can move itself, nor when put into *motion*, is this *Motion* absolutely essential to its Being, nor does depend upon itself; and therefore the *Preservation* of this *Motion* must have its Dependance on some other Cause. But there is no other Cause assignable besides the *omnipotent Cause*, who preserves the Being and Faculties of all natural Agents.

Great GOD, on the Behalf of all thy Creatures, I acknowledge in Thee we move and have our Being!

2

Experiments and Observations in Electricity

SOURCE: Benjamin Franklin to Peter Collinson, Philadelphia, April 29, 1749, in Leonard W. Labaree and others, eds., *The Papers of Benjamin Franklin*, III (New Haven: Yale University Press, 1961), 352-365. Reprinted with permission of The American Academy of Arts and Sciences.

To Peter Collinson

Sir   Philada. Apl. 29. 1749

I now send you some Further Experiments and Observations in Electricity made in Philadelphia 1748. viz.

§1. There will be the same Explosion and Shock if the electrified Phial is held in one Hand by the Hook, and the Coating touched by the other; as when held by the Coating and touched at the Hook.

§2. To take the charged Phial safely by the Hook, and not at the same Time diminish it's Force, it must first be set down on an Electric per se.

§3. The Phial will be electrified as strongly, if held by the Hook, and the Coating apply'd to the Globe, or Tube, as when held by the Coating and the Hook apply'd.

§4. But the Direction of the Electrical Fire being different in Charging, will also be different in the Explosion. The Bottle charged thro' the Hook will be discharged thro' the Hook. The Bottle charged thro' the Coating, will be discharged thro' the Coating and not otherwise: For the Fire must come out the same Way it went in.

§5. To prove this; Take two Bottles that were equally charg'd thro' the Hooks, one in each Hand; bring their Hooks near each other, and no Spark or Shock will follow; because each Hook is disposed to give Fire, and neither to receive it. Set one of the Bottles down on Glass, take it up by the Hook, and apply it's Coating to the Hook of the other; then there will be an Explosion and Shock, and both Bottles will be discharged.

§6. Vary the Experiment, by Charging two Vials equally, one thro' Hook, the other thro' the Coating: Hold that by the Coating which was charged thro' the Hook; and that by the Hook which was charged thro' the Coating. Apply the Hook of the first to the Coating of the other and there will be no Shock or Spark. Set that down on Glass, which you held by the Hook, take it up by the Coating, and bring the two Hooks together; a Spark and Shock will follow, and both Phials be discharged.

In this Experiment the Bottles are totally discharged, or the Equilibrium within them restored. The *Abounding* of Fire in one of the Hooks (or rather in the internal Surface of one Bottle) being exactly equal to the *Wanting* of the other: and therefore, as each Bottle has in itself the *Abounding* as well as the *Wanting*, the Wanting and Abounding must be equal in each Bottle. See §§8, 9, 10, 11. But if a Man holds in his Hands two Bottles, one fully electrified, the other not at all; and brings their Hooks together; he has but half a Shock, and the Bottles will both remain half electrified; the one being half discharged and the other half charged.

7. Farther, Place two Vials equally charged on a Table at 5 or 6 Inches Distance; Let a Cork Ball, suspended by a Silk Thread, hang between them. If the Vials were both charg'd thro' their Hooks, the Cork, when it has been attracted and repell'd by the one, will not be attracted but equally repell'd by the other. But if the Vials were charged, the one thro' the Hook and the other thro' the Coating,* the Ball when it is repell'd from one Hook will be as strongly attracted by the other, and play vigorously between them, till both Vials are nearly discharg'd.

8. When we use the Terms of *Charging* and *Discharging* the Phial, 'tis in Compliance with Custom, and for want of others more suitable: since We are of Opinion, that there is really no more electrical Fire in the Phial, after what is called it's *Charging* than before; nor less after it's *Discharging;* (excepting only the small Spark that might be given to and taken from the Non-electric Matter, if separated from the Bottle, which Spark may not be equal to a 500th. Part of what is called the Explosion) For, if on the Explosion, the Electrical Fire came out of the Bottle by one Part, and did not enter in again by another; then, if a Man standing on Wax and holding the Bottle in one Hand, takes the Spark by touching the Wire Hook with the other, the Bottle being thereby *discharg'd*, the Man would be *charg'd;* or, whatever Fire was lost by one, would be found in the other; since there is no Way for it's Escape. But the Contrary is true.

9. Besides, the Vial will not suffer what is called a *Charging*, unless as much Fire can go out of it one Way as is thrown in by another. A Phial can not be charged, standing on Wax, or Glass, or hanging on the prime Conductor, unless a Communication be form'd between it's Coating and the Floor.

10. But suspend two or more Phials on the prime Conductor, one hanging to the Tail of the other, and a Wire from the last to the Floor: an equal Number of Turns of the Wheel shall charge them all equally; and every one as much as one alone would have been. What is driven out at the Tail of the first, serving to charge the second; what is driven out of the second charging the third, and so on. By this Means, a great number of Bottles might be charged with the same Labour, and equally high with one alone, were it not that every Bottle receives new Fire and

---

*To charge a Bottle commodiously thro' the Coating, place it on a Glass Stand; form a Communication from the prime Conductor to the Coating, and another from the Hook to the Wall or Floor. When 'tis charg'd remove the latter Communication before you take hold of the Bottle; otherwise great Part of the Fire will escape by it.

loses it's old with some Reluctance, or rather gives some small Resistance to the Charging, which in a Number of Bottles becomes more equal to the Charging Power, and so repels the Fire back again on the Globe, sooner than a single Bottle would do.

11. When a Bottle is charg'd in the common Way, it's inside and outside Surfaces stand ready, the one to give Fire by the Hook, the other to receive it by the Coating: The one is full and ready to throw out, the other empty and extreamly hungry: yet as the first will not *give out,* unless the other can at the same Instant *receive in;* so neither will the latter *receive in,* unless the first can at the same Instant *give out.* When both can be done at once, 'tis done with inconceivable Quickness and Violence.

12. So a strait Spring (tho' the Comparison does not agree in every Particular) when forcibly bent, must, to restore itself contract that Side, which in the bending was extended, and extend that which was contracted; if either of these two Operations be hindered, the other can not be done. But the Spring is not said to be *charged* with Elasticity when bent, and *discharg'd* when unbent; it's Quantity of Elasticity is always the same.

13. Glass, in like Manner, has, within it's Substance always the same Quantity of Electrical Fire; and that, a very great Quantity in Proportion to the Mass of Glass, as shall be shewn hereafter. §26.

14. This Quantity, proportioned to the Glass, it strongly and obstinately retains, and will neither have more nor less; tho it will suffer a Change to be made in it's Parts and Situation; that is, We may take away Part of it from one of the Sides, provided we throw an equal Quantity into the other.

15. Yet when the Situation of the Electrical Fire is thus altered in the Glass, when some has been taken from one Side, and some added to the other; it will not be at Rest or in its natural State, till 'tis restored to it's original Equality. And this Restitution can not be made thro the Substance of the Glass, but must be done by a Non-electric Communication formed without, from Surface to Surface.

16. Thus the whole Force of the Bottle and Power of giving a Shock, is in the Glass itself; the Non-electrics in Contact with the two Surfaces serving only to give and receive to and from the several Parts of the Glass; that is, to give on one Side, and take away from the other.

17. This was discovered here in the following Manner. Purposing to analize the electrified Bottle, in Order to find where it's Strength lay; we placed it on Glass, and drew out the Cork and Wire, which, for that Purpose, had been loosly put in. Then taking the Bottle in one Hand, and bringing a Finger of the other near its Mouth, a strong Spark came from the Water, and the Shock was as violent as if the Wire had remained in it; which shew'd that the Force did not lie in the Wire. Then to find if it resided in the Water, being crowded into and condensed in it, as confined by the Glass; which had been our former Opinion; we electrified the Bottle again, and placing it on Glass, drew out the Wire and Cork as before, then taking up the Bottle, we decanted all its Water into an empty Bottle, which likewise stood on Glass; and taking up that other Bottle, we expected, if the Force resided in the Water, to find a

Shock from it; but there was none. We judged then, that it must either be lost in Decanting, or remain in the first Bottle. The latter we found to be true: For that Bottle on Trial gave the Shock, tho' filled up as it stood with fresh unelectrify'd Water from a Tea Pot. To find then whether Glass had this Property merely as Glass, or whether the Form contributed any Thing to it; we took a Pane of Sash Glass, and laying it on the Hand, placed a Plate of thin Lead on it's upper Surface; then electrified that Plate, and bring a Finger to it, there was a Spark and Shock. We then took two Plates of Lead of equal Dimensions, but less than the Glass by two Inches every Way, and electrified the Glass between them, by electrifying the uppermost Lead; then separated the Glass from the Lead; in doing which, what little Fire might be in the Lead was taken out; and the Glass being touched in the electrified Part with a Finger, afforded only very small pricking Sparks, but a great Number of them might be taken from different Places. Then dextrously placing it again between the Plates of Lead, and completing the Circle between the two Surfaces, a violent Shock ensu'd. Which demonstrated the Power to reside in the Glass as *Glass;* and that the Non-electrics in Contact served only like the Armature of the Loadstone, to unite the Forces of the several Parts, and bring them at once to any Point desired. It being a Property of a Nonelectric, that the whole Body instantly receives or gives what Electrical Fire is given to or taken from any one of its Parts.

18. Upon this We made what we call'd an *Electrical Battery,* consisting of eleven Panes of large Sash Glass, arm'd with thin leaden Plates, pasted on each Side, placed vertically, and supported at two Inches Distance on Silk Cords; with Hooks of thick Leaden Wire one from each Side standing upright, distant from each other; and convenient Communications of Wire and Chain from the giving Side of one Pane to the receiving Side of the other; that so the whole might be charg'd together, and with the same Labour as one single Pane; and another Contrivance to bring the giving Sides, after charging in Contact with one long Wire, and the Receivers with another; which two long Wires would give the Force of all the Plates of Glass at once thro' the Body of any Animal forming the Circle with them. The Plates may also be discharg'd separately, or any Number together that is required. But this Machine is not much used, as not perfectly answering our Intention with Regard to the Ease of Charging, for the Reasons given §10. We made also, of large Glass Panes, *Magical Pictures,* and self moving animated Wheels, presently to be described.

19. I perceive by the ingenious Mr. Watson's last Book, lately received, that Dr. Bevis had used Panes of Glass to give a Shock before us; tho' till that Book came to Hand, I thought to have communicated it to you as a Novelty. The Excuse for mentioning it here, is, that we try'd the Experiment differently, drew different Consequences from it (for Mr. Watson still seems to think the Fire accumulated on the Nonelectric that is in Contact with the Glass pag. 72) and, as far as we hitherto know, have carry'd it further.

20. The Magical Picture is made thus. Having a large Mezzotinto with a Frame and Glass (Suppose of the King, God preserve him) Take

out the Print, and cut a Pannel out of it, near two Inches all round distant from the Frame; if the Cut is thro' the Picture, 'tis not the Worse. With thin Paste or Gum Water, fix the Border, that is cut off, on the inside of the Glass, pressing it smoothe and close; then fill up the Vacancy by Gilding the Glass well with Leaf Gold or Brass; gild likewise the inner Edge of the Back of the Frame all round except the Top Part, and form a Communication between that Gilding and the Gilding behind the Glass: then put in the Board, and that side is finished. Turn up the Glass, and gild the foreside exactly over the Back Gilding; and when this is dry, cover it by pasting on the Pannel of the Picture that had been cut out, observing to bring the corresponding Parts of the Border and Picture together; by which the Picture will appear of a Piece as at first, only Part is behind the Glass and Part before. Hold the Picture horizontally by the Top, and place a little moveable gilt Crown on the Kings Head. If now the Picture be moderately electrified, and another Person take hold of the Frame with one Hand, so that his Fingers touch it's inside Gilding, and with the other Hand endeavour to take off the Crown, he will receive a terrible Blow and fail in the Attempt. If the Picture were highly charg'd, the Consequence might perhaps be as fatal as that of High Treason: For when the Spark is taken thro' a Quire of Paper laid on the Picture, by Means of a Wire Communication, it makes a fair Hole thro' every Sheet; that is thro' 48 Leaves (tho' a Quire of Paper is thought good Armour against the Push of a Sword, or even against a Pistol Bullet) and the Crack is exceeding loud. The Operator, who, to prevent its falling, holds the Picture by the upper End, where the inside of the Frame is not gilt, feels Nothing of the Shock, and may touch the Crown without Danger, which he pretends is a Test of his Loyalty. If a Ring of Persons take a Shock among them the Experiment is called the *Conspiracy*.

21. On the Principle in §7. That the Hooks of Bottles, differently charged, will attract and repel differently, is made an electrical Wheel, that turns with considerable Strength. A small upright Shaft of Wood passes at right Angles thro' a thin round Board of about a Foot Diameter, and turns on a sharp Point of Iron, fixt in the lower End, while a strong Wire in the upper End, passing thro' a small Hole in a thin Brass Plate, keeps the Shaft truly vertical. About 30 Radii of equal Length made of Sash Glass, cut in narrow Strips, issue Horizontally from the Circumference of the Board; the Ends most distant from the Center being about 4 Inches apart. On the End of everyone, a Brass Thimble is fixt. If now the Wire of a Bottle, electrified in the Common Way, be brought near the Circumference of this Wheel, it will attract the nearest Thimble, and so put the Wheel in Motion: That Thimble, in passing by, receives a Spark, and thereby being electrified is repell'd and so driven forwards, while a second, being attracted, approaches the Wire, receives a Spark and is driven after the first; and so on till the Wheel has gone once round, when the Thimbles, before Electrified, approaching the Wire, instead of being attracted, as they were at first, are repell'd; and the Motion presently ceases. But if another Bottle, which had been charg'd thro' the Coating be placed near the same Wheel, it's Wire will attract the Thimbles repell'd by the first, and thereby doubles the Force that

carries the Wheel round; and not only, taking out the Fire that had been communicated to the Thimbles by the first Bottle, but even robbing them of their natural Quantity, instead of being repell'd when they come again towards the first Bottle, they are more strongly attracted: so that the Wheel mends its Pace till it goes with great Rapidity, 12 or 15 Rounds in a Minute; and with such Strength, as that the Weight of 100 Spanish Dollars, with which we once loaded it, did not seem in the least to retard it's Motion. This is called an *Electrical Jack;* and if a large Fowl were spitted on the upright Shaft, it would be carried round before a Fire with a Motion fit for Roasting.

22. But this Wheel, like those driven by Wind, Water or Weights, moves by a foreign Force, viz. that of the Bottles. The *Selfmoving Wheel,* tho constructed on the same Principles, appears more surprizing. 'Tis made of a thin round Plate of Window Glass, 17 Inches Diameter, well gilt on both Sides, all but two Inches next the Edge. Two small Hemispheres of Wood are then fixt with Cement to the Middle of the upper and under Sides, centrally opposite, and in each of them a thick strong Wire 8 or 10 Inches long, which together make the Axis of the Wheel. It turns horizontally on a Point at the lower End of it's Axis which rests on a Bit of Brass, cemented within a Glass Salt-Seller. The upper End of it's Axis passes thro' a Hole in a thin Brass Plate, cemented to a long strong Piece of Glass, which keeps it 6 or 8 Inches Distant from any Non-electric, and has a small Ball of Wax or Metal on its Top to keep in the Fire. In a Circle on the Table, which supports the Wheel, are fixt 12 small Pillars of Glass, at about 4 Inches Distance, with a Thimble on the Top of each. On the Edge of the Wheel is a small leaden Bullet, communicating by a Wire with the Gilding of the upper Surface of the Wheel: and about 6 Inches from it, is another Bullet, communicating in like Manner with the under Surface. When the Wheel is to be charg'd by the upper Surface, a Communication must be made from the under Surface to the Table. When it is well chargd it begins to move; the Bullet nearest to a Pillar, moving towards the Thimble on that Pillar; and passing by, electrifies it, and then pushes itself from it: The succeeding Bullet, which communicates with the other Surface of the Glass, more strongly attracting that Thimble, on Account of it's being before electrified by the other Bullet: and thus the Wheel increases it's Motion, till it comes to such a Height, as that the Resistance of the Air regulates it. It will go half an Hour, and make, one Minute with another, 20 Turns in a Minute; which is 600 Turns in the whole: The Bullet of the upper Surface giving in each Turn 12 Sparks to the Thimbles, which makes 7200 Sparks, and the Bullet of the under Surface receiving as many from the Thimbles: these Bullets moving in the Time, near 2500 Feet. The Thimbles are well fixt, and in so exact a Circle, that the Bullets may pass within a very small Distance of each of them. If instead of 2 Bullets, you put 8, 4 communicating with the upper Surface, and four with the under Surface, placed alternately; which 8, at about 6 Inches Distance completes the Circumference; the Force and Swiftness will be greatly increased; the Wheel making 50 Turns in a Minute; but then it will not go so long. These Wheels may perhaps be apply'd to the Ringing of Chimes and Moving Orreries.

23. A small Wire bent circularly, with a loop at each End; Let one End rest against the under Surface of the Wheel, and bring the other End near the upper Surface, it will give a terrible Crack; The Force will be discharg'd, and the Wheel will stop.

24. Every Spark drawn in that Manner from the Surface of the Wheel, makes a round Hole in the Gilding, tearing off a Part of it in coming out; which shews that the Fire is not accumulated on the Gilding, but is in the Glass itself.

25. The Gilding being varnished over with Turpentine Varnish; the Varnish, tho' dry and hard, is burnt by the Spark drawn thro' it, gives a strong Smell and visible Smoke. And when the Spark is drawn thro' Paper, all round the Hole made by it, the Paper will be blackt by the Smoke, which Sometimes penetrates several of the Leaves. Parts of the Gilding, torn off, are also found forcibly driven into the Hole made in the paper by the Stroke.

26. 'Tis amazing to observe in how small a Portion of Glass a great Electrical Force may lie. A thin Glass Bubble about an Inch Diameter, weighing only six Grains, being half filled with Water, partly gilt on the outside, and furnished with a Wire Hook, gives when electrified, as great a Shock as a Man is willing to bear. As the Glass is thickest near the Orifice, I suppose the lower half, which being gilt, was electrified, and gave the Shock, did not exceed two Grains; for it appeared, when broke, much thinner than the upper half. If one of these thin Bottles be electrified by the Coating, and the Spark taken out thro the Gilding, it will break the Glass inwards, at the same Time that it breaks the Gilding outwards.

27. And allowing, for the Reasons before given §§8, 9, 10, that there is no more Electrical Fire in a Bottle after Charging than before, how great must the Quantity be in this small Portion of Glass! It seems as if it were of its very Substance and Essence. Perhaps if that due Quantity of Electrical Fire, so obstinately retain'd by Glass, could be separated from it, it would no longer be Glass, it might loose it's Transparency, or its Fragility, or Elasticity. Experiments may possibly be invented hereafter to discover this.

28. We are surprized at the Account given in Mr. Watson's Book, of a Shock communicated thro' a great Space of dry Ground, and suspect some metalline Quality in the Gravel of that Ground: having found, that simple dry Earth ramm'd in a Glass Tube open at both Ends, and a Wire Hook inserted in the Earth at each End; the Earth and Wires making Part of a Circle, would not conduct the least perceptible Shock. And indeed when one Wire was electrified, the other hardly shew'd any Signs of it's being in Connexion with it. Even a thoroughly wet Packthread sometimes fails of conducting a Shock, tho' it otherwise conducts Electricity very well. A dry Cake of Ice, or an Iceicle, held between two Persons in a Circle, likewise prevents the Shock, which one would not expect, as Water conducts it so perfectly well. Gilding on a new Book, tho' at first it conducts the Shock extreamly well; yet fails after 10 or a Dozen Experiments; tho' it appears otherwise in all Respects the same; which we can not account for.

29. There is one Experiment more, which surprizes us, and is hitherto

not satisfactorily accounted for. It is this. Place an Iron Shot on a Glass Stand, and let a damp Cork Ball, suspended by a Silk Thread hang in Contact with the Shot. Take a Bottle in each Hand, one that is electrified thro' the Hook, the other thro' the Coating. Apply the *giving* Wire to the Shot, which will electrify it positively, and the Cork shall be repell'd. Then apply the *requiring* Wire, which will take out the Spark given by the other, when the Cork will return to the Shot. Apply the same again, and take out another Spark, so will the Shot be electrified negatively, and the Cork in that Case shall be repell'd equally as before. Then apply the giving Wire, and give to the Shot the Spark it wanted, so will the Cork return: Give it another, which will be an Addition to it's natural Quantity, so will the Cork be repell'd again; And so may the Experiment be repeated, as long as there is any Charge remaining in the Bottles; Which shews that Bodies, having less than the common Quantity of Electricity, repel each other, as well as those that have more.

Chagrin'd a little that We have hitherto been able to discover Nothing in this Way of Use to Mankind, and the hot Weather coming on, when Electrical Experiments are not so agreable; 'tis proposed to put an End to them for this Season somewhat humorously in a Party of Pleasure on the Banks of SchuylKill, (where Spirits are at the same Time to be fired by a Spark sent from Side to Side thro' the River).† A Turky is to be killed for our Dinners by the Electrical Shock; and roasted by the electrical Jack, before a Fire kindled by the Electrified Bottle; when the Healths of all the famous Electricians in England, France and Germany, are to be drank in Electrified Bumpers,* under the Discharge of Guns from the Electrical Battery.

To Peter Collinson Esqr. F.R.S. London

---

†This was since done.

*An electrified Bumper is a small thin Glass Tumbler, near filled with Wine and electrified. This when brought to the Lips, gives a Shock; if the Party be close shaved, and does not breathe on the Liquor.

3

An Astronomical Description of the
Late Comet, 1664

SOURCE: Samuel Danforth, *An Astronomical Description of the Late Comet or Blazing Star, As it appeared in New England in the 9th, 10th, 11th and in the beginning of the 12th Moneth, 1664. Together with a brief Theological Application thereof.* (Cambridge, 1665). Readex Microprint Series, Evans No. 99.

I. *This Comet is no sublunary Meteor or sulphureous Exhalation, but a Celestial Luminary, moving in the starry Heavens.*

The Truth hereof may be demonstrated, 1 *By the vast Dimensions of it's body.* Some Comets have been observed by Astronomers to be halfe as big as the *Moon,* some bigger then the Moon, yea some bigger then the *Earth.* The exact Dimensions of this Comet, I may not presume to determine, but it seemeth not to be of the smallest size. Now 'tis not easy to imagine how the *Earth* should afford matter for a *Meteor* of such a huge magnitude, except we grant the greater part of the lower World, to be turned into an exhalation. 2. *By the smalness of it's Parallax.* The Parallax is the Distance between the *true* place of a *Planet* and the *apparent.* The lower and neerer any *Planet* is to the Earth, it hath the greater *Parallax.* The Moon's *Parallax* in her *Perige,* is one degree and six minutes. I could not by my Observation discerne that this Comet had any considerable *Parallax.* 3. *By it's large circular motion.* If it had moved in the upper Region of the *Aire,* it might have finished the whole visible *arch of it's Circle* in a few houres: but wee saw it perform it's proper motion with great constancy in a very large *Circle,* such as the aire is not capable of. 4. *By it's long duration and continuancie.* Had it been a Sulphureous *Vapor* kindled in the Aire; it might have been consumed in a short time; as other *fiery Meteors* are: but this continued about three months . . .

A Brief *Theological Application* of this strange
and notable *Appearance* in the *Heavens*

I. The Holy Scriptures, *which are the* Authentick *and unerring* Canon *of truth, teach us to look at* Comets, *as* Portentous *and* Signal of *great and notable Changes.*

Joel 2. 30, 31. I will shew wonders in the Heavens and in the Earth, Blood and Fire, and Pillars of Smoak. The Sun shall be turned into

Darkness and the Moon into Blood before the great and terrible day of the Lord come.

Luke 21. 25. There shall be signes in the Sun, and in the Moon, and in the Stars.

Acts 2. 19, 20. I will shew wonders in Heavens above, and figures in the Earth beneath: Blood, and Fire, and Vapors of Smoak. The Sun shall be turned into Darkness and the Moon into Blood before the great and notable day of the Lord come.

II. *The Histories of former Ages, do abundantly testifie that* Comets *have been many times Heralds of wrath to a secure and impenitent World.*

Take a few Instances.

A little before the *Achaick Warr* (as *Seneca* reports) there appeared a Comet fiery and ruddy, which cast a clear light, whereby the night was enlightened.

Anno Christi 56. There appeared a Comet, the same Year *Claudius* died, and bloody *Nero* succeeded, who slew his *Mother,* his *Wife* and his *Master Seneca,* and exercised a great deal of cruelty and wickedness.

Anno 323. There were diverse Comets which preceeded the *Pestilent Heresie* of *Arius.*

Anno 337. A Comet appeared before the death of *Constantine* the great, and innumerable evils followed.

Anno 602. A great Comet appeared, which preceded, if not presaged the slaughter of *Mauritius* the *Emperor,* and the *Supremacy* of the *Bishop of Rome.*

Anno 675, 676. There appeared a Comet 3 moneths, at which time the *Saracens* greatly afflicted the *Roman Empire.*

Anno 729. Two Comets appeared, and the same year a great *Plague* invaded the World.

Anno 814. A terrible Comet appeared before the death of *Charles the great.*

Anno 1066. A Comet appeared a long time to the whole World: the same Year *England* was many waies afflicted by *William Duke of Normandy,* and at length subdued.

Anno 1618. There appeared a great Comet: the same year brake forth the *Bloody Wars in Germany. Anno* 1652. There appeared a Comet at the beginning of Mr. Cottons sickness, and disappeared a few daies after his death. The next year strange and notable changes of state happened in *England.*

4

Observation of the Transit of Venus, 1761

SOURCE: John Winthrop, *Relation of a Voyage from Boston to
Newfoundland, for the Observation of the Transit of Venus,
June 6, 1761* (Boston, 1761). Readex Microprint Series,
Evans No. 9040.

The Transit of the Planet VENUS over the disc of the SUN, being a
most important as well as curious phaenomenon, has for a long time
imployed the consideration of Astronomers. The first notice that I find
taken of it was by the sagacious *Kepler,* who flourished not long after
the revival of the true astronomy by *Copernicus;* and in a work published in 1604, declared, that no such thing could happen in that century;
nor the next, till the year 1761. In this, however, that great man was
mistaken. For an English Astronomer, *Jeremiah Horrockes,* then no
more than 20 years of age, but of an admirable genius, having corrected
Kepler's Tables by some of his own observations, predicted and soon
after observ'd this most rare phaenomenon, on the 24th of November
O. S. in the Year 1639, at *Hoole,* a small village about 12 miles N. from
Leverpoole. Having waited several hours with great impatience, he had
at last the satisfaction to see the Planet as a black spot, just entring on
the Sun, at a quarter past three in the afternoon. He made three observations of its positions in half an hour, when he was depriv'd of a longer
sight of it by the setting of the Sun. He had given notice to an astronomical friend, Mr. *Crabtree,* who, at a few miles distance just got a
sight of it between the clouds, before Sun-set. These two were the only
persons that ever saw Venus in the Sun, before the present year.

These Transits became more generally known by a *Series,* which the
late Astronomer-Royal Dr. *Halley* publish'd, of all in a thousand years;
from which it appears that none could happen between the years 1639
and 1761. But what made this of June 6, 1761, most of all famous, was
a paper of the same learned author in the Philosophical Transactions
for the year 1705, wherein he explains an important use to be made of
it. Some uses of the transits of the inferior planets were obvious. They
serve much better than any other phaenomena, to perfect the theory of
these planets, which is more difficult to be settled than that of the
superiors; and did they happen frequently, would be of admirable use
in ascertaining the longitude of places on this globe. They likewise
demonstrate the truth of the Copernican System, so far as it relates to
these Planets, by making it evident that they respect the Sun, and not
the Earth, as the center of their motions. But Dr. *Halley* pointed out a

new and singular use to be made of the Transit of Venus; and to which no other phaenomenon in the heavens is near so well adapted. This is, in finding the Parallax of the Sun; which is so small that the Astronomers have never been able to discover it with exactness in any other method. If this were once known, the distance of the Sun, and of all the Planets, and of all the Comets, would be known too; and their magnitudes would also be known, from their apparent diameters. This would give us a just idea of the vast dimensions of the solar system, and of the mighty globes which compose it. Nor can we, but by such observations, know whether the Earth continues to revolve at the same distance from the Sun, or whether it gradually approaches him, as there is some reason to suspect; nor whether the Sun remains of the same magnitude, or consumes away and is diminish'd by the light which he is incessantly sending forth. The Parallax of the Sun is also an element that enters into the calculation of eclipses; and of what use these are in Astronomy, in Geography, in History and Chronology, is too well known to need being insisted on at this day. It would likewise determine the quantity of matter in the Earth, or the proportion which this bears to that in the Sun; and shew us precisely the amazing velocity with which light is darted from the Sun and other luminous Bodies; — and probably give us a deeper insight into many of the wonderful works of GOD. For such is the relation of the several branches of natural Philosophy to each other, and all of them to moral Philosophy, that whatever tends to the perfection of one tends to perfect the other, in proportion to the connection there is between them. And a capital point once adjusted, may serve for the determination of others, which were not at first thought of. Thus, the exact measure of a degree on the meridian enabled Sir *Isaac Newton* to demonstrate his Theory of universal Gravity, a scheme which had never enter'd into the minds of any, when the degree was proposed to be measured; by which means that great man laid open the constitution of the astronomical world, and pointed out the fundamental Law which the alwise CREATOR has established for regulating the several movements in this grand machine.

5

Account of the Transit of Venus, 1769

SOURCE: *"An Account of the* TRANSIT OF VENUS *over the*
SUN'S DISC, *as observed at* NORRITON, *in the County of*
Philadelphia, *and Province of Pennsylvania,* June 3d, 1769,"
*Transactions of the American Philosophical Society, Held at
Philadelphia, for Promoting Useful Knowledge,* I (Philadel-
phia, 1771), 8-12. Readex Microprint Series, Evans No.
11959.

Among the various public spirited designs, that have engaged the
attention of this *Society,* since its first Institution; none does them
more honor than their early resolution to appoint COMMITTEES, of
their own Members, to take as many observations, in different places,
of that *rare Phaenomenon,* the TRANSIT OF VENUS over the SUN'S
DISC, as they had any probability of being able to defray the expence
of, either from their own funds, or the public assistance they expected.

As the members of the *Norriton-Committee* live at some distance from
each other, I am, therefore, at their request, now to digest and lay before
you, in one view, the whole of our observations in that place; distinguishing, however, the part of each observer; and going back to the first
preparations. For I am persuaded that the dependence, which the learned
world may place on any particular Transit Account, will be in proportion
to the previous and subsequent care, which is found to have been taken
in a series of accurate and well conducted observations, for ascertaining
the *going* of the timepieces, and fixing the Latitude and Longitude of the
places of observation &c.

And I am the more desirous to be particular in these points, in order
to do justice to Mr. *Rittenhouse,* one of our Committee; to whose extraordinary skill and diligence is owing whatever advantage may be derived,
in these respects, to our observation of the *Transit* itself. It is further
presumed, that Astronomers, in distant countries, will be desirous to
have not only the work and results belonging to each particular *Transit-
Observation,* but the materials also, that they may examine and conclude for themselves. And this may be more particularly requisite, in a
new Observatory, such as *Norriton,* the name of which hath perhaps
never before been heard of by distant Astronomers; and therefore, its
latitude and longitude are to be once fixed, from principles that may be
satisfactory on the present, as well as on any future, occasion.

Our great discouragement, at our first appointment, was the want of
proper apparatus, especially good *Telescopes,* with *Micrometers.* The

generosity of our *Provincial Assembly* soon removed a great part of this discouragement, not only by their vote to purchase one of the best Reflecting Telescopes, with a *Dolland's* Micrometer; but likewise by their subsequent donation of *One Hundred Pounds*, for erecting Observatories, and defraying other incidental expences. It was foreseen that on the arrival of this Telescope, added to such private ones as might be procured in the city, together with fitting up the instruments belonging to the Honorable the Proprietaries of the Province, viz. the *equal Altitude* and *Transit Instruments*, and the large astronomical *Secler*, nothing would be wanting for the *City-Observatory* in the State-House Square, but a good Time-Piece, which was easily to be procured.

We remained however still at a loss, how to furnish the *Norriton Observatory*. But even this difficulty gradually vanished. Early in *September*, 1768, soon after the nomination of our *Committees*, I received a letter from that worthy and honorable Gentleman, THOMAS PENN, Esq, one of the Proprietaries of this Province, which he wrote at the desire of the Rev. Mr. *Maskelyne*, Astronomer Royal, expressing their desire, "That we should exert ourselves in observing the Transit, for which our situation would be so favourable"; and enclosing some copies of Mr. *Maskelyne's* printed directions for that purpose.

This gave me an opportunity, which I immediately embraced, of acquainting Mr. PENN what preparations we had already made; and what encouragement the Assembly had given in voting *One Hundred Pounds* Sterling, for the purchase of One Reflecting Telescope and Micrometer, for the City Observatory; but that we should be at a great loss for a telescope of the like construction for the *Norriton Observatory*, and requesting him to order a *Reflector* of two, or two and a half feets, with *Dolland's* Micrometer, to be got ready as soon as possible in *London*. It was not long before I had the pleasure to hear that Mr. PENN had ordered such a Telescope, which came to hand about the middle of *May*, with a most obliging letter, expressing the satisfaction he had in hearing of the spirit shewn at *Philadelphia*, for observing this curious Phaenomenon when it should happen, and concluding as follows —

"I have sent, by Capt. *Sparks*, a Reflecting Telescope with *Dolland's* Micrometer, exact to your request, which I hope will come safe to hand. After making your observation with it, I desire you will present it, in my name, to the College — Messrs. *Mason* and *Dixon* tell me, they never used a better than that which I formerly sent to the Library Company of *Philadelphia*, with which a good observation may be made, tho' it has no micrometer."

We were now enabled to furnish the *Norriton* Observatory, as follows, *viz.*

1. A GREGORIAN REFLECTOR about 2f. focal length, with a *Dolland's* Micrometer. This Telescope hath four different magnifying powers, viz. 55, 95, 130, and 200 times; by means of two Tubes containing eye-glasses that magnify differently, and two small Speculums of different focal distances.

Made by *Nairne*.   Used by Dr. SMITH.

2. A REFRACTOR of 42f. its magnifying power about 140. The glasses were sent from *London* with the large Reflector, and belonged to

Harvard College, *New England*; but as long as they did not arrive time enough to be sent to that place before the Transit, they were fitted up here, by Mr. *Rittenhouse*, and —

Used by Mr. LUKENS.

3. Mr. *Rittenhouse's* REFRACTOR, with an Object glass of 16f. focus, and a convex eye-glass of 3 inches, magnifying about 144 times

Used by HIMSELF.

Both these Refractors, as well as the Reflector, were in most exquisite order.

4. An *Equal-Altitude Instrument;* its telescope three and an half f. focal length, with two horizontal hairs, and a vertical one, in its focus, firmly supported on a stone pedestal, and easily adjusted to a plummet wire 4 feet in length, by 2 screws; one moving it in a North and South, the other in an East and West, direction.

5. A TRANSIT-TELESCOPE, fixed in the *Meridian* on an axis with fine steel points; so that the hair in its focus can move in no other direction than along the meridian; in which are two marks South and North, about 330 yards distance easy; to which it can be readily adjusted in a horizontal position by one screw, as it can in a vertical position by another screw.

6. AN excellent TIME-PIECE, having for its pendulum-rod a flat steel-bar, with a *bob* weighing about 12 lb. and vibrating in a small arch. It goes 8 days, does not stop when wound up, beats dead seconds, and is kept in motion by a weight of 5 pounds.

THESE three last articles were also Mr. *Rittenhouse's* property, and made by himself.

7. AN ASTRONOMICAL QUADRANT, two and an half f. radius, made by *Siffon*, the property of the *East-Jersey* Proprietors; under the care of the Right Hon. *William* Earl of *Stirling*, Surveyor-General of that Province; from whom Mr. *Lukens* procured the use of it, and sent it up to Mr. *Rittenhouse* for ascertaining the latitude of the Observatory. Thus we were at length compleatly furnished with every instrument proper for our work.

As Mr. *Rittenhouse's* dwelling at *Norriton* is about 20 miles North-West of *Philadelphia,* our other engagements did not permit Mr. *Lukens* or myself, to pay much attention to the necessary preparations; but we knew that we had entrusted to a gentleman on the spot, who had joined to a compleat skill in *Mechanics,* so extensive an *astronomical* and *mathematical* knowledge, that the use, management, and even the construction, of the necessary apparatus, were perfectly familiar to him. Mr. *Lukens* and myself could not set out for his house till *Thursday, June 1st*; but, on our arrival there, we found every preparation so forward, that we had little to do, but to examine, and adjust our respective telescopes to distinct vision. He had fitted up the different instruments, and made a great number of observations, to ascertain the going of his Time-Piece, and to determine the latitude and longitude *of his Observatory* . . .

6

An Oration Delivered February 4, 1774

SOURCE: Benjamin Rush, *An Oration, Delivered February 4, 1774, before the American Philosophical Society, held at Philadelphia, containing an Enquiry into Natural History of MEDICINE among the Indians in North-America, and A Comparative View of their Diseases and Remedies, with those of civilized Nations* (Philadelphia, 1774). Readex Microprint Series, Evans No. 13592.

The state of a country in point of population, temperance and industry, is so connected with its diseases, that a tolerable idea may be formed of it, by looking over its bills of mortality. HOSPITALS, with all their boasted advantages, exhibit at the same time monuments of the charity and depravity of a people. The opulence of physicians, and the divisions of their offices, into those of surgery, pharmacy and midwifery, are likewise proofs of the declining state of a country. In the infancy of the Roman Empire, the priest performed the office of a physician; so simple were the principles and practice of physic. It was only on the declension of the empire that physicians vied with the emperors of Rome in magnificence and splendor.

I am sorry to add in this place, that the number of patients in the HOSPITAL and incurables in the ALMSHOUSE of this city show, that we are treading in the enervated steps of our fellow subjects in Britain. Our bills of mortality likewise show the encroachments of British diseases upon us. The NERVOUS FEVER has become so familiar to us, that we look upon it as a natural disease. Dr. Sydenham so faithful in his history of fevers, takes no notice of it. Dr. Cadwallader informed me, that it made its first appearance in this city, about five and twenty years ago. It will be impossible to name the CONSUMPTION without recalling to our minds the memory of some friend, or relation, who has perished within these few years by that disorder. Its rapid progress among us has been unjustly attributed to the growing resemblance of our climate to that of Great-Britain. The HYSTERIC and HYPO-CHONDRIAC DISORDERS, once peculiar to the chambers of the great, are now to be found in our kitchens, and workshops. All these diseases have been produced by our having deserted the simple diet, and manners of our ancestors.

The blessings of literature, commerce and religion, were not *originally* purchased at the expence of health. The complete enjoyment of health is as compatible with civilization, as the enjoyment of civil liberty. We read of countries, rich in every thing that can form national happiness and national grandeur, the diseases of which are nearly as few and simple as those of the Indians. We hear of no diseases among the Jews, while they were under their democratical form of government, except such as were inflicted by a supernatural power. We should be tempted to doubt the accounts given of the populousness of that people, did we not see the practice of their simple customs, producing nearly the same populousness in Egypt, Rome, and other countries of antiquity. The empire of China, it is said contains more inhabitants than the whole of Europe. The political institutions of that country have exempted its Inhabitants from a large share of the diseases of other civilized nations. The inhabitants of Switzerland, Denmark, Norway and Sweden, enjoy the chief advantages of civilization without having surrendered for them the blessings of natural health. But it is unnecessary to appeal to antient or remote nations to prove, that health is not incompatible with civilization. The inhabitants of many parts of New-England, particularly the province of Connecticut, are strangers to artificial diseases. — Some of you may remember the time, and our fathers have told those of us who do not, when the diseases of PENNSYLVANIA were as few and as simple as those of the Indians. The food of the inhabitants was then simple: their only drink was water: their appetites were restrained by labor: religion excluded the influence of sickening passions: private hospitality supplied the want of a public hospital: nature was their only nurse: temperance their principal physician. But I must not dwell upon this retrospect of primeval manners: and I am too strongly impressed with a hope of such happy days, to pronounce them the golden age of our province.

Our esteem for the customs of our savage neighbours will be lessened when we add, that civilization does not preclude the honors of old age. The proportion of old people is much greater among civilized, then among savage nations. It would be easy to decide this assertion in our favor, by appealing to facts in the natural histories of Britain, Norway, Sweden, the province of Connecticut, and several of the West-India islands.

The laws of decency and nature, are not necessarily abolished by the customs of civilized nations. In many of these, we read of women among whom nature alone still performs the office of a mid-wife — and who feel the obligations of suckling their children, to be equally binding with the common obligations of morality.

Civilization does not render us less fit for the necessary hardships of war. We read of armies of civilized nations, who have endured degrees of cold, hunger and fatigue, which have not been exceeded by the savages of any country.

Civilization does not always multiply the avenues of death. It appears from the bills of mortality, of many countries, that fewer in proportion die among civilized, than among savage nations.

Even the charms of beauty are not necessarily given up in civilization. We read of stateliness, proportion, and fine complexions in both sexes, forming the principal outlines of national characters.

The danger of many diseases, is not proportioned to their violence, but to their duration. America has advanced but a few paces in luxury and effeminacy. There is yet strength enough in her vitals, to give life to those parts which are decayed. She may recall her steps. — For this purpose,

I. Let our children be educated in a manner more agreeable to nature.

II. Let the common people (who constitute the wealth and strength of our country) be preserved from the effects of intemperance. The increase of the price of spirituous liquors for this purpose, is a remedy as unequal to the design, as it is destructive to liberty and commerce. Sir William Temple tells us, that in Spain no man can be admitted as an evidence in court, who has once been convicted of drunkeness. I do not call for so severe a law in this country. Let us first try the force of severe manners. Lycurgus governed more by these, than by his laws. "Bonae mores non bonae leges," according to Tacitus, were the bulwarks of virtue among the ancient Germans.

III. Let us be cautious what kind of manufactures we admit among us. What is patriotism in one country may be treason in another. The same public spirit which leads a Hollander to promote all kinds of manufactories in his country overgrown with inhabitants, should lead us to oppose them, as hurtful to the true interest of our own. The rickets made their first appearance in the manufacturing towns in England. Dr. Fothergill informed me, that he had often observed, when a pupil, that the greatest part of the chronic patients in the London-Hospital were Spitalfield weavers. I would not be understood, from these facts, to discourage those manufactures which employ women and children: these suffer few inconveniencies from a sedentary life: nor do I mean to offer the least restraint to those manufactories among men, which admit of free air and the exercise of all their limbs.

IV. I despair of being able to call the votaries of Bacchus from their bottle, and shall therefore leave them to be roused by the more eloquent twinges of the gout.

V. I pass over likewise the ravages which TEA is making upon the health and populousness of our country. Had I a double portion of all that eloquence which has been employed in describing the political evils which lately accompanied this East-India herb, it would be too little to set forth the numerous and contemplated diseases which it has introduced among us. To encounter this hydra, requires an arm accustomed, like that of Hercules, to vanquish monsters.

The population of a country is not to be accomplished by rewards and punishments. And it is happy for America, that the universal prevalence of the protestant religion — the checks lately given to negro slavery — the general unwillingness among us to acknowledge the usurpations of primogeniture — the addition of Canada to the British empire — the universal practice of inoculation for the small-pox — and the absence of the plague, render the interposition of government for that purpose unnecessary.

These advantages can only be secured to our country by AGRICULTURE. This is the true basis of national health, riches and populousness. Nations, like individuals, never rise higher than when they are ignorant whither they are tending. It is impossible to tell from history, what will be the effects of agriculture — industry — temperance and commerce, urged on by the competition of colonies, united in the same general pursuits, in a country, which, for extent — variety of soil — climate — and number of navigable rivers, has never been equalled in any quarter of the globe. America is the theatre where human nature will probably receive her last and principal literary, civil and military honors.

But I recall myself from the ages of futurity. The province of Pennsylvania has already showed her sister colonies, the influence of agriculture and commerce upon the number and happiness of a people. It is scarcely an hundred years since our illustrious legislator, with a handful of men, landed upon these shores. Although the perfection of our government, the healthiness of our climate, and the fertility of our soil, seemed to ensure a rapid settlement of the province; yet it would have required a prescience bordering upon divine, to have foretold, that in such a short space of time, the province would contain above 300,000 inhabitants; and that near 30,000 of this number should compose a city, which should be the third, if not the second in commerce in the British empire. The pursuits of literature, require leisure and a total recess from clearing forests, planting, building, and all the common toils of settling a new country: But before these arduous works were accomplished, the SCIENCES, ever fond of the company of liberty and industry, chose this spot for the seat of their empire in this new world. Our COLLEGE, so catholic in its founding, and extensive in its objects, already sees her sons executing offices in the highest departments of society. I have now the honor of speaking in the presence of a most respectable number of philosophers — physicians — astronomers — botanists — patriots and legislators; many of whom have already seized the prizes of honor, which their ancestors had allotted to a much later posterity. Our first offering had scarcely found its way into the temple of fame, when the oldest societies of Europe turned their eyes upon us, expecting with impatience to see the mighty fabric of science, which like a well built arch, can only rest upon the whole of its materials, completely finished from the treasures of this unexplored quarter of the globe.

It reflects equal honor upon our society and the honourable assembly of our province, to acknowledge, that we have always found the latter willing to encourage by their patronage, and reward by their liberality, all our schemes for promoting useful knowledge. What may we not expect from this harmony between the sciences and government! Methinks I see canals cut — rivers once impassable, rendered navigable — bridges erected — and roads improved, to facilitate the exportation of grain. — I see the banks of our rivers vieing in fruitfulness with the banks of the river of Egypt. — I behold our farmers, nobles — our merchants, princes. — But I forbear — Imagination cannot swell with the subject.

I beg leave to conclude, by deriving an argument from our connection with the legislature, to remind my auditors of the duty they owe to the society. Patriotism and literature are here connected together; and a man cannot neglect the one, without being destitute of the other. Nature and our ancestors have completed their works amongst us; and have left us nothing to do, but to enlarge and perpetuate our own happiness.

7

An Oration, Delivered February 24, 1775

SOURCE: David Rittenhouse, *An Oration, Delivered February 24, 1775, before the American Philosophical Society, held at Philadelphia, for Promoting Useful Knowledge* (Philadelphia, 1775). Readex Microprint Series, Evans No. 14432.

Pardon these reflections; they rise not from the gloomy spirit of misanthropy. That being before whose piercing eye, all the intricate foldings and dark recesses of the human heart become expanded and illuminated, is my eyewitness with what sincerity, with what ardor, I wish for the happiness of the whole race of mankind: How much I admire that disposition of lands and seas, which affords a communication between distant regions, and a mutual exchange of benefits: How sincerely I approve of those social refinements which really add to our happiness, and induce us with gratitude to acknowledge our great creator's goodness. — How I delight in a participation of the discoveries made from time to time in nature's works, by our Philosophic brethren in Europe.

But when I consider, that *luxury* and her constant follower *tyranny*, who have long since laid in the dust, never to rise again, the glories of Asia, are now advancing like a torrent irresistible, whose weight no human force can stem, and have nearly compleated their conquest of Europe; luxury and tyranny, who by a vile affectation of virtues they know not, pretend at first to be the patrons of science and philosophy, but at length fail not effectually to destroy them; agitated I say by these reflections, I am ready to wish — vain wish! that nature would raise her everlasting bars between the new and old world; and make a voyage to Europe as impracticable as one to the moon. I confess indeed, that by our connections with Europe we have made most surprizing, I had almost said unnatural advances towards the meridian of glory; But by those connections too, in all probability, our fall will be premature. May the God of knowledge inspire us with wisdom to prevent it; Let our harbours, our doors, be shut against luxury. But I return to my subject, and will no longer indulge these melancholy thoughts.

Some have observed, that the wonderful discoveries of the microscope ought to go hand in hand with those of the telescope; lest while we contemplate the many instances of the wisdom and power of divine Providence, displayed in the great works of creation, we should be tempted to conclude that man, and other less important beings of this lower world, did not claim its attention. But I will venture to affirm, without at all derogating from the merits of those who have so greatly obliged the world with the success of their microscopical enquiries, that no such danger is to be apprehended. Nothing can better demonstrate the immediate presence of the deity in every part of space, whether vacant or occupied by matter, than astronomy does. It was from an astronomer St. Paul quoted that exalted expression, so often since repeated, *"In God we live, and move, and have our being."* His divine energy supports that universal *substratum* on which all corporeal substances subsist, that the laws of motion are derived from, and that wings *light* with angelic swiftness.

If the time would permit, how agreeable the talk to dwell on the praises of Astronomy: To consider its happy effects as a science, on the human mind. Let the sceptical writers forbear to lavish encomiums on their cobweb Philosophy, liable to be broken by the smallest incident in Nature. They tell us it is of great service to mankind, in banishing bigotry and superstition from amongst us. Is not this effectually done by Astronomy? The direct tendency of this science is to dilate the heart with universal benevolence, and to enlarge its views. But then it does this without propagating a single point of doctrine contrary to common sense, or the most cultivated reason. It flatters no fashionable princely device, or national depravity. It encourages not the libertine by relaxing any of the precepts of morality; nor does it attempt to undermine the foundations of religion. It denies none of those attributes, which the wisest and best of mankind, have in all ages ascribed to the deity: Nor does it degrade the human mind from that dignity, which is ever necessary to make it contemplate itself with complacency. None of these things does Astronomy pretend to; and if these things merit the aim of Philosophy, and the encouragement of a people, then let scepticism flourish and Astronomy lie neglected; then let the names of Berkeley and Hume become immortal, and that of Newton be lost in oblivion.

I shall conclude this part of my discourse with the words of Dr. Barrow — It is to Astronomy we owe "that we comprehend the huge fabric of the universe, admire and contemplate the wonderful beauty of the divine workmanship, and so learn the invincible force and sagacity of our own minds, as to acknowledge the blessings of heaven with a pious affection."

I now come, in the last place, to point out some of the defects of Astronomy at this day. Which I am induced to undertake by the hopes I entertain that some of those defects may be removed under the auspices of this society and of you my fellow citizens who have so zealously promoted its institution. "The advantages arising from Astronomy, the pleasure attending the study of it, the care with which it was cultivated by many great men among the ancients, and the extraordinary attention paid to it in Europe by the present age," all contribute to recommend it to your protection, under which we have the best reason to expect that it will flourish.

The mildness of our climate and the serenity of our atmosphere, perhaps not inferior to that of Italy, and likewise our distant situation from the principal observatories in the world (whence many curious phenomena must be visible here that are not likely to be observed any where else) are so many circumstances greatly in our favour.

And I trust there will not be wanting men of genius, to arise in this new world, whose talents may be particularly adapted to astronomical enquiries.

LAWRENCE H. LEDER

Colonial Political Thought

T HOMAS PAINE CLEARLY SPOKE for the eighteenth century when he announced that "government even in its best state is but a necessary evil; in its worst state an intolerable one. . . . Government, like dress, is the badge of lost innocence; the palaces of kings are built on the ruins of the bowers of paradise." Colonial Americans looked back fondly on the bowers of paradise, on the state of nature in which they had had no need for government. Yet they knew that their too-recent fall from divine grace ill-prepared them for the angelic luxury of absolute, uncontrolled liberty, that their own perversities would soon convert liberty into license and would make men like beasts feeding upon one another. They understood that neither men nor liberty itself could long survive without order, without clearly defined limits to prevent men's abuse of liberty.

How to curb men's bestial instincts, while at the same time allowing them maximum enjoyment of their God-given liberty, became the conundrum of eighteenth-century political thought, especially in colonial America. All human societies needed order, and men established government for that purpose. However, the New World placed a premium on order because of its raw, unstructured state, because it presented men with the grossest uncertainties on every hand. For the adventuresome few, these

uncertainties offered great opportunities; for the timid majority,
they created great fears.

As a people living on civilization's frontier and facing an untamed and unknown wilderness whose very dimensions remained
a mystery to them, colonial Americans had a deeper appreciation
of the state of nature's significance than did their contemporaries
in Europe. The latter from the moment of their birth found themselves in a traditional and highly organized society. However,
when the first settlers arrived in Jamestown, New Amsterdam, or
Plymouth — and each generation repeated the sensation as it
moved to the newest frontier — they found themselves truly living
in a state of nature, in an arrangement which had no structure
or order other than that which they carried in their own minds.

By their move to the New World Americans acquired a greater
degree of liberty than their contemporaries ever knew. And they
venerated their liberty, but it also scared them because they understood their own inadequacies better than they did their new milieu.
Rather than resolve their dilemma by purposefully restricting
their liberty, they moved instead to curb their own evil propensi-
ties by creating government. They recognized that men needed to
impose an artificial structure and rationality on themselves and
thereby sacrifice a minimum of liberty in order to preserve as
much of that attribute as they could safely utilize.

As a consequence of their view of the role of government,
eighteenth-century men had different expectations of that institution than we do today. They saw it solely as an instrument to control men's baser instincts; we view it as a mechanism to better
men's lot. Government in that era had a negative and static function, not the positive and dynamic one that we have given it.
Thomas Paine succinctly expressed this when he defined "the true
design and end of government" as security. "It unanswerably follows," he continued, "that whatever form thereof appears most
likely to ensure it to us, with the least expence and greatest benefit,
is preferable to all others." Indeed, apart from the elitist group
which led the Enlightenment and popularized the concept of progress, eighteenth-century men thought in terms of tradition, custom, order, and stability and viewed government as a device to
preserve those qualities.

However, those who created and administered government were
imperfect men and they possessed antisocial passions. This meant
that government and those who governed had the potential to
abuse their authority and thereby destroy all liberty, something

against which mankind had to guard. Eighteenth-century thinkers tried to balance liberty and authority, to determine the permissible maximum of liberty which men could enjoy and the absolute minimum of government which they required. Too much liberty led to license and chaos, too much authority to tyranny and repression. Since liberty came from God (or nature), men could not alter it but could only ponder how much of it they could safely use; since men created government, they could change it as often as necessary so that it would best fulfill its proper function. Consequently, eighteenth-century political thought focused on the structure of government rather than the dimensions of liberty. Modern society has reversed those priorities largely because it has emphasized man's perfectibility rather than his imperfections.

Colonial Americans, in their discussions of the proper institutionalization of authority, looked backward to the wisdom of the ancient Greeks. They found the Greek idea of the cyclical development of power congenial, and they accepted the specific Greek concept that authority tended to degenerate from democracy to aristocracy to tyranny. Each form had its beneficial as well as its deleterious aspects, but Americans did not resignedly accept the constant transition from one form to another. They tried to capture the better elements of each and to bind them together in a static equilibrium. Maintenance of this balance became all-important, for otherwise society would quickly descend into the chaos of absolute liberty or escalate into the rigidity of absolute tyranny.

The key to the desired balance lay in structuring matters so that one element of authority counterbalanced another, thereby preventing each from dominating and destroying the others. To maintain the beneficial aspects of democracy, aristocracy, and monarchy, colonial Americans sought to tie them together in a contractual relationship, preferably in a written form so that they could constantly match performance against the ideal. A written constitution — whether called a fundamental frame, a charter, or even merely recorded customs and traditions — thus became the key to colonial political thought.

Eighteenth-century Americans, busy until the revolution in carving a civilization out of the wilderness, had little time for abstract speculations. Thus no cohesive body of political thought emerged within the covers of one volume until the famous *Federalist* papers appeared in 1787-88. Yet, Americans did speculate about their political system, often in response to immediate problems. Their theoretical constructs, admittedly on an *ad hoc* basis, do in retrospect possess enough consistency to constitute a coherent body of thought. Repeated often enough over the years, this thought became a common possession of the Americans.

Americans who considered the theoretical aspects of politics often dealt first with the nature of the British constitution. This topic had a compelling practicality for colonials trying to define their place within the empire. By beginning with an understanding of Great Britain's basic frame of government, they could determine their own position with greater precision. Moreover, given the general adulation of things British by eighteenth-century Americans, their use of the mother country's constitution as a guide for their own governmental arrangements made perfectly good sense to all concerned.

Initial American views of the British constitution fluctuated between two extremes: they either accepted Parliament as the constitution, thereby making the document flexible and changeable, or they insisted that the constitution consisted of rigidly fixed principles and rules, thereby making it unchangeable. Each approach, of course, led to a totally different conclusion. If the constitution had no fixed limits, if Parliament had absolute discretionary power, the colonists were at its mercy and that of its agents. Certainly they would have had little ability to maintain the powers they claimed for themselves. However, if the constitution were fixed beyond the ability of Parliament or the monarch to make independent alterations, the Americans could by imitation substantiate certain claims for themselves.

The first evidence of colonial concern about constitutionalism — about the limits of governmental authority — appeared as early as 1715, but Americans did not begin to ask appropriate questions of the British constitution until the 1720s. That decade saw increasing controversy between American legislatures and imperial administrators over expansions of local power, particularly as British policy-makers took a more rigid and formalistic approach toward colonial affairs, while American social and governmental institutions began to mature. As colonials took upon themselves a larger share of policy-making, they became concerned with defining the ultimate authority that controlled their destinies.

For a variety of reasons political commentators in the middle colonies first attempted definitions of the British constitution. Having been founded late as British colonies — New York in 1664, New Jersey at the same time, and Pennsylvania in 1683 — they reached political and social maturity later than the New England and southern colonies. Moreover, they reached maturity at a time of increasing British involvement in colonial affairs, at a time consequently of greater disagreements between the mother country and its colonies.

An effort to moderate a typical Anglo-American conflict appeared in James Logan's charge to the Philadelphia grand jury in 1723. To make his fellow subjects aware of their benefits from imperial membership, he explicated the British constitution. He praised the British for combining the best aspects of monarchy, aristocracy, and democracy within their governmental system. He then described the king as the supreme governor, but one limited in his powers by law. Most important, Logan stipulated that law depended upon the combined efforts of the monarch, the aristocracy, and the commons, and that no one element could alter the law without the consent of the other two. Without derogating the executive, Logan had reemphasized the assembly's importance, a key factor in colonial politics. The Pennsylvania legislature fully utilized this point a few years later when it lectured Governor Patrick Gordon on his proper relationship with the assembly. Governor William Burnet even used the same idea when he lectured the Massachusetts General Court, but he insisted that the executive had a role of equal importance with the assembly, a point conveniently forgotten on many occasions by colonial politicians.

Americans gave constant reaffirmation to the view that the excellence of the British constitution lay in the even balance of authority between each branch of government. During the New York trial of John Peter Zenger for seditious libel in 1735, the ensuing controversy included theoretical discussions of the nature of power and its distribution. Critics of Governor William Cosby's repressive policies warned him of the importance of balanced government and of limits upon executive authority. "The property of the people is fenced," one newspaper essayist boasted, "and the power of the prince bounded with received and established laws." The mutual dependence of the several branches of government, another essayist suggested, meant that "the power of the sovereign is moderated, and the liberty of the people is secured."

Admiration for balanced government did not go unchallenged. John Webbe, writing under the pseudonym "Z," presented a contrary approach in a series of newspaper essays in Philadelphia. He limited the sovereign's power, noting as had Bracton centuries before that the king could do no wrong because if he did he would no longer be king. However, Webbe created a major difficulty for his fellow colonials by his answer to the question of who could determine when the king had forfeited his power by his abuse of it. Webbe answered that that belonged exclusively to Parliament, which had limitless authority — "they could do anything," he suggested, "but turn a man into a woman." Webbe said that no past parliamentary action remained sacrosanct, that each session of Parliament by majority vote could undo the work of its predecessors. The uncertainties embodied in this view carried countless dangers for colonial Americans.

Indeed, Americans desperately required a fixed British constitution that allocated limited powers to each branch of government, and since it did not exist they set about to construct it as a myth. As colonial legislatures expanded their activities, often at the expense of gubernatorial power, they justified themselves by claiming that they simply tried to reproduce the British constitution in America. But for it to serve their purposes, that constitution had to place limits upon all forms of power, whether monarchical, aristocratic, or democratic. By fixing limits to the king's power, they limited the governor; by fixing limits to Parliament's power, they limited the assemblies. Of course, the colonial argument contained an unstated premise: local assemblies had not yet attained the same powers as the House of Commons. Thus they could cast their aggressive expansion of their own power within an acceptable context — that of duplicating the British constitution as they defined it.

Time and again, colonial Americans justified themselves in this way and constantly reaffirmed their belief in the need to limit authority. A Boston essayist in 1748 stipulated that the monarch had all necessary powers, but he was "so restrained by the fundamental laws of the constitution as that the subject is in no danger of oppression and tyranny." No one, not even the king, stood above the law; if the monarch violated the law "he ought to be deemed an enemy to the community." An extended series of essays published in Maryland in 1748 fully explored the whole problem, with one essayist defending the Webbe approach and another refuting it. The final article in the series admitted that Parliament did have great power and could change anything passed by its predecessors, but it warned of "some fundamentals which it would not be *safe* for a parliament to alter." Any tampering with the rights of persons or property authorized the people to resist, to return to the state of nature, and to reconstitute government in a safer fashion.

Americans by the mid-eighteenth century did not openly challenge the idea of a firmly fixed British constitution. Indeed, some in the 1750s even suggested that a law could be "unconstitutional." However, the colonial emphasis upon a clearly defined fundamental law which restricted all governmental power begged the question of where Americans could find that law. They turned, perhaps in desperation, to Magna Carta and the 1707 Act of Union between England and Scotland as examples of fundamental law. The Great Charter, one colonial announced without fear of contradiction, "is only declaratory of the principal grounds, of the fundamental laws and liberties of England." Magna Carta only affirmed a set of preexisting principles, which therefore remained beyond the power of any governmental agency to contradict or modify, whether or not Magna Carta continued in effect. Another colonial, with equally firm conviction, declared that not even Parliament could violate the Act of Union, for to do so would "destroy [the people's] obligations to obedience." Indeed, he suggested that British judges exercised judicial review by measuring subsequent parliamentary statutes against the Act of Union.

Development of the idea that the British government operated under the limits of a fixed and easily defined constitution seemed harmless enough as long as neither Crown nor Parliament seriously interfered in internal colonial affairs. This condition held until the end of the French and Indian War. After 1763, however, the British moved to reform their empire, at first by tightening up on traditional practices and, when that failed, by innovative approaches to the financial, military, and political problems of the empire. Once the British authorities took that latter step, the myth of the British constitution created by the Americans suddenly became meaningless. The British government had done things which Americans had convinced themselves it could not do. Americans protested against these violations of the mythical British constitution, but their pleas fell on deaf ears. In the 1760s and especially in the 1770s, as the American myth finally confronted British reality, Britain and its colonies came to a parting of the ways.

At the same time Americans created their own definition of the British constitution, they struggled to define the colonial constitution, to apply those imperial standards to their local situations. They meant to limit the power of their governors and to enhance the power of their legislatures. However, in doing so, Americans had to deal with the reality of an immediate situation rather than the imagery of a remote one.

One reality with which colonials had to deal was the extraordinary diversity of their constitutions. Some colonies (Connecticut and Rhode Island, and to a lesser degree, Massachusetts) had royal charters given to the people of the colony legally joined together as a corporation. These charters easily lent themselves to constitutional interpretations and — provided no one delved too deeply into the power which initially created them and which therefore could alter them — could be viewed as permanent and immutable. Other colonies (Pennsylvania and Maryland) had royal charters granted to proprietors. These offered some protection to the people of those colonies, who viewed them as binding contracts which limited the authority of both the grantor and the recipient. Thus these colonists could claim protection against both king and proprietor. Finally, most colonies were governed directly under Crown authority, and these usually could not claim protection from any written document, although some minor exceptions existed. Thus the evaluation by Americans of their own constitutions led to most uneven results.

Debates within each colony over the nature of its constitution usually emerged from traditional legislative-executive disputes over finances. Since those living in Crown colonies most often felt the threat of royal authority, the dispute over popular as opposed to gubernatorial or royal power most often centered in them. As early as 1711 the New York assembly insisted that its exclusive right to dispose of the people's money came "from the free choice and election of the people, who ought not to be divested of their property (nor justly can) without their consent." When a New York attorney, Joseph Murray, defined the situation in 1734, he made an even stronger statement: Assemblies gain their power "from the common custom and laws of England, claimed as an Englishman's birthright, and as having been such by immemorial custom in England." Thus the origin and authority of New York's assembly owed nothing to either the Crown or the governor, but emerged from an authority independent of both.

Royal governors did not take kindly to such claims, and Governor Lewis Morris of New Jersey warned his assembly that only the king's letters patent to him established "the constitution of government here." Since governors took as pragmatic an attitude as did their legislatures, they often compared the colonial situation with the British one when it served their interests. This was their mistake. By doing so they hoped to emphasize the regal nature of their authority, but they could not avoid conceding that the assembly most closely resembled the House of Commons, and

thus they played right into the legislators' hands. Governor George
Clarke did just this in 1739, when he announced that the New
York constitution resembled the British "as nearly . . . as the
nature of the thing would admit of." "Why would you not tread in
the steps of a British Parliament?" he asked his assembly.

No question could have pleased the colonials more. Although
they refused to apply this logic to the immediate problem as Clarke
desired, they gratefully agreed to the parallel. Some governors
realized the dangers implicit in this parallelism and tried to avoid
giving the colonials such a wide opening. Governor Lewis Morris
continually lectured the New Jersey assembly on its responsibili-
ties. On several occasions he warned them that the colonial constitution was patterned on the British, but only "by virtue of his
Majesty's letters patent . . . and instructions . . . by which solely
we have the power of legislation." He claimed that the king had
invested him with the exclusive power to call, adjourn, prorogue,
and dissolve assemblies, and they "are bound on their allegiance
to obey."

Governors often began their administrations in the fond expectation of cooperation, and they would urge the assemblymen
to "understand and love the English constitution." Governor
George Clinton delivered that injunction to his first assembly in
New York, but he soon found himself sternly lecturing the legislators. They sat and acted only by the authority of the king's commission to the governor, and the Crown could alter that grant at
pleasure. Moreover, he added, "every branch of the legislature . . .
may be criminal in the eyes of the law, and there is a power able to
punish you."

As the dispute heated up in New York between Clinton and his
assembly, still more interesting comments appeared in the public
prints. One critic of the governor suggested that the British constitution firmly fixed rules upon monarch and people alike, that
while he could not presume to compare a governor to the king, a
council to the House of Lords, or an assembly to the House of
Commons, each colonial institution should aim at imitating the
merits of its English counterpart. This evoked a more moderate
response from Clinton's supporters, who now suggested that the
beauty of the New York constitution, like that of the English constitution, consisted "in the due balance between the several
branches of the legislature." As always, the opponents disagreed
as to who had been aggressively upsetting that balance.

Controversies in royal colonies between governors and assemblies over their respective powers and the sources of those powers continued throughout the colonial period. The only specific documents to which either side could point did little to resolve the disputes. The royal commission and instructions to a colonial governor clearly gave him greater power than any colonial assembly would ever accept. To find a superior source of authority which would override the governor's claims, assemblies frequently resorted to such speculative devices as parallels between English and colonial forms, and eventually to the nebulous concept of the rights of Englishmen.

Proprietary and corporate colonies had far less difficulty in determining the nature of their constitutions, for they could point to a specific document, a charter, which the issuing authority could not alter without either the consent of the inhabitants or proof that they had broken the contract. English law gave a special status to charters as property rights, which English officials had hesitated to attack (except in due course of law) ever since the reigns of Charles I and James II, both of whom had illegally interfered with such rights to their regret. However, these documents were subject to interpretation, and that led to serious questions about their permanence, the relationship between English and colonial forms, and the applicability of English laws in the colonies.

Pennsylvanians and Marylanders referred to specific documents when they claimed constitutional privileges. The royal charters to the Penn and Baltimore families placed limits upon the powers of the proprietors and guaranteed certain rights to those who settled on their lands; a contractual relationship between proprietors and settlers thus resulted, and the judiciary could enforce this relationship. Indeed, colonists in these provinces often found it advantageous to deny any parallel between their situation and that of England; they sometimes recognized that they possessed a major advantage — a written constitution — over other Englishmen. In Pennsylvania one essayist deplored those who "cry up the necessity of reducing the form of this government to the British model," and referred to the attempt as "a design almost as wicked, as was the attempt to change the English constitution into a democracy." A similar rejection of the "British model" occurred in Maryland when the assembly denied the council's authority to participate in legislation, since that effectively gave the governor, who was a mere subject, the right to appoint legislators over his fellow subjects without their consent.

Colonists in proprietaries did not limit themselves to attacks upon the council; they also took on the proprietary governor. As one essayist declared in 1757; "If then it be dangerous and destructive to the liberties of our mother country to invest a sovereign who knows no interest but his people's . . . with a power of making laws independent of his parliaments, how much more so is it to invest the temporary governor of a colony, a stranger to such sacred connections . . . with such an uncontrolled power?" This particular argument also found its use in royal colonies every time a governor tried to extend his authority at the expense of the popularly-elected assembly.

The two proprietary colonies of Pennsylvania and Maryland each went their own way, making the best possible use of their own individual charters. While both opposed all parallels with the English situation and attacked proprietary power, they produced no overarching principle which other colonies could use. As a matter of fact, Pennsylvania and Maryland challenged the very principle of parallelism on which royal colonies had to rely.

Corporate colonies, on the other hand, enjoyed a far greater degree of freedom from British control during the eighteenth century than did either royal or proprietary provinces. The property rights of their charters inhered in the people, rather than in the third party of a proprietor, and this made all the difference in the world. As the *New England Weekly Journal* phrased it, "Our charter is the great hedge which Providence has planted around our natural rights, to guard us from an invasion." Royal authorities found it extremely difficult to make their will effective in Massachusetts (which had only some of the attributes of a chartered colony) and almost impossible to do so in Connecticut or Rhode Island. The latter two colonies differed from Massachusetts, which had a royal governor, in that they even elected their own executives.

One consequence of this was the absence of serious discussions in either Rhode Island or Connecticut over the nature of their constitutions. No need existed to debate the issue, for no one within the colony challenged their complete autonomy. Lacking any effective royal authority within their borders, the inhabitants of those two provinces went about their business largely unhindered. Only in Massachusetts, where the external authority of a royal governor intruded to break the pattern of autonomy, did the issue get aired in a series of continuous and acrimonious debates.

A bitter dispute between Governor William Burnet and the General Court erupted almost as soon as he set foot in the colony in 1728. The Crown had instructed him to secure a permanent revenue and had directed the General Court to pay him a specific salary. Both of these matters, the legislature insisted, rested exclusively within its jurisdiction, and it pointed to the royal charter as justification. Burnet ended up by lecturing the General Court on its resemblance to the British model, but the legislators rejected any parallel between king and governor, noting that the king's interest was inseparable from that of his people, but the same could not be said for every governor. Unfortunately for Burnet, he could not hold his temper effectively and he possessed a streak of stubbornness. The dispute raged on until his death, only to be renewed on the arrival of Governor Jonathan Belcher.

Indeed, the Massachusetts legislature opportunistically adopted the governor's arguments about parallels between English and colonial situations and turned it against Belcher. It took him to task for threatening the General Court, a parliamentary body, with dire consequences for failing to obey the dictates of the Crown. The last monarch to have done so was Charles I, they reminded the governor, and that king had paid a heavy penalty for his mistake.

In viewing the acrimonious controversies in Massachusetts, a Rhode Islander took comfort in the fact that, "By our charter, our legislature and executive power are more agreeable to the equality of nature and do better serve the true ends of government than any other form or method whatever." Other New Englanders envied Rhode Island's autonomy. Indeed, when a Massachusetts essayist sought to publish his views, he found that he had to turn to a Rhode Island printer because the governor had intimidated all the Boston printers. This testified to the beneficial effects of Rhode Island's charter which excluded from the colony the external authority of a royal appointee.

Out of the turmoil that racked its politics came a clear understanding within Massachusetts by mid-eighteenth century of the nature and significance of its charter. One conservative essayist explored the powers of the legislature and found the executive so cowed that he uttered the traditional warning that the security of a free state depended upon the proper balance between the several parts of its government. Another essayist, not quite so conservative, examined the position of the royal governor and realistically concluded that it depended wholly on his ability to maneuver in a system of factional politics. After listing all of his formal powers, the essayist acknowledged that the governor's real authority came from the political influence he wielded among judges, sheriffs, and militia officers who, in turn, influenced the attitudes of the representatives in General Court. Beyond that, he also had the power of logic if he could harangue the legislators often and long enough to make an impression.

Clearly, the diversity of colonial governments by the 1760s led to an equally great diversity in their definitions of their own constitutions. Connecticut and Rhode Island remained silent while enjoying the blessings of autonomy, Massachusetts engaged in bitter internicine warfare with its governors and usually won, Maryland and Pennsylvania opportunistically and individually resolved their own problems with their proprietors, while the royal colonies floundered and came up with no clear-cut defense of their claims to authority.

Although the question of internal constitutional authority remained in flux by the early 1760s, succeeding events would force the colonists to reassess their positions and to realize that charter rights were indeed weak reeds upon which to rely. Colony after colony finally reconciled itself to this fact, beginning with the royal colonies, but soon including even those which had thought themselves fully protected by a royal charter. It was not mere coincidence that much of the prerevolutionary skirmishing between local authority and royal power took place in Massachusetts, a colony which had consistently beaten back Crown efforts to exercise control over its internal polity. The successful concentration of English power against the Bay Colony suggested the wisdom of finding broader ideas to oppose British policy innovations.

Some broader-based ideas had circulated in the colonies in the early eighteenth century, but only in the vaguest terms and almost never dealing with the kind of issue facing the Americans in the 1760s and 1770s. Colonists simply had no reason, prior to 1776, to develop a revolutionary philosophy. To fend off British incursions against their rights, they utilized such devices as Magna Carta, claiming that its guarantees extended across the Atlantic. However, they never offered any definition of it nor did they spell out just how it fitted their situations. Such imprecision had certain advantages, for Americans could challenge any British claim by alleging that it violated Magna Carta, thereby forcing the problem of definition on royal officials who sought to exercise their claims to authority. Indeed, this was entirely in keeping with eighteenth-century view of liberty, which as an absolute never needed definition, and of government, which as a positive, man-made factor always had to prove itself.

As early as 1721 Jeremiah Dummer summed up the rights of New England by simply stating that "the subjects abroad claim the privilege of Magna Carta," without ever once indicating the meaning of that phrase. This slogan found reiteration in colony after colony. In New York, when two prominent attorneys controverted an especially important case, both premised their arguments on Magna Carta and both defined it in the same simplistic manner. William Smith announced that New Yorkers had "a right to Magna Carta" and other ancient English statutes; Joseph Murray, who rebutted Smith's conclusions, agreed on the point that "our American abode has put no limitation on these rights." The "Watch Tower" essays in 1755 argued that Magna Carta also confirmed the right to jury trials, "this excellent bulwark of our liberties."

Beyond the vagaries of Magna Carta, American polemicists often recited "the great birthright of Englishmen." Just what they meant by this they never specified, except in dealing with the two topics of jury trials and taxation only by consent. The former included a continuing controversy in most colonies over the appointment of judges during the king's pleasure rather than during good behaviour. Uncertain tenure for judges left them dependent on the whim of royal officials, and only in this area did Americans completely fail to gain control. They never managed to make the judiciary independent of gubernatorial control; if they had done so they probably might have been much better equipped to resist all British policy. On the other hand, consensual taxation became at a very early date a key idea in the American political lexicon. In 1708 the New York assembly enunciated this principle and parroted the great lessons of seventeenth-century English history. Forty years later, a Marylander referred to this as "the great hinge upon which liberty hangs." This, too, was in keeping with eighteenth-century views of government, for only by controlling government's fiscal power could the people curb its authority and challenge its excesses.

Americans in the eighteenth century clearly understood the interplay between liberty and property. Liberty came in an absolute form from the state of nature, but its survival in society depended on the sanctity of property. In 1735 one essayist stipulated: "As for property, it is so interwoven with liberty that whenever we perceive the latter weakened, the former cannot fail of being impaired." This involved the view that only a financially secure people could afford to resist encroachments upon their liberty. Thus a tyrant first endeavored to undermine property rights; having done this, he could more readily move upon the people's liberty.

The blending of the "immediate gifts of God" (life and liberty), with property — "as absolutely essential to human happiness as even life or liberty" — made necessary government and imposed restrictions upon liberty. However, men had to frame those restrictions with utmost care so as to preserve a maximum of the "immediate gifts of God." As one minister put it in mid-century, "this I rest on as certain, that no more natural liberty or power is given up than is necessary for the preservation of person and property." A New York newspaper summed up the argument with brevity: "In all disputes between power and liberty, power must always be proved, but liberty proves itself; the one being founded on positive law, the other upon the law of nature."

Americans' failure to discuss their liberties in any detail, while perfectly in keeping with the ethos of the eighteenth century, presented them with a predicament once Anglo-American relations began to deteriorate in the 1760s and collapsed in the 1770s. They had forced the British to define the power they wanted to exercise, but until the 1760s the British had done so very hesitantly. However, after 1763, they became less and less reticent about rebutting colonial arguments and denying colonial pretensions. As British aggressiveness increased, Americans found their evocation of Magna Carta, the rights of Englishmen, and similar vagaries of little or no effectiveness. Such techniques left colonials at the mercy of British interpretations, and royal authorities now willingly defined them to the colonists' disadvantage. Thus Americans turned in the 1770s, once they had seen the flaws in their previous approach, to an even broader concept, which they could define as well as anyone else. They turned to the universal principles of the rights of man which overrode those peculiar to the colonials or the English.

Bernard Bailyn has defined the paradox of eighteenth-century American politics as the conflict between "a presumptuous prerogative and an over-great democracy." This kind of conflict existed throughout Anglo-America except for the isolated and insulated corporate colonies of Connecticut and Rhode Island. In all others, politicians opposed royal or proprietary authority almost as a matter of principle. In doing so, they tried to defend and apply to the colonial scene the Glorious Revolution Settlement of 1688. When Parliament ousted James II and installed William and Mary on the throne, it created the constitutional monarchy to which Americans so fervently gave their allegiance. Eighteenth-century colonials, like seventeenth-century Englishmen, feared the constant expansion of regal power. In the eighteenth century this no longer really bothered the majority of English politicians, but Americans continued to look for lustful enemies of liberty in every nook and cranny of government. Constantly reiterated fears of executive power-grabs, of efforts to weaken popularly-elected legislatures, of attempts to elevate hand-picked governor's councils to positions of preeminence — all these spelled perversions of the ideal balance which hypothetically made up the British constitutional system.

The resulting hysteria — a basic characteristic of the political system in colonial America — remained under control until 1763, largely because no one had challenged the American understanding of the system. The generally accepted context of British constitutionalism gave colonials a rational way of viewing their irrational world, a means of measuring themselves and the events around them. When the British abandoned that structure, they dealt Americans the cruelest possible blow because it set them adrift in the strange sea of presumed despotism.

For three-quarters of a century Americans had idealized Britain as the last stronghold of good and proper government. Suddenly, they discovered that that nation had become the source of all evil policies. They explained that constitutional virtue had been overwhelmed by the devil in the persons of George Grenville, then Charles Townshend, then Lord Hillsborough, and finally George III himself, especially after he rejected all American appeals for a return to reason. Americans continued to seek those in England who would overthrow the designing men around the throne and return the nation to its proper path. They put their faith in their champion during the French and Indian War, William Pitt, only to watch the Great Commoner sink into the peerage as Earl of Chatham. More than that, he brought about no reversal of policy as the king's first minister. Perhaps alone among all English political leaders Edumund Burke understood the Americans, but his pleas for reconciliation were only cries in the wilderness.

When the British Parliament passed the Declaratory Act in 1766 and enunciated its full authority over the empire, it cast the die. Americans refused to accept that clear and concise statute at face value, thereby striving to maintain a now meaningless fabric of empire. Instead, they spent the next decade vainly seeking to convince the British that the Americans's idealized image of the Old Empire should control the shape of the New. Their task was hopeless, especially for a people so bemused by their own myths.

Americans after 1766 had to confront reality, not myths. They had to deal directly with the issue of the locus of power within the empire; that is, they had to accept or reject without equivocation the terms of the Declaratory Act. By ignoring that document, they evaded the real issue more or less successfully for a decade, but the time of reckoning came soon enough. By 1776, they could no longer ignore the true problem, but even then they approached it within an ideological context as exemplified by the preamble to the Declaration of Independence. Not until they put together the Articles of Confederation did the Americans finally deal with the question of what should have been the political structure of the British Empire. By then, of course, it was too late, and the structure they erected in 1781 proved inadequate for their own use, even outside the Old Empire.

FOR FURTHER READING

Bailyn, Bernard. *The Ideological Origins of the American Revolution.* Cambridge: Harvard University Press, 1967.
————. *The Origins of American Politics.* New York: Vintage Books, 1968.
Colbourn, H. Trevor. *The Lamp of Experience: Whig History and the Intellectual Origins of the American Revolution.* Chapel Hill: University of North Carolina Press, 1965.
Douglass, Elisha P. *Rebels and Democrats: The Struggle for Equal Political Rights and Majority Rule During the American Revolution.* Chapel Hill: University of North Carolina Press, 1955.
Greene, Jack P. *The Quest for Power: The Lower House of Assembly in the Southern Royal Colonies, 1689-1776.* Chapel Hill: University of North Carolina Press, 1963.
Leder, Lawrence H. *Liberty and Authority: Early American Political Ideology, 1689-1763.* Chicago: Quadrangle Books, 1968.
McIlwain, Charles H. *The American Revolution: A Constitutional Interpretation.* New York: Macmillan, 1923.

1

Charles I's Answer to the 19 Propositions of Parliament, June 18, 1642

SOURCE: J. Rushworth, ed., *Historical Collections* (8 vols., London; 1659-1701), V, 730-32.

There being three kinds of government among men, absolute monarchy, aristocracy and democracy, and all these having their particular conveniences and inconveniences, the experience and wisdom of your ancestors hath so moulded this out of a mixture of these as to give to this kingdom (as far as human prudence can provide) the conveniences of all three, without the inconveniences of any one, as long as the balance hangs even between the three estates, and they run jointly on in their proper channel (begetting verdure and fertility in the meadows on both sides) and the overflowing of either on either side raise no deluge or inundation. The ill of absolute monarchy is tyranny, the ill of aristocracy is faction and division, the ills of democracy are tumults, violence and licentiousness. The good of monarchy is the uniting a nation under one head to resist invasion from abroad and insurrection at home; the good of aristocracy is the conjunction of counsel in the ablest persons of a state for the public benefit; the good of democracy is liberty, and the courage and industry which liberty begets.

In this kingdom the laws are jointly made by a king, by a house of peers, and by a House of Commons chosen by the people, all having free votes and particular privileges. The government, according to these laws, is [en]trusted to the King; power of treaties of war and peace, of making peers, of choosing officers and councillors for state, judges for law, commanders for forts and castles, giving commissions for raising men, to make war abroad, or to prevent or provide against invasions or insurrections at home, benefit of confiscations, power of pardoning, and some more of the like kind are placed in the King. And this kind of regulated monarchy, having this power to preserve that authority without which it would be disabled to preserve the laws in their force and the subjects in their liberties and properties, is intended to draw to him such a respect and relation from the great ones, as may hinder the ills of division and faction, and such a fear and reverence from the people as may hinder tumults, violence and licentiousness.

Again, that the prince may not make use of this high and perpetual power to the hurt of those for whose good he hath it, and make use of the name of public necessity for the gain of his private favourites and followers, to the detriment of his people, the House of Commons (an excellent convener of liberty, but never intended for any share in government, or the choosing of them that govern) is solely entrusted with the first propositions concerning the levy of money (which is the sinews as well of peace as of war), and the impeaching of those who for their own ends, though countenanced by any surreptitiously gotten command of the King, have violated the law, which he is bound (when he knows it) to protect; and to the prosecution of which they are bound to advise him, at least not to serve him to the contrary. And the Lords, being trusted with a judicatory power, are an excellent screen and bank between the prince and people, to assist each against any encroachments of the other, and by just judgements to preserve that law which ought to be the rule of every one of the three. . . .

Since therefore the power, legally placed in both houses, is more than sufficient to prevent and restrain the power of tyranny, and without the power which is now asked from us we shall not be able to discharge that trust which is the end of monarchy, since this would be a total subversion of the fundamental laws, and that excellent constitution of this kingdom which hath made this nation so many years both famous and happy to a great degree of envy, since to the power of punishing (which is already in your hands according to law) if the power of preferring be added, we shall have nothing left for us but to look on, since the encroaching of one of these estates upon the power of the other is unhappy in the effects, both to them and all the rest, since this power of at most a joint government in us with our councillors (or rather, our guardians) will return us to the worst kind of minority, and make us despicable both at home and abroad, and beget eternal factions and dissensions (as destructive to public happiness as war) both in the chosen, and in the houses that chose them, and the people who chose the choosers, since so new a power will undoubtedly intoxicate persons who were not born to it, and beget not only divisions among them as equals, but in them contempt of us, as become an equal to them, and insolence and injustice toward our people, as now so much their inferiors, which will be the more grievous unto them, as suffering from those who were so lately of a nearer degree to themselves, and being to have redress only from those that placed them, and fearing they may be inclined to preserve what they have made, both out of kindness and policy, since all great changes are extremely inconvenient, and almost infallibly beget yet greater changes, which beget yet greater inconveniences.

Since as great a one in the Church must follow this of the Kingdom, since the second estate would in all probability follow the fate of the first, and by some of the turbulent spirits jealousies would soon be raised against them, and the like propositions for reconciliation of differences would then be sent to them as they now have joined to send to us till (all power being vested in the House of Commons, and their number making them incapable of transacting affairs of state with the necessary service and expedition, these being retrusted to some close committee) at last the common people (who in the meantime must be flattered, and to whom licence must be given in all their wild humours, how contrary soever to established law, or their own real good) discover this *arcanum imperii,* that all this was done by them, but not for them, and grow weary of journey-work, and set up for themselves, call parity and independence liberty, devour that estate which had devoured the rest, destroy all rights and properties, all distinctions of families and merit, and by this means this splendid and excellently distinguished form of government end in a dark, equal chaos of confusion, and the long line of our many noble ancestors in a Jack Cade or a Wat Tyler.

2

Men Need Government

SOURCE: John Wise, *A Vindication of the Government of New-England Churches* (Boston, 1717), 33-46.

I shall consider man in a state of natural being, as a free-born subject under the crown of heaven, and owing homage to none but God himself. It is certain civil government in general, is a very admirable result of providence, and an incomparable benefit to mankind, yet must needs be acknowledged to be the effect of humane free-compacts and not of divine institution; it is the product of man's reason, of humane and rational combinations, and not from any direct orders of infinite wisdom, in any positive law wherein is drawn up this or that scheme of civil government. Government (says Lord Warrington) is necessary — in that no society of men can subsist without it; and that particular form of government is necessary which best suits the temper and inclination of a people. Nothing can be God's ordinance, but what he has particularly declared to be such; there is no particular form of civil government described in God's words, neither does nature prompt it. The government of the Jews was changed five times. Government is not formed by nature as other births or productions; if it were, it would be the same in all countries; because nature keeps the same method, in the same thing, in all climates. If a common wealth be changed into a monarchy, is it nature that forms and brings forth the monarch? Or if a royal family be wholly extinct (as in Noah's case, being not heir apparent from descent from Adam) is it nature that must go to work (with the king bees who themselves alone preserve the royal race in that empire) to breed a monarch before the people can have a king, or a government sent over them? And thus we must leave kings to resolve which is their best title to their crowns, whether natural right, or the constitution of government settled by humane compacts, under the direction and conduct of reason. . . .

The prime immunity in man's state, is that he is most properly the subject of the law of nature. He is the favourite animal on earth; in that this part of God's image, viz. Reason is congenate with his nature, wherein by a law immutable, instampt upon his frame, God has provided a rule for all men in all their actions, obliging each one to the performance of that which is right, not only as to justice, but likewise as to all other moral virtues, the which is nothing but the dictate of right reason founded in the soul of man. . . . That which is to be drawn from man's reason, flowing from the true current of that faculty, when unperverted, may be said to be the law of nature; on which account, the Holy Scriptures declare it written on men's hearts. . . . When we acknowledge the law of nature to be the dictate of right reason, we must mean that the understanding of man is endowed with such a power, as to be able, from the contemplation of humane condition to discover a necessity of living agreeably with this law: And likewise to find some principle, by which the precepts of it, may be clearly and solidly demonstrated. The way to discover the law of nature in our own state, is by a narrow watch, and accurate contemplation of our natural condition, and propensions. . . .

And to give such sentiments the force of law, we must suppose a God who takes care of all mankind, and has thus obliged each one, as a subject of higher principles of being, than mere instincts. For that all law properly considered, supposes a capable subject, and a superior power; and the law of God which is binding, is published by the dictates of right reason as other ways: . . . But moreover that God has established the law of nature, as the general rule of government, is further illustrable from the many sanctions in providence, and from the peace and guilt of conscience in them that either obey, or violate the law of nature. But moreover, the foundation of the law of nature with relation to government may be thus discovered, *scil.* Man is a creature extreamly desirous of his own preservation; of himself he is plainly exposed to many wants, unable to secure his own safety, and maintenance without the assistance of his fellows; and he is also able of returning kindness by the furtherance of mutual good; but yet man is often found to be malicious, insolent, and easily provoked, and as powerful in effecting mischief, as he is ready in designing it. That such a creature may be preserved, it is necessary that he be sociable; that is, that he may be capable and disposed to unite himself to those of his own species, and to regulate himself towards them, that they may have no fair reason to do him harm; but rather incline to promote his interests, and secure his rights and concerns. This then is a fundamental law of nature, that every man as far as in him lies, do maintain a sociableness with others, agreeable with the main end and disposition of humane nature in general. For this is very apparent, that reason and society render man the most potent of all creatures. And finally, from the principles of sociableness it follows as a fundamental law of nature, that man is not so wedded to his own interest, but that he can make the common good the mark of his aim: And hence he becomes capacitated to enter into a civil state by the law of nature; for without this property in nature, viz. sociableness, which is for the cementing of parts, every government would soon moulder and dissolve.

The second great immunity of man is an original liberty instampt upon his rational nature. He that intrudes upon this liberty, violates the law of nature. . . .

The internal native liberty of man's nature in general implies a faculty of doing or omitting things according to the direction of his judgement. But in a more special meaning, this liberty does not consist in a loose and ungovernable freedom, or in an unbounded license of acting. . . . The true natural liberty of man, such as really and truely agrees to him, must be understood, as he is guided and restrained by the tyes of reason, and laws of nature; all the rest is brutal, if not worse.

Man's external personal, natural liberty, antecedent to all humane parts, or alliances must also be considered. And so every man must be conceived to be perfectly in his own power and disposal, and not to be controuled by the authority of any other. And thus every man, must be acknowledged equal to every man, since all subjection and all command are equally banished on both sides; and considering all men thus at liberty, every man has a prerogative to judge for himself, viz. what shall be most for his behoof, happiness, and well-being.

The third capital immunity belonging to man's nature, is an equality amongst men; which is not to be denied by the law of nature, till man has resigned himself with all his rights for the sake of a civil state; and then his personal liberty and equality is to be cherished, and preserved to the highest degree, as will consist with all just distinctions amongst men of honour, and shall be agreeable with the publick good. For man has a high valuation of himself, and the passion seems to lay its first foundation (not in pride, but) really in the high and admirable frame and constitution of humane nature. . . .

Every man considered in a natural state, must be allowed to be free, and at his own dispose; yet to suit man's inclinations to society, and in a peculiar manner to gratify the necessity he is in of publick rule and order, he is impelled to enter into a civil community; and divests himself of his natural freedom, and puts himself under government; which amongst other things comprehends the power of life and death over him; together with authority to injoyn him some things to which he has an utter aversation, and to prohibit him other things, for which he may have as strong an inclination; so that he may be often under this authority, obliged to sacrifice his private, for the publick good. So that though man is inclined to society, yet he is driven to a combination by great necessity. For that the true and leading cause of forming governments and yielding up natural liberty, and throwing man's equality into a common pile to be new cast by the rules of fellowship; was really and truly to guard themselves against the injuries men were lyable to interchangeably; for none so good to man as man, and yet none a greater enemy. So that,

The first humane subject and original of civil power is people. For as they have a power every man over himself in a natural state, so upon a combination they can and do bequeath this power unto others; and settle it according as their united discretion shall determine. For that this is very plain, that when the subject of sovereign power is quite extinct, that power returns to the people again. And when they are free they may set up what species of government they please; or if they rather incline to it, they may subside into a state of natural being, if it be plainly for the best. . . .

The formal reason of government is the will of a community, yielded up and surrendered to some other subject, either of one particular person, or more, conveyed in the following manner.

Let us conceive in our mind a multitude of men, all naturally free and equal; going about voluntarily to erect themselves into a new commonwealth. Now their condition being such to bring themselves into a political body, they must needs enter into divers covenants.

They must interchangeably each man covenant to joyn in one lasting society, that they may be capable to concert the measures of their safety by a publick vote.

A vote or decree must then nextly pass to set up some particular species of government over them. And if they are joyned in their first compact upon absolute terms to stand to the decision of the first vote concerning the species of government; then all are bound by the majority to acquiesce in that particular form thereby settled, though their own private opinion, incline them to some other model.

After a decree has specified the particular form of government, then there will be need of a new covenant, whereby those on whom authority is conferred, engage to take care of the common peace, and welfare. And the subjects on the other hand, to yield them faithful obedience. In which covenant is included that submission and union of wills, by which a state may be conceived to be but one person. So that the most proper definition of a civil state, is this, viz. A civil state is a compound moral person, whose will (united by those covenants before passed) is the will of all; to the end it may use, and apply the strength and riches of private persons towards maintaining the common peace, security and well being of all. Which may be conceived as tho' the whole state was now become but one man; in which the aforesaid covenants may be supposed under God's providence to be the divine fiat, pronounced by God, let us make man. . . .

3

Rights Under the Charter

SOURCE: Anon., *Question: Are We Obliged in This Government of the Massachusetts, By Charter, To Settle a Salary Upon the Governour?* (Boston, 1729), 1, 2.

We are a dependent government, and are incorporated into one political body by charter, and all our power is derivative from thence; We may as well of our selves extend our bounds beyond the limits circumscribed to us in our charter, as our power beyond the charter limitations. Some indeed understand so little about politicks that they say, our general Assembly have got a parliamentary power, and can do as they will; or as the parliament of Great Britain can do; but that is a great mistake: The Parliament of Great Britain is a superior court, accountable to none but God alone: But our General Assembly is a body incorporated by charter, as before hath been said, and we have not an inch of power but what is contained in the charter: In the charter there is no power given the general assembly to provide neither for the defence of the governor, nor the support of the governing power, but by some act of law made by the legislature; . . .

It doth plainly appear by the charter that their Majesties King William and Queen Mary, did by charter frame our constitution so that the legislature should consist of three branches, either of which had a negative voice in all laws, &c. In it it did cloath the Governor the King's representative with several royal prerogatives, and the other two branches of the legislature with many ample privileges (and indeed such a government when it is kept in a due poize and ballance I think to be the best of governments) and then can any man imagine seeing plainly their Majesties design in the charter that they were guilty of such folly, or ignorance, that in the same charter they should put it into the hands of one branch of the legislature, viz. the Representatives, to cramp the first branch of the legislature, viz. the Governor, by withholding his support? . . .

4

The Necessity of Government

SOURCE: *The Universal Instructor in All Arts and Sciences: And the Pennsylvania Gazette,* April 3, 1729 (#15).

If men did punctually observe that excellent law of nature, to do as we would be done by, I think all the positive institutions of civil government would be entirely useless; but since this is rather to be made the subject of our most sanguine wish, than of any regular or well grounded expectation; and since by experience we know that men differ not only from one another in their opinions, but often very widely from themselves, this infinite variety in our natural constitutions, points out the beauties of vertue, social life and order; for some men, thro' negligence, or want of understanding, can no more judge of their own welfare, than children who would forfeit any future advantage for a present glittering toy: And as all cannot be immediately active in legislation, a trust is necessary to be reposed in such whose station, abilities and justice have given them time and inclination on the one hand, to guard us against the encroachments of power, and on the other hand, to secure a barrier against the insolence of popular fury. Hence government arises with all its beauties, when that trust is discharged with honour; but as power is of an encreasing nature thro' the weakness and imperfections of human kind, what was designed to support us in our rightful liberties, sometimes springs up into unlimited prerogative, where the will of the prince is made the measure of right and wrong. Some of these shackles, when once imposed, are uncomfortable, some grievous, and others intolerable; altho' I cannot conceive on what foundation absolute governments exercised with tyranny, can expect a full submission from their oppressed subjects, since such submission implies a renouncing their reason, which is really to renounce our characteristick, our very nature, and the only true measure of our allegiance; for men expect from the reasons of instituting government, to enjoy some advantages under it, which they cannot possess in a state of nature, as order and proportion take place in the moral as well as in the natural world. Now 'tis impossible there should be an absolute subjection in the state of nature, and consequently this oppression being a disadvantageous change, 'tis against the very end we propose in submitting to government; while on the other hand, the subjects of free well-regulated governments are happy in several degrees of liberty, in proportion to the excellence of their constitution. Some are tolerably happy, others are extreamly so: But as bodies filled with too much blood are in continual danger of the most fierce and raging distempers, an excess of liberty has often degenerated into licentious riots, and oppressed the common cause with insuperable convulsions.

Among the antients, the most unbounded liberties were allowed by the Lacedamonians in their government; for the administration was lodged equally in the different estates that composed the whole; their Kings had the executive powers in war, and their magistrates were annually elected to fill the courts of justice, while the legislative authority was lodged with the senate, who were chosen by the people, to whom also belonged the choice of officers of honour and trust, who were elected by ballot; and thus these officers made up an equal magistracy by an annual and just rotation; for he who executed or filled any post for the present, could not possess the same the ensuing year, because their constitution enjoyed that some small time at least should intervene. And thus in those early days they aimed at perfection of government, which they judged to consist in governing, so as men might seem to determine themselves freely while they were guided by laws, and the subject had just reason to believe his own advantage consisted in obedience to them.

5

Thoughts of Pretended Patriotism and Publick Spirit

SOURCE: *The New York Gazette,* March 11-18, 1733/34 (#438).

A Form of Government neither purely Monarchical, nor entirely Republican, is the most compleat and regular, that has ever been contrived by the Wisdom of Man. This was the primitive Form in all the Nations of Europe, I may say, in all Wise Nations, and is at this Day the happy Constitution of the English alone. Their Zeal and public Spirit, their Integrity, and disinterested Minds, their steady Attachment to their fundamental Constitution are the generous means, by which it has always been preserved, and by which it does still subsist. . . .

The Excellency of this Constitution lies in that even Ballance of Authority resulting from the mutual Dependence of its several Parts; whereby the Power of the Sovereign is moderated, and the Liberty of the People secured. Thus Power and Liberty are reconciled and stand in perfect Agreement with one another. Thus we are removed at an equal distance from the Inconvenience of Absolute Rule, and the Disorder and Confusion of Popular; the two Precipices with which the Path of just Policy is on both sides border'd. The Prince is entrusted with no Power, but that of doing good, which is properly the Perfection of Power; the Licentiousness of the People is restrained without taking away their Liberty; but wherever it would be incompatible with their Liberty, to restrain an Abuse of it, the Abuse rather to be permitted, than the Liberty itself abridged.

A free Government cannot but be subject to Parties, Cabals, and Intrigues. This perhaps may be formed into an Objection against free Governments by the Advocates for absolute Power, but for that Reason it is of no weight. I have somewhere seen Opposition of Interests call'd a Curse attending free Governments, because it is inseparable from them; when it tends to sap the Foundations of the Constitution, then indeed it properly deserves that Name, but to pronounce the Opposition of those a Curse, who from a just Zeal and Jealousy for their Liberty endeavour to defeat Schemes of Power destructive of Liberty, is the dialect and language of Tools of Power, and Sycophants. . . . Parties are a check upon one another, and by keeping the Ambition of one another within Bounds, serve to maintain the public Liberty. Opposition is the Life and Soul of public Zeal, which without it would flag, and decay. . . .

The People of this Province live under the happy Influence of a free Government; it is no wonder therefore if those in the Administration meet with Opposition, since it is the Effect of free Government. . . .

6

Rhode Island—The Ideal Colony

SOURCE: William Freeborn to Timothy Truman, *The Rhode Island Gazette*, January 11, 1733 (#15).

When I consider the liberties left in the English nation, when almost the whole world besides those fortunate islands is enslaved, it fills my heart with gratitude to God, and those illustrious heroes, who, under him, were the happy means of its preservation. . . .

When I reflect on our happy condition in this colony, and the most valuable privileges we enjoy at the easiest and cheapest rate imaginable, I cannot sufficiently admire the wisdom and felicity of our Constitution, nor enough applaud the discretion and frugality with which our affairs have all along been managed.

By our charter, our legislature and the executive power are more agreeable to the equality of nature, and do better serve the true ends of government, than any other form or method whatever. The annual choice of magistrates, and all other officers, is a wise provision to keep them honest and faithful, and makes way for that rotation in government which has always been sound and acknowledged the surest support and defence of a just liberty. . . . The distribution of lands at first, and the preservation of property in so many hands, is a great bulwark to our constitution. And so has been our custom of changing, and varying several officers, which has procured us more men capable of those offices, and at the same time, they have so many checks upon one another. And from hence has proceeded, above all, the cheapness of our administration, the easiness of our taxes of all sorts, which I apprehend has in the greatest degree preserved to us the intire use of the original plan of government the Crown was most graciously pleased, with so much wisdom and goodness, at first to give us.

7

English Rights in the Colonies

SOURCE: William Smith, *Mr. Smith's Opinion Humbly Offered to the General Assembly of the Colony of New York, on the Seventh of June, 1734 At Their Request* (New York, 1734), 12-13, 33-34.

I conceive that in the main, we are under the same constitution with the people of England. That the prerogatives of the Crown and the liberties of the people are the same here as there. 'Tis very evident that we have but one king, who bears the same relation to all his subjects, as their common head and father, who deals not with one as a son, and with another as a slave, but with all as children. And as the bonds of duty and allegiance equally oblige them all, so all have an equal share in his paternal care and protection.

It is but one oath that the King takes at his coronation, with respect to the government of the people of England, and people here. By which oath, according to the act of Parliament, he promises and swears, *To govern the people of England, and the dominions thereunto belonging according to the statutes in Parliament agreed on, and the laws and customs of the same.*

Hence the subjects inhabiting the remotest dominions, belonging to

England, are to be governed by the same laws, as the people inhabiting within the realm. And as the people of this colony, are governed by the same prince, according to the same laws, with the people of England, it seems clearly to follow from thence, That the King cannot erect a Court of Chancery within this Colony, without consent of the legislature, because by the laws of England, he cannot erect such a Court there, without such consent. . . .

To affirm this power in the Crown, without an act of the legislature, in my humble opinion, supposes his Majesty to be vested with an arbitrary authority over his American subjects, with power to impose new laws, without their consent; which would be to alter the constitution, and deprive us of one of the chief privileges, which we justly glory in, as the birth-right of Englishmen. . . .

From all which it seems, that the government in England does, and always has, look'd upon the plantations as having the same privileges with the people of England; and that the prerogatives of the Crown, and the people's liberty, are regulated by and under the protection of the same laws here as in England.

Hence it seems undeniably to follow, that we in this colony, have a right to Magna Charta, the effect of which in part is, That no man shall lose his life, liberty, or estate, but by the judgment of his peers, and the law of the land. . . .

If we in this colony are entitled to the privileges of Englishmen, then we also share in all the benefits contained in the petition of right, by which the liberties contained in the Great Charter, and other ancient statutes, are declared to be the right of the subject. . . .

But tho' the same courts cannot conveniently extend, yet the same laws which declare the rights of freemen do extend. We hold under the same grand charter with the people of England: We have the same fundamental rights, privileges, and liberties as they have. Hence we have a right to choose the laws by which we will be governed; we have also a right to be governed only by such laws. These are the birth-right of Englishmen. These summarily comprehend those felicities which distinguish us from all other people. Our American abode has put no limits on these rights, but what necessarily flows from our dependence; a dependence vastly to our advantage, which conveys to us the protection and superiour wisdom of an indulgent parent. Hence we have a right to choose every law that is not repugnant to the laws of England; and to choose every law of England, that suits our convenience; and to refuse every law of England that in its original institution was not intended to oblige us.

8

Essay by "Z" (John Webbe)

SOURCE: *The Pennsylvania Gazette,* April 8-15, 1736 (#384).

Freedom is the birthright of every man. We are all born naturally equal. I should be justly accused of impudence to tell another animal like myself, that I came into the world his superior. He might reasonably demand by what divine authority; and, that failing, put me upon proving that my outward vessel was made of finer clay than his own.

'Tis certain nature has made no distinction; from the same clod of dirt she forms a monarch and a cobbler.

Reason and revelation oblige us to pay obedience to magistrates, but to whom is left to our own choice; since they are not particularly pointed out, and that none is born with a right to controul another.

But no man relinquishes part of his natural liberty, except on a more valuable consideration, as protection from injuries, security of property, mutual defence, &c. If those ends are not obtained, of which none can be judges but the people, the compact is void, *frustratione finis,* as the lawyers phrase it, because the design is frustrated.

Therefore a magistrate cannot justly complain when he's turned out of his office; besides he might have refused or quitted when he pleased, no man is obliged to take the reins of government into his hand against his will. But should he be desired to resign, and he maintain himself in his post, it must be by force, which is tyranny. If he wants a specious pretext, let him apply to Mr. Hobbes, who will tell him, that when a nation chuses a prince, they confer on him all their power; but as the same nation can dispense with any promises that may be made them, and as all their authority is transferred to the prince; therefore he may give himself absolutism. This is bravely resolved considering the coward that was author of it. Yet it is not the only wilful mistake that wretched philosopher has been guilty of. A condition implies a power in each party to compel the other that fails to make good his promise, as it's expressed by Grotius in the motto; and no contract can tie up the hands of a people from repelling wrongs received from a prince conditionally chosen.

As a nation make their own agreements under which they promise to be governed, so they always retain in themselves a power of altering the old and of enacting new laws according to the change of circumstances.

Nor can it be otherwise: A law receives its sanction from the consent of a people, or at least of a majority, who are under no obligation to obey any order where they have not declared their concurrence.

The edicts of the French tyrant are of no force till they are enregistered by the Parliament; tho' at present this is only a piece of formality in France . . . yet it's a confession that no people can be bound but by their own agreement. Hence arises the sacred veneration due to laws. No man can be obliged but by his own act, and if he's punished he has no room for complaint, because he himself has fixed the penalty. The disagreement of a few does not invalidate the general rule; yet if they receive protection from the law, it's a tacit acknowledgement that they ought to submit themselves to the rigours of the law.

These principles are agreeable to reason and the eternal nature of things, supported by the authority of the great ancients and best moderns, and entirely conformable to the English constitution. . . .

At the coronation of an English King, the Arch-Bishop pronounces four times on the four sides of the scaffold, Will you have this man to reign? and then he's crowned upon conditions which are expressed in his oath: He swears he will govern according to the laws of the land, and pass all laws that the people chuse; and that (upon supposition of not performing the agreement) the Barons and commonalty of the land may streighten and compel him by all means possible, as by seizing his towns, lands and possessions, or any other way till satisfaction be made according to their pleasure; and that it shall be lawful for all men in the kingdom to rise up against him, and to do all things that may be grievous to him, as if they were absolutely free from any engagement to his person.

The Parliament are the only judges whether these conditions are performed. They are interpreters of the law, otherwise a wicked King might refine away the meaning of magna charta. By the statute of 35 Edward III. the judges are ordered to defer the decision of doubtful cases to the Parliament. Our monarchy is under a great many other limitations, that put it out of the power of any prince to destroy the constitution.

A King in conjunction with his Council, cannot enact any new law, nor can he sit in any court in person, and determine causes. The stile *coram Rege Domino* is not sufficient to support a contrary opinion. . . .

The King seems to have no negative voice, since he's sworn to pass all such laws as the people chuse. His Majesty in Council may advise with the Parliament, and if the bill is dropped, 'tis because the House will not exert their authority. . . .

The King cannot pardon a criminal impeached by the House of Commons; and the Parliament are so jealous of the King's meddling in judicial proceedings, that the judges who formerly might be turned out at pleasure, are by an act of William III to enjoy their offices for life, *quam diu se bene gesserint*: and by another of George I their salaries are raised and fixed, that they may not be byassed by the influence of the Court from a due discharge of their office.

On the other hand, the power of the Parliament is so great, that Burleigh used to say, they could do any thing but turn a man into a woman; and Sir Thomas More when in the Tower, being asked by Rich the King's Solicitor, if the Parliament had an authority to make Richard Rich King? answered, that was *levis casus*; taking it for granted, that they might make and unmake whom they please. This is asserted by the Statute of 13 Queen Elizabeth, denouncing the most grievous punishments against all such as should dare to contradict it. It appears from hence that an Act of Parliament may be good tho' it has not the Royal assent, as that which raised the Prince of Orange to the Throne; but this is not the only instance which proves that a Parliament may bestow the Crown on whom they please. They empowered H[enry] VIII to dispose of it by his will, and he left it to a bastard; for Mary and Elizabeth could not both be legitimate; and by the same authority he might have given it to his secretary or valet de chambre.

9

Pennsylvania's Unique Constitution

SOURCE: Anon. Essay, *The Pennsylvania Gazette*, March 21-28, 1737/38 (#485) [reprinted in *The American Magazine*, I (January 1740/41), 26].

It is a laudable partiality in Britons, to prefer their own constitution, as the most perfect. . . . But some among us have argued from thence, that the government of this province is defective, as far as it wants an exact resemblance to that of our mother country; not considering, that it is altogether as absurd, to prescribe the same form of government to people differently circumstanced, as to pretend to fortify all sorts of places on the same model. . . .

After the founder of Pennsylvania, (a man whose actions as well as writings were influenced by a spirit of liberty and universal benevolence) had obtained of King Charles II, a grant of this province, that those of his persuasion, or of any other persuasion, might enjoy that liberty of conscience, which was DENIED them in their native country; they entered into a MUTUAL COMPACT, for the maintenance of civil and religious liberty. They had seen and felt the effects of DESPOTISM at home and therefore endeavoured by the wisest regulations to guard against it abroad. The whole legislative power was lodged, where it is always safest lodged, in the hands of the people; and the laws they enacted were to be executed and put in force by magistrates of their own chusing. In short the original frame of government (a copy of which is now before me) was raised on the principles of reason and equality, and suited to the sober dispositions and independent circumstances of the first adventurers. Tho' it has since received some rude shocks and alterations from the enemies of liberty, yet if we can maintain the ground that is left us, we have no reason to envy the condition of our neighbours.

The laws of a free society must, nay will, be always conformable to the circumstances, the genius and humours of the society. For want of this observation, bookish and speculative men, who have never studied human nature but in their books, have vainly amused themselves, in chalking out chimerical schemes of government, which could not possibly have any other existence, but in their own imaginations. These are harmless animals, whose writings are as useless and insignificant as themselves. But there are others amongst us, who take all opportunities, to cry up the necessity of reducing the form of this government to the British model; a design almost as wicked, as was the attempt to change the English constitution into a democracy. But the thing is palpably absurd and impracticable; and no step can be made towards it, without throwing a greater share of power into the Governor's hands, than is consistent with our liberties. The design therefore of those gentlemen, in pleading for such an alteration, is evident; They wish the supream magistrate as absolute as the Grand Turk in expectation that they shall be his Bashaws or Under-Tyrants.

Others again say, that the King's representatives ought not to be restrained, hampered or fettered by our provincial laws. But who can refrain from laughter who hears professed Jacobites argue after this manner. . . . No nation ever sent forth colonies but with an eye to her own advantage. The view of the British in placing and protecting so many settlements, at so great an expence, on this side of the globe, was to extend her trade and vend her manufactures. These we consume in proportion to the number of our inhabitants. Now it is an allowed maxim, that wherever liberty shines, there people will naturally flock to bask themselves in its beams. The great acquisitions we have made from Germany and other parts of Europe, which we annually drain of their people, is a pregnant proof of the foregoing observation. . . . It is therefore an undeniable consequence, that we cannot more effectually promote the interest of England, than by maintaining our liberties.

10

On Liberty

SOURCE: Samuel Chew, *The Speech of Samuel Chew, Esq.; Chief Justice of the Government of New Castle, Kent, and Sussex Upon Delaware* (Philadelphia, 1742), p. 2.

The end of all civil government being happiness, that happiness consists in the security and protection of the lives, liberties and properties of the people who form or constitute the community. The security of life and property is commonly well enough understood, and therefore needs no explanation. But to know wherein true liberty consists, and what is meant by the security of it, requires more consideration. "True and impartial liberty has been justly defined to be the right of every man to pursue the natural, reasonable and religious dictates of his own mind; to think what he will, and act as he thinks, provided he acts not to the prejudice of another." This right is inherent to all men: Every man is born with it, nor can he be debarred the exercise of it but by the means of tyranny and usurpation. And so dear is it to mankind, that they will frequently risque all other things for its sake, and sacrifice even life itself rather than part with it. To secure this invaluable blessing, was, as has been said, one of the main ends of the institution of civil government. And whenever those who are intrusted with the execution of the powers of government, go about to deprive the people of the free exercise of this liberty, they cease to be properly governors, and are tyrants; and that government may justly be pronounced the most perfect, where the preservation of the lives of the people, the right of every man to dispose of the produce of his own labour, and to be of that religion he thinks best, are the most effectually secured from the attempts of such as would take them away. And it is for this reason that the constitution of our mother-country claims the preference of all others, and has ever been the glory of Englishmen, and the admiration and envy of foreigners.

11

On Power's Limits

SOURCE: Charles Chauncy, *Civil Magistrates Must be Just, Ruling in Fear of God* (Boston, 1747), 14-16.

Whatever power any are vested with, 'tis delegated to them according to some civil constitution. And this, so long as it remains the constitution, they are bound in justice to conform themselves to: To be sure, they ought not to act in violation of any of its main and essential rights. Especially, is this an important part of justice; where the constitution is branched into several parts, and the power originally lodged in it, is divided, in certain measures, to each part, in order to preserve, a ballance in the whole. Rulers, in this case, in either branch of the government, are bound by the constitution, and obliged to keep within the proper limits assigned to them; never clashing in the exercise of their power, never encroaching upon the rights of each other, in any shape, or under any pretence whatever. They have severally and equally a right to that power which is granted to them in the constitution, and to wrest it out of each other's hands, or to obstruct one another in the regular legal exercise of it, is evidently unjust. As in the British constitution, which devolves the power of the state, in certain proportions, on King, Lords, and Commons, they have neither of them a right to invade the province of the other, but are required, by the rule of righteousness, to keep severally within their own boundaries, acting in union among themselves, and consistency with the constitution. If the prerogatives of the king are sacred, so also are the rights of the Lords and Commons: And if it would be unjust in Lords or Commons, to touch, in any instance, the prerogative of the Crown; so would it be in the Crown, to invade the rights, which are legally settled in the Lords and Commons. . . .

And the case is just the same in all dependent governments, as in those whose power originates in themselves: Especially where the derived constitution, like that of Great Britain, is divided into several ruling parts, and distributes the granted power and privileges severally among these ruling parts, to each their limited portion. The constitution is here evidently the grand rule to all cloathed with power, or claiming privilege, in either branch of the government. And 'tis indeed a fundamental point of justice, that they keep respectively within the bounds marked out to them in the constitution. Rulers in one branch of the state should not assume powers delegated to those in another.

12

A Debate on Power

SOURCE: A Freeholder, *The Maryland Gazette*, February 10, 1747/48 (#146), March 16, 1747/48 (#151), Philanthropos, April 27, 1748 (#157), Native of Maryland, May 11, 1748 (#159), Americano-Britannus, June 4, 1748 (#162).

I had thought it had been a thing notoriously known by every man who thought himself qualified to act in a public capacity that it was one of the most distinguishing marks of British liberty, nay the very soul and essence of it, for the people, or (which is the same thing), the representatives of the people, to be possess'd of a power of keeping their purse in their own hands, to be the sole judges of how much is necessary to be raised upon them, and to direct the disposal of it. . . . If this then be a fundamental part of the constitution, as I think won't be denied, a question will arise, whether a parliament (or in America, an assembly, for I presume none will pretend to make any material distinction) has a power, i.e., a right to enact anything contrary to a fundamental part of the British constitution? For my own part, I would not take upon me to answer this great question, if it had not been often resolved in the negative by some of the greatest statesmen England ever saw. They say it is a vulgar mistake to imagine that a parliament is omnipotent, or may do anything for that they can't alter the constitution. There are certain powers, rights, and privileges invested in every branch of the legislature, by the constitution; no part of which can be given up by any of them without breaking thro' that constitution, which is the basis of the whole. To instance in the case in hand: As all money to be raised for the use of the public must come from the people, the wisdom of our ancestors thought it but reasonable that the power of judging the sum necessary and directing the application of it should be lodged in the people; and after many brave and bloody struggles in opposition to arbitrary impositions, they have handed down that inestimable privilege to us. But seeing the people cannot act collectively in a legislative capacity, they are obliged to choose men to represent them, and act for their interest in exercising the people's share in the legislative power. Is it in the power then of these representatives to give up this antient privilege of the people? By no means for this evident reason, because in that case, they would not act for the interest of their constituents, but expressly against it, which is absurd to suppose their constitution gave them any power to do. They sit as representatives of the people, not to destroy their just rights, but to preserve them. . . . In such a case the original compact (which in the very nature of free governments must be supposed) would be broken, the people loos'd from all tyes of obedience (so much power being granted, and so much obedience due, only on condition of so many privileges enjoy'd); and as a very great author expresses it, the government dissolved. . . .

•   •   •   •   •

What was said . . . concerning that right inherent in the people by the constitution to judge (by their representatives) of their own taxes may be carp'd at, but can never be over thrown. It is the great hinge upon which liberty hangs, and whenever that is weakened or thrown down, liberty must be proportionably weakened or fall with it. By this alone it is that the great powers yielded to magistrates of all sorts, from the supream magistrate to the county justice, suffer any control. For the most expensive and pernicious schemes may be projected under a maladministration, as the people have no check on their councils, but while they are masters of their own money they may keep from them the means of putting such schemes as they do not approve in execution. On the other hand, should ever this power be lodged in any set of men besides those who are the immediate trustees of the people, and appointed by them, it must be evident to every man of common sense that all liberty would soon be at an end. There would be no further occasion for parliaments or assemblies. . . .

I have all along taken it for granted that we in America have a just claim to the hereditary rights of British subjects, and I believe no man will dispute it, at least no man worth regarding. In consequence of this, I say that our constitution is plainly an original contract betwixt the people and their rulers. . . . We may safely venture to defy the warmest stickler for arbitrary power to produce one point of time since which we know anything of our constitution wherein the whole scheme of it wou'd not have been one monstrous absurdity unless an original contract had been supposed. This was the case as well before Magna Charta as after it, for the Lord Coke (that oracle of the law) in diverse places asserts, and all lawyers know, that this charter is for the most part declaratory of old rights, and not a grant of new ones. . . . But whatever disputes may formerly have been concerning the original contract, there is not the least room left for any such, since the settlement made at the late revolution [of 1688-89], which was an express renewal of it. From that happy period our constitution has taken a new aura, not that the people acquired at that time any new rights, but that their old ones were more explicitly acknowledged and ascertained. . . .

•   •   •   •   •

I shall now humbly and with great deference to the community, offer my opinion of the constitution: I take the basis, or foundation, of it to be the great law of reason, the rules whereof are deducible from the nature of things; but would be ineffectual for the purposes of government, without the best and wisest of the community to explain and apply them impartially, to the exigencies and necessities of the whole. The dictates of reason, then, directed our ancestors to that mixed form of government, that we now have, which secures to the body of the people the legislative power, and lodges the executive in a single person, under limitations; and this has been improved into what we call a parliament, consisting of king, lords, and commons; who regularly meet, and enact laws agreeable to the nature of things, for the well ordering, directing, and governing the whole community. To them belong the explication and application of the law of reason, for the purposes of government. I know of no essential or fundamental of the constitution, but parliaments; their existence was before the law, their origin cannot be founded in any law; we have laws for the choice and regulation of them, but not for their existence: An essential or fundamental must be before, or at least coeval to the thing, of which it is essential or fundamental: Now, if this be the case, that there are no other essentials of our constitution but parliaments, they must have an unlimited and absolute power, and may do whatever is fitting and necessary to be done, in all cases: And so may a Maryland assembly, for I presume none will pretend to make any material distinction, and I think it notorious, that they have always assumed such an unlimited power: The Parliament of Great Britain independent, the assembly of Maryland dependent. Parliaments then, are the very constitution itself. It would be absurd to say, they can or would alter the constitution; that is, themselves: But there is nothing dependent upon the constitution, but what they can and may alter. There is no power on earth superior to them. . . .

•   •   •   •   •

I should be glad to be informed by this cunning statesman [A Freeholder], what part of the constitution the Parliament cannot alter? Or whether every new law made, or old one repealed, is not an alteration of the constitution, for the better or worse? What is our constitution at present, but a series of alterations made by parliaments; or whether the power of parliaments, at this day, is not as ample and extensive as was that of their predecessors? It is true, there are some fundamentals which it would not be safe for a parliament to alter. For in the constitution of Great Britain, we are to consider, not only the constituent powers, but the things constituted; which are the fundamental laws of the kingdom, the great barrier and security of person and property; so that if the constituent powers should abolish any old laws, or make new, which either take away or weaken the general security of person and property, they would then act against the spirit or design of the constitution. Thus, had the lords and commons, as King James wished and designed, enacted a law, that the kings of England had a right to suspend or dispense with laws, to levy money, or raise an army, without the consent of any future parliaments, or that the parliaments should be perpetual and chuse one another as members died off: This tho' done by the constituent powers, would have been a traitorous delivering up of the constitution: And the people would have had the same reason to resist all the powers as to resist one, and to return to their original state of nature, and chuse a new government, or resume the old one. All the fundamentals, essentials, and basis's therefore that I know of, which the parliament have no just power to alter, centers in this, that they cannot give up any of those powers, which by the joint consent of the community, in order to keep up their mixt form of government, the several branches of the legislature are invested with; that is, they can't make new legislators, or transfer the power of making laws, or place it otherwise than where the people have.

•   •   •   •   •

From what has been said it will appear, that parliaments are not the constitution . . . but that they take their form, powers, and existence from it: That they cannot alter that form, or alienate those powers, either from one branch of the legislature to another, or to any other distinct body of men whatever, without breaking thro' that agreement of the society (to be govern'd after such a particular manner) which constituted them. . . . I expect to be told, that this is taking upon me to dictate to the assembly what they cannot do: But, Sir, I am warranted by that greater authority, which has never yet been disputed, to say, that "it is a mistake to think that the supreme legislative power of any commonwealth can do what they will; their power, in the utmost bounds of it, being limited to the public good of the society." . . . The representatives of the people, having only a delegated power for a certain time, are bound to deliver over all that power they were entrusted with, at the expiration of that time, back again to the people; who may intrust the same men again, or others, if they think proper: Now it being a fundamental part of that agreement which constituted the society under the present form of government, that the people should not be taxed without their own consent, or their representatives; should their representatives agree to put that power of taxing on any other footing, how could they deliver back that power to their constituents, at the expiration of the stated time, which was the very condition of their being intrusted with it?

13

Governments Compared

SOURCE: T---s W---t, *The South-Carolina Gazette, Supplement,* May 23, 1756 (#1142).

Our constitution is no way altered by his Majesty's being vested with the estate of the lords proprietors [of Carolina]; it ought to be as near as possible like that of England (by our charter) ; but the scheme form'd by the late lords proprietors, for making a nobility in this province to represent an upper house, failing, hitherto none but his majesty's rights and those of the people seem to constitute the legislative power in this province; for, since there is no nobility, the government cannot here be similar or like that of England, one estate or part of the British constitution being wanted, and therefore we come as near to the practice of Great Britain, by passing our laws in the assembly, and those confirmed or assented to by the governor, as the situation and circumstances of our province will admit. The parliament of England is composed of king, lords, and commons; the two houses agreeing and uniting, are a proper balance of power between the crown and people: But, if his majesty's authority is represented by his governor, which constitutes one estate of our legislature, and his majesty should further appoint a council, to preside in the nature of an upper house or house of peers, and these appointed only *durante bene placito regis,* such an appointment must necessarily destroy the balance, and be contrary to the usage of our mother-country. I dare venture to affirm, no instruction from his majesty to any governor, ever called the council an upper house, nor can the council produce any instruction to any governor, wherein any words can imply them to be a house of peers. The council have not any correspondence with his majesty's ministers, or with the lords for trade and plantations, as council. They have no commission or patent for their places, but are only named by his majesty, or by his majesty's order to his governor to appoint them. . . . Their power lives, moves, and has being, only from the governor's instructions [from the king]: How far such a council is, from the nature of an upper house, or house of peers, will easily be discerned from a little inquiry: But first it will be proper, to consider the council as assistants to the governor, and named by his majesty for that end, lest the weighty affairs of government be too ponderous for the judgment of every governor, and that the advice of council might help the governors in arduous affairs, and support the rights of his majesty, as well as promote the good of his people in the colonies. If the council were in the nature of an upper house or house of peers, then the governor would have no counsellors; for, having, as an upper house, given their opinion, he would be precluded asking their advice, they having already determined, and consequently, in most or many cases, will be without council. . . . The lords of parliament are called by writ every parliament, as well as the commons, to consult about the arduous affairs of the kingdom. The lords have no vote for electing parliament-men. The lords are independent and not to be displaced at pleasure of a minister. The peers are hereditary counsellors to the king and kingdom. The counsellors in Carolina are dependent, and hold their places during pleasure. The counsellors in Carolina vote for members of assembly, and have their representatives: Can they represent themselves, and be represented? The members of the Council can be suspended by the governor: Can a peer of England be suspended? The members of the council are summoned, by the governor's order, upon every important occasion: Does his majesty summon the peers of the realm? Surely, no person can draw the least similitude between the council in Carolina, and the house of peers in England. . . .

I imagine from hence, no addition or diminution can be made to our constitution; and altho' his majesty should be pleased, by his ministers, to give instructions to his governor, for erecting or making an upper house of assembly, I conceive, such an upper house could not have a legal establishment, without an act of parliament of Great Britain, or an act of assembly of this province; for, if any instructions from his majesty can substitute an upper house, or make an addition to our legislature, by the same rule, his majesty's instructions can lessen the rights of assembly, or totally take away all their privileges — Instructions from his majesty, to his governor, or the council, are binding to them, and esteem'd as laws or rules; because, if either should disregard them, they might immediately be displaced: But, if instructions should be laws and rules to the people of this province, then there would be no need of assemblies, and all our laws and taxes might be made and levied by an instruction. . . .

14

Benjamin Franklin's
Rules by Which a Great Empire
May Be Reduced to a Small One

Presented to a late Minister, when he entered
upon his Administration

SOURCE: The *Gentleman's Magazine,* Sept., 1773.

An ancient Sage boasted, that, tho' he could not fiddle, he knew how to make a *great city* of a *little one.* The science that I, a modern simpleton, am about to communicate, is the very reverse.

I address myself to all ministers who have the management of extensive dominions, which from their very greatness are become troublesome to govern, because the multiplicity of their affairs leaves no time for *fiddling.*

I. In the first place, gentlemen, you are to consider, that a great empire, like a great cake, is most easily diminished at the edges. Turn your attention, therefore, first to your *remotest* provinces; that, as you get rid of them, the next may follow in order.

II. That the possibility of this separation may always exist, take special care the provinces are never incorporated with the mother country; that they do not enjoy the same common rights, the same privileges in commerce; and that they are governed by *severer* laws, all of *your enacting,* without allowing them any share in the choice of the legislators. By carefully making and preserving such distinctions, you will (to keep to my simile of the cake) act like a wise ginger-bread-baker, who, to facilitate a division, cuts his dough half through in those places where, when baked, he would have it *broken to pieces.*

III. Those remote provinces have perhaps been acquired, purchased, or conquered, at the *sole expence* of the settlers, or their ancestors, without the aid of the mother country. If this should happen to increase her *strength,* by their growing numbers, ready to join in her wars; her *commerce,* by their growing demand for her manufactures; or her *naval power,* by greater employment for her ships and seamen, they may probably suppose some merit in this, and that it entitles them to some favour; you are therefore to *forget it all,* or *resent it,* as if they had done you injury. If they happen to be zealous whigs, friends of liberty, nurtured in revolution principles, *remember all that* to their prejudice, and resolve to punish it; for such principles, after a revolution is thoroughly established, are of *no more use;* they are even *odious* and *abominable.*

IV. However peaceably your colonies have submitted to your government, shewn their affection to your interests, and patiently borne their grievances; you are to *suppose* them always inclined to revolt, and treat them accordingly. Quarter troops among them, who by their insolence may *provoke* the rising of mobs, and by their bullets and bayonets *suppress* them. By this means, like the husband who uses his wife ill *from suspicion,* you may in time convert your *suspicions* into *realities.*

V. Remote provinces must have *Governors* and *Judges,* to represent the Royal Person, and execute everywhere the delegated parts of his office and authority. You ministers know, that much of the strength of government depends on the *opinion* of the people; and much of that opinion on the *choice of rulers* placed immediately over them. If you send them wise and good men for governors, who study the interest of the colonists, and advance their prosperity, they will think their King wise and good, and that he wishes the welfare of his subjects. If you send them learned and upright men for Judges, they will think him a lover of justice. This may attach your provinces more to his government. You are therefore to be careful whom you recommend for those offices. If you can find prodigals, who have ruined their fortunes, broken gamesters or stock-jobbers, these may do well as *governors;* for they will probably be rapacious, and provoke the people by their extortions. Wrangling proctors and pettifogging lawyers, too, are not amiss; for they will be for ever disputing and quarrelling with their little parliaments. If withal they should be ignorant, wrong-headed, and insolent, so much the better. Attornies' clerks and Newgate solicitors will do for *Chief Justices,* especially if they hold their places *during your pleasure;* and all will contribute to impress those ideas of your government, that are proper for a people *you would wish to renounce it.*

VI. To confirm these impressions, and strike them deeper, whenever the injured come to the capital with complaints of maladministration, oppression, or injustice, punish such suitors with long delay, enormous expence, and a final judgment in favour of the oppressor. This will have an admirable effect every way. The trouble of future complaints will be prevented, and Governors and Judges will be encouraged to farther acts of oppression and injustice; and thence the people may become more disaffected, and at length desperate. . . .

VIII. If, when you are engaged in war, your colonies should vie in liberal aids of men and money against the common enemy, upon your simple requisition, and give far beyond their abilities, reflect that a penny taken from them by your power is more honourable to you, than a pound presented by their benevolence; despise therefore their voluntary grants, and resolve to harass them with novel taxes. They will probably complain to your parliaments, that they are taxed by a body in which they have no representative, and that this is contrary to common right. They will petition for redress. Let the Parliaments flout their claims, reject their petitions, refuse even to suffer the reading of them, and treat the petitioners with the utmost contempt. Nothing can have a better effect in producing the alienation proposed; for though many can forgive injuries, *none ever forgave contempt.*

IX. In laying these taxes, never regard the heavy burthens those remote people already undergo, in defending their own frontiers, supporting their own provincial governments, making new roads, building bridges, churches, and other public edifices, which in old countries have been done to your hands by your ancestors, but which occasion constant calls and demands on the purses of a new people. . . . But remember to make your arbitrary tax more grievous to your provinces, by public declarations importing that your power of taxing them has *no limits;* so that when you take from them without their consent one shilling in the pound, you have a clear right to the other nineteen. This will probably weaken every idea of *security in their property,* and convince them, that under such a government they *have nothing they can call their own;* which can scarce fail of producing the *happiest consequences!*

X. Possibly, indeed, some of them might still comfort themselves, and say, "Though we have no property, we have yet *something* left that is valuable; we have constitutional *liberty,* both of person and of conscience. This King, these Lords, and these Commons, who it seems are too remote from us to know us, and feel for us, cannot take from us our *Habeas Corpus* right, or our right of trial *by a jury of our neighbours;* they cannot deprive us of the exercise of our religion, alter our ecclesiastical constitution, and compel us to be Papists, if they please, or Mahometans." To annihilate this comfort, begin by laws to perplex their commerce with infinite regulations, impossible to be remembered and observed; ordain seizures of their property for every failure; take away the trial of such property by Jury, and give it to arbitrary Judges of your own appointing, and of the lowest characters in the country, whose salaries and emoluments are to arise out of the duties or condemnations, and whose appointments are *during pleasure.* Then let there be a formal declaration of both Houses, that opposition to your edicts is *treason,* and that any person suspected of treason in the provinces may, according to some obsolete law, be seized and sent to the metropolis of the empire for trial; and pass an act, that those there charged with certain other offences, shall be sent away in chains from their friends and country to be tried in the same manner for felony. Then erect a new Court of Inquisition among them, accompanied by an armed force, with instructions to transport all such suspected persons; to be ruined by the expence, if they bring over evidences to prove their innocence, or be found guilty and hanged, if they cannot afford it. And, lest the people should think you cannot possibly go any farther, pass another solemn declaratory act, "that King, Lords, Commons had, hath, and of right ought to have, full power and authority to make statutes of sufficient force and validity to bind the unrepresented provinces IN ALL CASES WHATSOEVER." This will include *spiritual* with temporal, and, taken together, must operate wonderfully to your purpose; by convincing them, that they are at present under a power something like that spoken of in the scriptures, which can not only *kill their bodies,* but *damn their souls* to all eternity, by compelling them, if it pleases, to *worship the Devil.* . . .

XIII. If the people of any province have been accustomed to support their own Governors and Judges to satisfaction, you are to apprehend that such Governors and Judges may be thereby influenced to treat the people kindly, and to do them justice. This is another reason for applying part of that revenue in larger salaries to such Governors and Judges, given, as their commissions are, *during your pleasure* only; forbidding them to take any salaries from their provinces; that thus the people may no longer hope any kindness from their Governors, or (in Crown cases) any justice from their Judges. And, as the money thus misapplied in one province is extorted from all, probably *all will resent the misapplication.*

XIV. If the parliaments of your provinces should dare to claim rights, or complain of your administration, order them to be harassed with *repeated dissolutions.* If the same men are continually returned by new elections, adjourn their meetings to some country village, where they cannot be accommodated, and there keep them *during pleasure;* for this, you know, is your PREROGATIVE; and an excellent one it is, as you may manage it to promote discontents among the people, diminish their respect, and *increase their disaffection....*

XX. Lastly, invest the General of your army in the provinces, with great and unconstitutional powers, and free him from the controul of even your own Civil Governors. Let him have troops enow under his command, with all the fortresses in his possession; and who knows but (like some provincial Generals in the Roman empire, and encouraged by the universal discontent you have produced) he may take it into his head to set up for himself? If he should, and you have carefully practised these few *excellent rules* of mine, take my word for it, all the provinces will immediately join him; and you will that day (if you have not done it sooner) get rid of the trouble of governing them, and all the *plagues* attending their *commerce* and connection from henceforth and for ever.

Q. E. D.

15

Gov. Thomas Hutchinson's Speech to Massachusetts General Court, Jan. 6, 1773

SOURCE: J. K. Hosmer, *The Life of Thomas Hutchinson* (Boston, 1896), pp. 363-68.

When our predecessors first took possession of this plantation, or colony, under a grant and charter from the Crown of England, it was their sense, and it was the sense of the kingdom, that they were to remain subject to the supreme authority of Parliament. This appears from the charter itself, and from other irresistible evidence. This supreme authority has, from time to time, been exercised by Parliament, and submitted to by the colony, and hath been, in the most express terms, acknowledged by the Legislature, and, except about the time of the anarchy and confusion in England, which preceded the restoration of King Charles the Second, I have not discovered that it has been called in question, even by private or particular persons, until within seven or eight years last past. Our provincial or local laws have, in numerous instances, had relation to acts of Parliament, made to respect the plantations in general, and this colony in particular, and in our Executive Courts, both Juries and Judges have, to all intents and purposes, considered such acts as part of our rule of law. Such a constitution, in a plantation, is not peculiar to England, but agrees with the principles of the most celebrated writers upon the law of nations, that "when a nation takes possession of a distant country, and settles there, that country, though separated from the principal establishment, or mother country, naturally becomes a part of the state, equally with its ancient possessions."

So much, however, of the spirit of liberty breathes through all parts of the English constitution, that, although from the nature of government, there must be one supreme authority over the whole, yet this constitution will admit of subordinate powers with Legislative and Executive authority, greater or less, according to local and other circumstances. Thus we see a variety of corporations formed within the kingdom, with powers to make and execute such by-laws as are for their immediate use and benefit, the members of such corporations still remaining subject to the general laws of the kingdom. We see also governments established in the plantations, which, from their separate and remote situation, require more general and extensive powers of legislation within themselves, than those formed within the kingdom, but subject, nevertheless, to all such laws of the kingdom as immediately respect them, or are designed to extend to them; and, accordingly, we, in this province have, from the first settlement of it, been left to the exercise of our Legislative and Executive powers, Parliament occasionally, though rarely, interposing, as in its wisdom has been judged necessary.

Under this constitution, for more than one hundred years, the laws both of the supreme and subordinate authority were in general, duly executed; offenders against them have been brought to condign punishment, peace and order have been maintained, and the people of this province have experienced as largely the advantages of government, as, perhaps, any people upon the globe; and they have, from time to time, in the most public manner expressed their sense of it, and, once in every year, have offered up their united thanksgivings to God for the enjoyment of these privileges, and as often, their united prayers for the continuance of them.

At length the constitution has been called in question, and the authority of the Parliament of Great Britain to make and establish laws for the inhabitants of this province has been, by many, denied. What was at first whispered with caution, was soon after openly asserted in print; and, of late, a number of inhabitants, in several of the principal towns in the province, having assembled together in their respective towns, and having assumed the name of legal town meetings, have passed resolves, which they have ordered to be placed upon their town records, and caused to be printed and published in pamphlets and newspapers. I am sorry that it is thus become impossible to conceal, what I could wish had never been made public. I will not particularize these resolves or votes, and shall only observe to you in general, that some of them deny the supreme authority of Parliament, and so are repugnant to the principles of the constitution, and that others speak of this supreme authority, of which the King is a constituent part, and to every act of which his assent is necessary, in such terms as have a direct tendency to alienate the affections of the people from their Sovereign, who has ever been most tender of their rights, and whose person, crown, and dignity, we are under every possible obligation to defend and support. In consequence of these resolves, committees of correspondence are formed in several of those towns, to maintain the principles upon which they are founded.

I know of no arguments, founded in reason, which will be sufficient to support these principles, or to justify the measures taken in consequence of them. It has been urged, that the sole power of making laws is granted, by charter, to a Legislature established in the province, consisting of the King, by his representative the Governor, the Council, and the House of Representatives; that, by this charter, there are likewise granted, or assured to the inhabitants of the province, all the liberties and immunities of free and natural subjects, to all intents, constructions and purposes whatsoever, as if they had been born within the realms of England; that it is part of the liberties of English subjects, which has its foundation in nature, to be governed by laws made by their consent in person, or by their representative; that the subjects in this province are not, and cannot be represented in the Parliament of Great Britain, and, consequently, the acts of that Parliament cannot be binding upon them.

I do not find, gentlemen, in the charter, such an expression as sole power, or any words which import it. The General Court has, by charter, full power to make such laws, as are not repugnant to the laws of England. A favorable construction has been put upon this clause, when it has been allowed to intend such laws of England only, as are expressly declared to respect us. Surely then this is, by charter, a reserve of power and authority to Parliament to bind us by such laws, at least, as are made expressly to refer to us, and consequently, is a limitation of the power given to the General Court. Nor can it be contended, that, by the limits of free and natural subjects, is to be understood an exemption from acts of Parliament, because not represented there, seeing it is provided by the same charter, that such acts shall be in force; and if they that make the objection to such acts, will read the charter with attention, they must be convinced that this grant of liberties and immunities is nothing more than a declaration and assurance on the part of the Crown, that the place, to which their predecessors were about to remove, was, and would be considered as part of the dominions of the Crown of England, and, therefore, that the subjects of the Crown so removing, and those born there, or in their passage thither, or in their passage from thence, would not become aliens, but would, throughout all parts of the English dominions, wherever they might happen to be, as well as within the colony, retain the liberties and immunities of free and natural subjects, their removal from, or not being born within the realm notwithstanding. If the plantations be part of the dominions of the Crown, this clause in the charter does not confer or reserve any liberties, but what would have been enjoyed without it, and what the inhabitants of every other colony do enjoy where they are without a charter. If the plantations are not the dominions of the Crown, will not all that are born here, be considered as born out of the liegeance of the King of England, and, whenever they go into any parts of the dominions, will they not be deemed aliens to all intents and purposes, this grant in the charter notwithstanding?

They who claim exemption from acts of Parliament by virtue of their rights as Englishmen, should consider that it is impossible the rights of English subjects should be the same, in every respect, in all parts of the dominions. It is one of their rights as English subjects, to be governed by laws made by persons, in whose election they have, from time to time, a voice; they remove from the kingdom, where, perhaps, they were in the full exercise of this right, to the plantations, where it cannot be exercised, or where the exercise of it would be of no benefit to them. Does it follow that the government, by their removal from one part of the dominions to another, loses its authority over that part to which they remove, and that they are freed from the subjection they were under before; or do they expect that government should relinquish its authority because they cannot enjoy this particular right? Will it not rather be said, that by this, their voluntary removal, they have relinquished for a time at least, one of the rights of an English subject, which they might, if they pleased, have continued to enjoy, and may again enjoy, whensoever they will return to the place where it can be exercised?

They who claim exemption, as part of their rights by nature, should consider that every restraint which men are laid under by a state of government, is a privation of part of their natural rights; and of all the different forms of government which exist, there can be. no two of them in which the departure from natural rights is exactly the same. Even in case of representation by election, do they not give up part of their natural rights when they consent to be represented by such person as shall be chosen by the majority of the electors, although their own voices may be for some other person? And is it not contrary to their natural rights to be obliged to submit to a representative for seven years, or even one year, after they are dissatisfied with his conduct, although they gave their voices for him when he was elected? This must, therefore, be considered as an objection against a state of government, rather than against any particular form.

If what I have said shall not be sufficient to satisfy such as object to the supreme authority of Parliament over the plantations, there may something further be added to induce them to an acknowledgment of it, which, I think, will well deserve their consideration. I know of no line that can be drawn between the supreme authority of Parliament and the total independence of the colonies; it is impossible there should be two independent Legislatures in one and the same state; for, although there may be but one head, the King, yet the two Legislative bodies will make two governments as distinct as the kingdoms of England and Scotland before the union. If we might be suffered to be altogether independent of Great Britain, could we have any claim to the protection of that government, of which we are no longer a part? Without this protection, should we not become the prey of one or the other powers of Europe, such as should first seize upon us? Is there any thing which we have more reason to dread than independence? I hope it never will be our misfortune to know, by experience, the difference between the liberties of an English colonist, and those of the Spanish, French, or Dutch.

If, then, the supremacy of Parliament over the whole British dominions shall no longer be denied, it will follow that the mere exercise of its authority can be no matter of grievance. If it has been, or shall be exercised in such way and manner as shall appear to be grievous, still this cannot be sufficient ground for immediately denying or renouncing the authority, or refusing to submit to it. The acts and doings of authority, in the most perfect form of government, will not always be thought just and equitable by all the parts of which it consists; but it is the greatest absurdity to admit the several parts to be at liberty to obey, or disobey, according as the acts of such authority may be approved, or disapproved of by them, for this necessarily works a dissolution of the government. The manner, then, of obtaining redress, must be by representations and endeavors, in such ways and forms, as the established rules of the constitution prescribe or allow, in order to make any matters, alleged to be grievances, appear to be really such; but, I conceive it is rather the mere exercise of this authority, which is complained of as a grievance, than any heavy burdens which have been brought upon the people by means of it.

As contentment and order were the happy effects of a constitution, strengthened by universal assent and approbation, so discontent and disorder are now the deplorable effects of a constitution, enfeebled by contest and opposition. Besides divisions and animosities, which disturb the peace of towns and families, the law in some important cases cannot have its course; offenders ordered, by advice of his Majesty's Council, to be prosecuted, escape with impunity, and are supported and encouraged to go on offending; the authority of government is brought into contempt, and there are but small remains of that subordination, which was once very conspicuous in this colony, and which is essential to a well regulated state.

When the bands of government are thus weakened, it certainly behoves those with whom the powers of government are entrusted, to omit nothing which may tend to strengthen them.

16

Edmund Burke's Speech on Reconciliation, March 22, 1775

SOURCE: *The Writings and Speeches of Edmund Burke* (6 vols., Boston, 1906), II, 99-186.

But there is still behind a third consideration concerning this object, which serves to determine my opinion on the sort of policy which ought to be pursued in the management of America, even more than its population and its commerce: I mean its *temper and character*.

In this character of the Americans a love of freedom is the predominating feature which marks and distinguishes the whole: and as an ardent is always a jealous affection, your colonies become suspicious, restive, and untractable, whenever they see the least attempt to wrest from them by force, or shuffle from them by chicane, what they think the only advantage worth living for. This fierce spirit of liberty is stronger in the English colonies, probably, than in any other people of the earth, and this from a great variety of powerful causes; which, to understand the true temper of their minds, and the direction which this spirit takes, it will not be amiss to lay open somewhat more largely.

First, the people of the colonies are descendants of Englishmen. England, Sir, is a nation which still, I hope, respects, and formerly adored, her freedom. The colonists emigrated from you when this part of your character was most predominant; and they took this bias and direction the moment they parted from your hands. They are therefore not only devoted to liberty, but to liberty according to English ideas and on

English principles. Abstract liberty, like other mere abstractions, is not to be found. Liberty inheres in some sensible object; and every nation has formed to itself some favorite point, which by way of eminence becomes the criterion of their happiness. It happened, you know, Sir, that the great contests for freedom in this country were from the earliest times chiefly upon the question of taxing. Most of the contests in the ancient commonwealths turned primarily on the right of election of magistrates, or on the balance among the several orders of the state. The question of money was not with them so immediate. But in England it was otherwise. On this point of taxes the ablest pens and most eloquent tongues have been exercised, the greatest spirits have acted and suffered. In order to give the fullest satisfaction concerning the importance of this point, it was not only necessary for those who in argument defended the excellence of the English Constitution to insist on this privilege of granting money as a dry point of fact, and to prove that the right had been acknowledged in ancient parchments and blind usages to reside in a certain body called an House of Commons: they went much further: they attempted to prove, and they succeeded, that in theory it ought to be so, from the particular nature of a House of Commons, as an immediate representative of the people, whether the old records had delivered this oracle or not. They took infinite pains to inculcate, as a fundamental principle, that in all monarchies the people must in effect themselves, mediately or immediately, possess the power of granting their own money, or no shadow of liberty could subsist. The colonies draw from you, as with their life-blood, these ideas and principles. Their love of liberty, as with you, fixed and attached on this specific point of taxing. Liberty might be safe or might be endangered in twenty other particulars without their being much pleased or alarmed. Here they felt its pulse; and as they found that beat, they thought themselves sick or sound. I do not say whether they were right or wrong in applying your general arguments to their own case. It is not easy, indeed, to make a monopoly of theorems and corollaries. The fact is, that they did thus apply those general arguments; and your mode of governing them, whether through lenity or indolence, through wisdom or mistake, confirmed them in the imagination, that they, as well as you, had an interest in these common principles.

They were further confirmed in this pleasing error by the form of their provincial legislative assemblies. Their governments are popular in an high degree: some are merely popular; in all, the popular representative is the most weighty; and this share of the people in their ordinary government never fails to inspire them with lofty sentiments, and with a strong aversion from whatever tends to deprive them of their chief importance.

If anything were wanting to this necessary operation of the form of government, religion would have given it a complete effect. Religion, always a principle of energy, in this new people is no way worn out or impaired; and their mode of professing it is also one main cause of this free spirit. The people are Protestants, and of that kind which is the most adverse to all implicit submission of mind and opinion. This is a persuasion not only favorable to liberty, but built upon it. I do not think, Sir, that the reason of this averseness in the dissenting churches from all that looks like absolute government is so much to be sought in their religious tenets as in their history. Every one knows that the Roman Catholic religion is at least coeval with most of the governments where it prevails, that it has generally gone hand in hand with them, and received great favor and every kind of support from authority. The Church of England, too, was formed from her cradle under the nursing care of regular government. But the dissenting interests have sprung up in direct opposition to all the ordinary powers of the world, and could justify that opposition only on a strong claim to natural liberty. Their very existence depended on the powerful and unremitted assertion of that claim. All Protestantism, even the most cold and passive, is a sort of dissent. But the religion most prevalent in our northern colonies is a refinement on the principle of resistance: it is the dissidence of dissent, and the protestantism of the Protestant religion. This religion, under a variety of denominations agreeing in nothing but in the communion of the spirit of liberty, is predominant in most of the northern provinces, where the Church of England, notwithstanding its legal rights, is in reality no more than a sort of private sect, not composing, most probably, the tenth of the people. The colonists left England when this spirit was high, and in the emigrants was the highest of all; and even that stream of foreigners which has been constantly flowing into these colonies has, for the greatest part, been composed of dissenters from the establishments of their several countries, and have brought with them a temper and character far from alien to that of the people with whom they mixed.

Sir, I can perceive, by their manner, that some gentlemen object to the latitude of this description, because in the southern colonies the Church of England forms a large body, and has a regular establishment. It is certainly true. There is, however, a circumstance attending these colonies, which, in my opinion, fully counterbalances this difference, and makes the spirit of liberty still more high and haughty than in those to the northward. It is, that in Virginia and the Carolinas they have a vast multitude of slaves. Where this is the case in any part of the world, those who are free are by far the most proud and jealous of their freedom. Freedom is to them not only an enjoyment, but a kind of rank and privilege. Not seeing there, that freedom, as in countries where it is a common blessing, and as broad and general as the air, may be united with much abject toil, with great misery, with all the exterior of servitude, liberty looks, amongst them, like something that is more noble and liberal. I do not mean, Sir, to commend the superior morality of this sentiment, which has at least as much pride as virtue in it; but I cannot alter the nature of man. The fact is so; and these people of the southern colonies are much more strongly, and with an higher and more stubborn spirit, attached to liberty, than those to the northward. Such were all the ancient commonwealths; such were our Gothic ancestors; such in our days were the Poles; and such will be all masters of slaves, who are not slaves themselves. In such a people, the haughtiness of domination combines with the spirit of freedom, fortifies it, and renders it invincible.

Permit me, Sir, to add another circumstance in our colonies, which contributes no mean part towards the growth and effect of this untractable spirit: I mean their education. In no country, perhaps, in the world is the law so general a study. The profession itself is numerous and powerful, and in most provinces it takes the lead. The greater number of the deputies sent to the Congress were lawyers. But all who read, and most do read, endeavor to obtain some smattering in that science. I have been told by an eminent bookseller, that in no branch of his business, after tracts of popular devotion, were so many books as those on the law exported to the plantations. The colonists have now fallen into the way of printing them for their own use. I hear that they have sold nearly as many of Blackstone's "Commentaries" in America as in England. General Gage marks out this disposition very particularly in a letter on your table. He states, that all the people in his government are lawyers, or smatterers in law — and that in Boston they have been enabled, by successful chicane, wholly to evade many parts of one of your capital penal constitutions. The smartness of debate will say, that this knowledge ought to teach them more clearly the rights of legislature, their obligations to obedience, and the penalties of rebellion. All this is mighty well. But my honorable and learned friend on the floor, who condescends to mark what I say for animadversion, will disdain that ground. He has heard, as well as I, that, when great honors and great emoluments do not win over this knowledge to the service of the state, it is a formidable adversary to government. If the spirit be not tamed and broken by these happy methods, it is stubborn and litigious. *Abeunt studia in mores.* This study renders men acute, inquisitive, dexterous, prompt in attack, ready in defence, full of resources. In other countries, the people, more simple, and of a less mercurial cast, judge of an ill principle in government only by an actual grievance; here they anticipate the evil, and judge of the pressure of the grievance by the badness of the principle. They augur misgovernment at a distance, and snuff the approach of tyranny in every tainted breeze.

The last cause of this disobedient spirit in the colonies is hardly less powerful than the rest, as it is not merely moral, but laid deep in the natural constitution of things. Three thousand miles of ocean lie between you and them. No contrivance can prevent the effect of this distance in weakening government. Seas roll, and months pass, between the order and the execution; and the want of a speedy explanation of a single point is enough to defeat an whole system. You have, indeed, winged ministers of vengeance, who carry your bolts in their pounces to the remotest verge of the sea: but there a power steps in, that limits the arrogance of raging passions and furious elements, and says, "So far shalt thou go, and no farther." Who are you, that should fret and rage, and bite the chains of Nature? Nothing worse happens to you than does to all nations who have extensive empire; and it happens in all the forms into which empire can be thrown. In large bodies, the circulation of power must be less vigorous at the extremities. Nature has said it. The Turk cannot govern Egypt, and Arabia, and Kurdistan, as he governs Thrace; nor has he the same dominion in Crimea and Algiers which he has at Brusa and Smyrna. Despotism itself is obliged to truck and huckster. The Sultan gets such obedience as he can. He governs with a loose rein, that he may govern at all; and the whole of the force and vigor of his authority in his centre is derived from a prudent relaxation in all his borders. Spain, in her provinces, is perhaps not so well obeyed as you are in yours. She complies, too; she submits; she watches times. This is the immutable condition, the eternal law, of extensive and detached empire.

Then, Sir, from these six capital sources, of descent, of form of government, of religion in the northern provinces, of manners in the southern, of education, of the remoteness of situation from the first mover of government — from all these causes a fierce spirit of liberty has grown up. It has grown with the growth of the people in your colonies, and increased with the increase of their wealth: a spirit, that, unhappily meeting with an exercise of power in England, which, however lawful, is not reconcilable to any ideas of liberty, much less with theirs, has kindled this flame that is ready to consume us.

I do not mean to commend either the spirit in this excess, or the moral causes which produce it. Perhaps a more smooth and accommodating spirit of freedom in them would be more acceptable to us. Perhaps ideas of liberty might be desired more reconcilable with an arbitrary and boundless authority. Perhaps we might wish the colonists to be persuaded that their liberty is more secure when held in trust for them by us (as their guardians during a perpetual minority) than with any part of it in their own hands. But the question is not, whether their spirit deserves praise or blame — what, in the name of God, shall we do with it? You have before you the object, such as it is — with all its glories, with all its imperfections on its head. You see the magnitude, the importance, the temper, the habits, the disorders. By all these considerations we are strongly urged to determine something concerning it. We are called upon to fix some rule and line for our future conduct, which may give a little stability to our politics, and prevent the return of such unhappy deliberations as the present. . . . Until very lately, all authority in America seemed to be nothing but an emanation from yours. Even the popular part of the colony constitution derived all its activity, and its first vital movement, from the pleasure of the crown. We thought, Sir, that the utmost which the discontented colonists could do was to disturb authority; we never dreamt they could of themselves supply it, knowing in general what an operose business it is to establish a government absolutely new. But having, for our purposes in this contention, resolved that none but an obedient assembly should sit, the humors of the people there, finding all passage through the legal channel stopped, with great violence broke out another way. Some provinces have tried their experiment, as we have tried ours; and theirs has succeeded. They have formed a government sufficient for its purposes, without the bustle of a revolution, or the troublesome formality of an election. Evident necessity and tacit consent have done the business in an instant. . . . Obedience is what makes government, and not the names by which it is called: not the name of Governor, as formerly, or Committee, as at present. This new government has originated directly from the people, and was not transmitted through any of the ordinary artificial media of a positive constitution. It was not a manufacture ready formed, and transmitted to them in that condition from England. The evil arising from hence is this:

that the colonists having once found the possibility of enjoying the advantages of order in the midst of a struggle for liberty, such struggles will not henceforward seem so terrible to the settled and sober part of mankind as they had appeared before the trial.

17

Articles of Confederation
November 15, 1777

To all to whom these Presents shall come, we the undersigned Delegates of the States affixed to our Names send greeting.

WHEREAS THE DELEGATES of the United States of America in Congress assembled did on the fifteenth day of November in the year of our Lord One Thousand Seven Hundred and Seventy-seven, and in the Second Year of the Independence of America agree to certain articles of Confederation and perpetual Union between the States of Newhampshire, Massachusetts-bay, Rhodeisland and Providence Plantations, Connecticut, New York, New Jersey, Pennsylvania, Delaware, Virginia, North-Carolina, South-Carolina and Georgia in the Words following, viz.

"ARTICLES OF CONFEDERATION AND PERPETUAL UNION BETWEEN THE STATES OF NEWHAMPSHIRE, MASSACHUSETTS-BAY, RHODEISLAND AND PROVIDENCE PLANTATIONS, CONNECTICUT, NEW-YORK, NEW-JERSEY, PENNSYLVANIA, DELAWARE, MARYLAND, VIRGINIA, NORTH-CAROLINA, SOUTH-CAROLINA AND GEORGIA."

ARTICLE I. The stile of this confederacy shall be "The United States of America."

ARTICLE II. Each State retains its sovereignty, freedom and independence, and every power, jurisdiction and right, which is not by this confederation expressly delegated to the United States, in Congress assembled.

ARTICLE III. The said States hereby severally enter into a firm league of friendship with each other, for their common defence, the security of their liberties, and their mutual and general welfare, binding themselves to assist each other, against all force offered to, or attacks made upon them, or any of them, on account of religion, sovereignty, trade, or any other pretence whatever.

ARTICLE IV. The better to secure and perpetuate mutual friendship and intercourse among the people of the different States in this Union, the free inhabitants of each of these States, paupers, vagabonds and fugitives from justice excepted, shall be entitled to all privileges and immunities of free citizens in the several States; . . . .

ARTICLE V.   For the more convenient management of the general interest of the United States, delegates shall be annually appointed in such manner as the legislature of each State shall direct, to meet in Congress on the first Monday in November, in every year, with a power reserved to each State, to recall its delegates, or any of them, at any time within the year, and to send others in their stead, for the remainder of the year. . . .

ARTICLE VI.   No State without the consent of the United States in Congress assembled, shall send any embassy to, or receive any embassy from, or enter into any conference, agreement, alliance or treaty with any king, prince or state; . . . .

No two or more States shall enter into any treaty, confederation or alliance whatever between them, without the consent of the United States in Congress assembled, specifying accurately the purposes for which the same is to be entered into, and how long it shall continue.

No State shall lay any imposts or duties, which may interfere with any stipulations in treaties, entered into by the United States in Congress assembled, with any king, prince or state, in pursuance of any treaties already proposed by Congress, to the courts of France and Spain. . . .

ARTICLE VIII.   All charges of war, and all other expenses that shall be incurred for the common defence or general welfare, and allowed by the United States in Congress assembled, shall be defrayed out of a common treasury, which shall be supplied by the several States, in proportion to the value of all land within each State, granted to or surveyed for any person, as such land and the buildings and improvements thereon shall be estimated according to such mode as the United States in Congress assembled, shall from time to time direct and appoint.

The taxes for paying that proportion shall be laid and levied by the authority and direction of the Legislatures of the several States within the time agreed upon by the United States in Congress assembled.

ARTICLE IX.   The United States in Congress assembled, shall have the sole and exclusive right and power of determining on peace and war, except in the cases mentioned in the sixth article — of sending and receiving ambassadors — entering into treaties and alliances, provided that no treaty of commerce shall be made whereby the legislative power of the respective States shall be restrained from imposing such imposts and duties on foreigners, as their own people are subjected to, or from prohibiting the exportation or importation of any species of goods or commodities whatsoever — of establishing rules for deciding in all cases, what captures on land or water shall be legal, and in what manner prizes taken by land or naval forces in the service of the United States shall be divided or appropriated — of granting letters of marque and reprisal in times of peace — appointing courts for the trial of piracies and felonies committed on the high seas and establishing courts for receiving and determining finally appeals in all cases of captures, provided that no member of Congress shall be appointed a judge of any of the said courts. . . .

M. L. BRADBURY

Loyalism and Allegiance

I N ONE OF THE STRIKING PHRASES for which he became famous, Carl Becker announced in 1909 that the movement for independence, at least in New York, had involved two questions – one of home rule and the other of who should rule at home.[1] By this distinction Becker meant that the incidents leading up to the revolution in New York were dominated by a dispute between Great Britain and America over the nature of the imperial connection and by a struggle between radical and conservative groups in America for Whig political leadership. Historians quickly used Becker's analysis of New York politics to explain the divisions of the revolutionary struggle in the rest of the colonies.

Although Becker's argument still has some merit, it illustrated a common error in American historical writing. His formula slighted the role played by the Loyalists in the revolution. Victors in any war habitually rewrite history in their own terms, and the vanquished commonly lack satisfactory spokesmen for their cause. The writing of the history of the United States confirmed this statement, for until the twentieth century the Loyalists found relatively few serious students of their part in the revolution.[2]

---

[1]Carl Becker, *The History of Political Parties in the Province of New York: 1760-1776* (Madison, 1909), 5.

[2]See Lawrence H. Leder, ed., *The Colonial Legacy, vol. I: Loyalist Historians* (New York, 1971), for an analysis of some spokesmen of the vanquished.

Admittedly the revolution and the chain of events that produced it involved political and military conflict between Britons and Americans, and also among Americans. But, contrary to Becker's contention, much of the struggle among Americans turned on the question of whether they should continue in their allegiance to the Crown or assert their independence. In this respect the revolution was the first American civil war. For those Americans who remained loyal to Britain in the revolution, Becker's two disputes — home rule and the determining of who should rule at home — were one and the same.

The argument for the revolution as a civil war gains support from estimates of Loyalist strength. All such figures are at best approximations and depend for their accuracy on definitions of what constituted allegiance to Great Britain. In estimating Loyalist numbers, the fidelity of some can be determined with far greater ease than that of others. Out of a total population of 2,500,000, roughly 100,000 Americans left their homes during the war and went into exile with the British. In 1780, some 8,000 Americans served as regular soldiers of the king, while at the same time approximately 9,000 native inhabitants served with Washington's army. Those who suffered exile or fought for Britain may be classed as Loyalists with some degree of safety. But the allegiance to Britain of many equally legitimate Loyalists, for one reason or another, did not take such obvious forms. These less thoroughgoing and consistent Loyalists are much less readily numbered, particularly since they merge, at times imperceptibly, into the sizable body of neutral or passive Americans during the revolution. In a letter to Jedidiah Morse in 1815, John Adams wrote that "nearly one third of the people of the colonies remained loyal to Great Britain."[3] The best estimates of modern scholars do not diverge too widely from Adams's figure. Wallace Brown has recently calculated the Loyalists during the revolution as comprising from 13 to 30 per cent of the entire population and 15 to 36 per cent of the white population of America.[4] Brown's percentages leave considerable allowance for error, but they do demonstrate that Loyalists existed in considerable numbers among the population. Clearly the revolution was as much a civil war as a conflict between America and Great Britain.

---

[3]John Adams to Jedidiah Morse, 22 December, 1815, in Charles Francis Adams, ed., *The Works of John Adams* (Boston, 1856), X, 193.

[4]Wallace Brown, *The Good Americans: The Loyalists in the American Revolution* (New York, 1969), 227.

Recitation of the statistics of Loyalism helps to establish its dimensions as a popular movement, but it ignores the far more interesting question of motivation — what led certain men to become Loyalists and others to become Whigs. In a sense, even to frame the question in these terms can be seriously misleading. The Loyalists did not so much become as simply remain as they were. On the whole the course of events left them behind. Though often participants in the whirl of protests against Britain in the 1760s and early 1770s, they could not go the final distance with other Americans and advocate or accept independence. Their failure to change their political convictions and allegiance sufficiently resulted in Whig denunciation of them as traitors to America. From the perspective of 1770 the Loyalists were often patriotic Americans. But what constituted patriotism in 1770 did not automatically do so in 1780, at least not in the eyes of Whig leaders. Thus, to understand why some Americans remained loyal to Britain requires the historian to begin at a time when no Loyalists existed, or rather, when all Americans to some degree accepted loyalty to the Crown. Surprisingly, no clear and consistent line existed between Whig and Loyalist as late as the early 1770s.

The series of events that precipitated the division into Whig and Loyalist, and that culminated in the revolution, began in 1760 with the accession to the English throne of George III. His coming to power placed great pressures on long-standing channels of influence between England and America, channels whose existence had made possible the peaceful accommodation of differences between the two countries. Probably his accession would not have produced armed revolt had it not coincided with the ending of the Seven Years' War. The Treaty of Paris of 1763 gave the British government most of the former French possessions in North America and left a substantial war debt. Almost inevitably Britain decided to deal with these consequences of the war by introducing some government into the new territories and by forcing the colonists to bear some part of the financial burden of the imperial establishment.

These policies produced numerous concrete changes in the traditional British governance of America in the 1760s and 1770s. They led to the stationing of 10,000 regular troops in the colonies after 1763 and to continuing efforts to tighten up the customs service. They led to the passage of various laws to increase the revenue from America. The Revenue Act of 1764 attempted to stop the smuggling of molasses and placed a duty of three pence per gallon on all foreign molasses imported into the colonies. The Stamp Act of 1765 required the use of revenue stamps on numerous items. The Townsend Acts of 1767 put import duties on glass, lead, paper, paints, and tea. Though for the most part of short duration, these acts and others that threatened to change the familiar pattern of Anglo-American relations spawned vigorous colonial protests. Among other forms, these involved the writing of pamphlets and newspaper articles, the sending of petitions to England, and rioting in the streets as a direct confrontation with royal authority.

The struggles of the 1760s, on whatever level they took place, did not produce a sharp division between future Whig and Loyalist. Of course, some preliminary indications of later paths did exist in those events. By the end of the decade Thomas Hutchinson — lieutenant governor of Massachusetts and in later years Loyalist *par excellence* — had become more or less permanently isolated in Massachusetts politics. His public support of British policies had already made him the object of vicious attacks by such Whig leaders as James Otis, Jr., and Samuel Adams. Yet, though certainly important, Hutchinson was by no means a typical Loyalist. In the 1760s many future Loyalists found dissatisfaction with the changes in British policy toward North America as did future Whigs, and the two groups remained firmly allied. William Smith, Jr., of New York — eventually an exile and chief justice of Quebec — was known in the 1760s as "Patriotic Billy" for his opposition to British tax policies.

The line between Whig and Loyalist was not drawn with any precision or finality until after 1773. In 1773 the British government decided to allow the East India Company to export tea directly to America and to sell it through its own agents at a lower price than normal. Many colonists disapproved of the Tea Act, but the Whig leaders of Boston took the step of first expressing this disapproval in violent form on the night of December 16, 1773, by dumping the tea overboard. The British government responded swiftly to the Boston Tea Party. In 1774 it passed the Coercive Acts to bring Boston and Massachusetts to heel and to assert royal authority there clearly and unequivocally. Unfortunately for the fate of the empire, Britain's extreme reaction probably gained more support for Boston, and finally for independence, than would otherwise have been the case. In September, 1774, delegates from twelve colonies assembled in Philadelphia in the First Continental Congress to consider united resistance to the Coercive Acts and to British authority.

The calling of the Continental Congress set in motion public measures that politically isolated most Loyalists and in the end produced a concept of patriotism that left no room for allegiance to both America and the Crown. On October 18, 1774, the Congress agreed to the Continental Association — a pledge that the colonies would cut off their trade with Great Britain and create local machinery to enforce the Association. These committees firmly entrenched Whig authority in most colonies. In some instances they entirely replaced the institutions of royal government. Whig organizations quickly swung into action and harrassed, coerced, and ostracized those who disagreed with their understanding of patriotism. For some Americans, not participating in the Association represented their first public display of the badge of Loyalism.

Yet, other future Loyalists did sign the Association, either voluntarily or under duress. For most of these the gap between Great Britain and America did not become too great to bridge until 1775 or 1776. After Concord, Lexington, and Bunker Hill, Whig opposition to the established government became increasingly militant. Whig authorities on different levels launched a concerted effort to resist future British aggression and to silence those still loyal to Britain. In the various colonies they drew up lists for a patriot militia and also disarmed and forced oaths of allegiance on those whom they regarded as disaffected to the Whig cause. Finally, on July 2, 1776, the Continental Congress approved the Declaration of Independence in its final form.

For most Loyalists the decision to maintain their allegiance to Great Britain came in the period from 1774 to 1776. It might come as a public refusal to obey the Continental Association, to enroll in the Whig militia, or possibly to take an oath of allegiance to the new Whig governments. Often they made the decision to remain loyal at considerable cost, particularly after the states began systematically to confiscate and sell Loyalist property. The choosing of sides could also result in some risk to life and limb. The Whig authorities willingly used violence against their opponents, as did the Loyalists against the Whigs when they had the opportunity. One day in 1776 Seth Seeley, a Connecticut farmer, paid the price of his loyalty when he was caught by a mob. Its members rode him on a rail, put him into the stocks while smearing him with eggs, and then robbed him of his money. As evidence of his service to the British cause, John Malcolm retained a dried piece of his skin with the tar and feathers still attached, the souvenir of his treatment by a Boston mob. Undoubtedly, the very real danger to life and property kept some Americans silent who might otherwise have been Loyalists.

The decisions of the period 1774 to 1776, however, were not always final or irrevocable. Some Loyalists of 1776 later switched sides as the cause of the British became militarily less attractive. Others, far removed geographically from the sources of British authority and surrounded by Whig enclaves, did not become openly Loyalist until the British Army passed by in the course of one of its revolutionary campaigns. If the British Army did not come through, then Loyalists of this variety might remain passive throughout the revolution. For some Americans the decision to exhibit their Loyalism after 1776 occurred at unexpected or unpredictable times. It might spring from such a relatively trivial source as a dispute with neighbors or, as in the case of Benedict Arnold, from thwarted ambition on the Whig side. For others, capture by the British triggered an avowal of Loyalism. Some captured soldiers and sailors promptly chose Loyalism and fought for the British rather than remain confined in a military prison for the duration of the war.

Devising a formula to explain Loyalist motivations, no matter when they made their choice, presents great difficulties. Most made their decisions on an individual basis, and their motives differed in as many ways as their numbers were plentiful. Nor did they uniformly react in the way that personal interest dictated. Loyalists could be patriotic Americans — at least in their meaning of the term — and display a capacity for self-sacrifice and disinterested zeal that rivaled any exhibited on the Whig side. The life of William Franklin — last royal governor of New Jersey and bastard son of Benjamin Franklin — revealed this aspect of the Loyalist character. In an address to the New Jersey legislature in 1775 he defined his attitude toward the issues between Britain and America — "Who has been most in the right or most in the wrong can never be satisfactorily decided. Many Things will ever happen, in the Course of a long continued Dispute, which good Men of both Parties must reflect on with Pain, and wish to have buried in Oblivion."[5] Franklin fully understood the deficiencies of British rule, but his appreciation of America's true public good left him with no easy alternative to loyalty to Great Britain. His refusal to take the path toward independence eventually cost

---

[5]Frederick W. Ricord and William Nelson, eds., *Documents Relating to the Colonial History of the State of New Jersey* (Newark, N.J., 1886), 1st series, X, 629.

him the friendship of his father and much of his fortune. He ended life in England in 1813, a bitter and lonely man. With such a diverse group as the Loyalists, possibly it is better not to attempt a comprehensive analysis of the sources of their motivations, but simply to suggest some of the different motives that might produce a Loyalist. Even such a limited task requires great care, for when confronted with almost identical circumstances, some Americans remained loyal to Britain while others became Whigs.

Crude and unabashed pursuit of self-interest undoubtedly accounted for the British sympathies of some Americans. The career of Benjamin Church afforded one of the most notorious examples of this species of Loyalist. Church was a prominent Boston physician, active in the Whig leadership of Massachusetts. At the same time he served the British as a double agent and kept their commander in Boston, Thomas Gage, informed of Whig deliberations and decisions. Exposed as a traitor in October 1775, Church at first had his liberty restrained and then in 1778 was allowed to sail for the West Indies. His vessel disappeared while en route there. Church's motives in selling out his former friends were closely related to his need for money. He lived extravagantly and required ready cash to finance an elaborate house and the demands of a mistress. Loyalty of this kind, moreover, was not confined to men. The mistress of John Hancock, another Massachusetts Whig leader, abandoned him for a British officer. Eventually she landed in England, where she received a British pension for her act of self-sacrifice.

To be effective, however, the appeal of self-interest did not have to be as raw as in the case of Church or Hancock's mistress. Calculations of personal gain helped to make Loyalists out of many royal officials in the colonies. As a group they could expect little profit by severing their British connection. Their activities before 1776 had badly compromised and limited their authority in American society. If not already predisposed to favor British rule, most of them probably would have abandoned their offices in the divisive controversies of the 1770s. Their isolation from popular bases of support and their association with the British blocked one road that lay open to other Americans — remaining neutral or passive during the revolution. Most royal officials in America had few practical alternatives to British loyalty.

Commonly, the cause of Great Britain attracted those Americans with little expectation of gain from political change or with little reason for dissatisfaction with their current situation. This consideration explained the elitist bias among the Loyalists. Of course, the division between Whig and Loyalist did not follow any simple social or economic cleavage. Both existed among the upper-class groups in colonial society — among its merchants, landowners, lawyers, and clergymen. A useful distinction can be made, however. Many members of these elite groups owed their success to the favors of the British government, and those in this category usually remained allied with the Crown, though they by no means comprised all the Loyalists. Large grants of land had been one reward for those who enjoyed political influence. Landowners whose titles depended on their British ties had little incentive to support the Whig cause. In the North, mercantile success went most readily to the participants in the profitable trade between England and America. Entry into this commerce often hinged on good English connections. For a merchant, favorable association with the British drastically reduced his difficulties with customs officials. In addition, the representatives of royal authority sometimes had lucrative contracts to dispense to particularly well-disposed merchants. Not surprisingly, many merchants remained loyal to Britain during the revolution.

The connection between political success and legal prominence requires little exploration as a source of Loyalism among many lawyers. Yet other kinds of bonds could bring lawyers, and also doctors, to side with Great Britain. Many leading men in these professions had taken their training in Britain — at the Inns of Court in the case of lawyers, and at the hospitals and universities of England and Scotland in the case of doctors. Possibly this early exposure to Great Britain made many of them more sympathetic to Britain politically and contributed to their later inclination toward Loyalism. Probably, if they had not had some sense of identification with Britain, most of them would not have gone abroad in the first place.

Americans, however, did not have to be members of an elite to have a stake in preserving the *status quo* and to have a predisposition toward Loyalism. An act of the Massachusetts legislature of 1778 indicated the diverse social appeal of allegiance to the Crown. It prohibited Loyalists who had previously fled to the British from returning to Massachusetts, listing these exiles by name and trade or profession. Approximately one-third of the men on the list were members of the upper classes, one-third farmers, and one-third various kinds of artisans, laborers, or small businessmen. Other lists of Loyalists exist, and although they yield different fractions, they all attest to the varied social and economic composition of the Loyalists. Richard Walsh has recently studied the artisans of Charleston, S.C., and concluded that some of them turned Loyalist because of their reliance on British trade. These artisans had ample economic reason for not wanting a split between Britain and America.[6] Some of the same incentives toward Loyalism prevailed in the province of New York, where a landed aristocracy dominated the colony's political and economic life. Its members employed large numbers of tenants to farm their estates. Many of New York's landed proprietors became Loyalists, and their tenants often followed their political lead — possibly from coercion, lack of political awareness, or simple contentment with their lot. In fact, New York's tenants furnished a substantial proportion of the Loyalist farmers in all the colonies in the revolution.

Accounts of Loyalist motivations often omit those of two significant groups — the Indians and the Negroes. The Indians of the western territory mostly supported the British cause and willingly fought against the Americans. Previously they had relied upon the British as the source for many of their supplies. British agents had worked among them, and in many instances the Indians had come to accept and trust their leadership. After the Declaration of Independence the British organized the Indians to take up arms against the Whigs. Self-interest, too, contributed to Indian support of the British. Indians all too often associated the Whigs with attempts to extend the frontier further into their lands. Efforts to stop the course of westward expansion had been largely ineffectual in the past, but the British had made the only efforts to do so. The Indian had little to gain from an independent America.

Substantial numbers of Negroes responded to the American Revolution in the same manner as the Indians, though many also sided with the Whigs. The Negro slave customarily had his choice of political persuasion made for him by his master. And Loyalist slaveowners, even those fleeing from the Whigs, ordinarily tried to keep their slaves since they had no intention of losing their human capital for their allegiance to the Britain. For other Negroes, however, the British lines did represent freedom, and that lure furnished the motive for their Loyalism. In 1779, Gen-

---

[6]Richard Walsh, *Charleston's Sons of Liberty: A Study of the Artisans, 1763-1789* (Columbia, S.C., 1959), 93.

eral Sir Henry Clinton openly proclaimed the previously unofficial practice and offered freedom to all slaves who would desert their Whig masters for the British. When campaigning in an area, British troops often carried slaves off with them, and this capture by a new set of masters also made Loyalists of many Negroes. On leaving Boston for Halifax in 1776 some of the British sought to convince Scipio Fayerweather, a free Negro, to come with them. After his refusal they destroyed his house and furniture. The number of Negroes who fled to the British cannot be precisely estimated, but it certainly ran into the tens of thousands. A few of these escaped or captured Negroes saw active service with the British army and navy, but the British valued most of them for their contribution to the labor supply. They used Negro laborers, for example, at the siege of Yorktown. Because of the unsanitary conditions under which they worked, they suffered a higher death rate than the British soldiers.

The diversity and individuality of the Loyalists' motives handicaps all efforts to discuss them in general terms, but William Nelson has sought to overcome this difficulty by using the insights of the social sciences. He found the Loyalists concentrated in two geographic areas — the sparsely populated frontier running from Georgia to Vermont and the maritime parts of the Middle Atlantic region (Long Island, the lower Hudson Valley, southern New Jersey, the Philadelphia area, and the Delmarva peninsula). Nelson also noted Loyalists in substantial numbers in certain sea coast towns — in Charleston, S.C., Wilmington, Del., Norfolk, Va., Newport, R.I., and Portsmouth, N.H. He concluded that these regions shared the common experience of being threatened or dominated by nearby, more prosperous areas, which were often Whiggish in their politics. In Nelson's terms, the Loyalists existed on the economic and political peripheries of America. They lived in places undergoing political or economic decline, or in areas not yet important.[7]

Nelson also discovered an incentive for Loyalism in membership in cultural minorities. Often, cultural minorities tended to favor the British and cultural majorities the Whigs. For example, when already anglicized, the Dutch and the Germans usually upheld the Whig cause, but where members of these immigrant groups had retained their native language and customs, they largely remained loyal. Nelson accounted for the religious line between

---

[7]William H. Nelson, *The American Tory* (Oxford, 1961), 87.

Whig and Loyalist in minority terms as well. In the South the Anglicans constituted a major religious denomination, and most were Whigs. In the North, the less numerous Anglicans often depended on royal support for their existence, and they were more commonly Loyalists. Conversely, few northern Presbyterians and Congregationalists were Loyalists, but in the South, as a much less influential group, many often were.[8] Though Nelson's arguments cannot be regarded as conclusive, he has identified important geographic and cultural elements in the creation of Loyalism.

The multiplicity of Loyalist motives and their diverse social and geographic location in America produced a similar multiplicity and diversity in their contributions to the war effort. Some Loyalists lived openly in the midst of predominantly Whig areas, and, if well-accepted by their neighbors and if they did nothing to aid the British, remained secure. Of course, others in almost identical situations found themselves expelled and their property confiscated. As active Loyalists, Negro laborers, tenant farmers, or merchant princes played quite different parts directly related to their race and social position. For example, merchant princes did not fight as enlisted men, nor did tenant farmers ordinarily become high-ranking Loyalist officers. Silent or passive British sympathizers had little direct effect on the war, other than the fears they aroused in the minds of the Whig leaders. Any assessment of the Loyalist role in the revolution must confine itself primarily to those who openly aided the British. That evaluation must begin with the expectations the British government and military commanders had of the Loyalists since they never proved particularly effective at organizing themselves. British attitudes and plans did much to give formal structure to the Loyalist contribution to the war.

At the beginning of the revolution the British made two errors in exploiting the military potential of the Loyalists. They miscalculated the numbers of the British sympathizers and did little to organize them. From the British perspective of 1776, the Whig forces appeared an ill-organized and motley mob with little staying power in the field and without deep roots in most parts of America. The British conceived their task principally as one of dispersing the armed Whig minority. Then, Americans would voluntarily return to their allegiance to the Crown. The British thought their problem more military than political: once they

---

[8]*Ibid.*, 89-90.

defeated the Whigs, they expected the automatic reestablishment of their political control. Thus, organizing and arming the Loyalists had little attraction and offered certain dangers. Giving weapons to the Loyalists and turning them against their neighbors might stiffen moderate Whig resistance to British rule. The British did want to defeat the Whigs militarily, but to do so in a way that reconciled, rather than alienated, the mass of Americans whether Loyalist or Whig.

In 1778 the entire character of the revolution changed for the British, and they then sought to make more effective use of the Loyalists. After the British defeat in the Battle of Saratoga, France joined the war on the side of the United States. For the first time in the eighteenth century, Britain had not a single ally on the European continent while involved in a conflict against France. With its forces thinly spread around the globe and inadequately equipped to fight a world war, Britain had to use whatever resources lay at hand, including the Loyalists. Also, by 1778 the war had seemingly reached a stalemate in the North, and British leaders decided to take advantage of the substantial Loyalist population in the South by actively campaigning there. Because of limited shipping and manpower, not until 1780 could they fit out a major expedition, which successfully laid siege to Charleston, S.C. After the capture of Charleston, Lord Cornwallis launched the series of operations that led the British from South to North Carolina, and finally in 1781 to Yorktown.

British plans for the southern campaign of 1780-81 hinged on Loyalist contributions. Loyalist militia would not only fight alongside Cornwallis's army, but would also serve to police conquered areas. For a time this strategy seemed to work, particularly after the Battle of Camden in August 1780, when all South Carolina apparently returned to its allegiance to Great Britain. Many southern Loyalists did fight in the way that the British had expected. In fact, the South saw some of the most bitter and bloody fighting among Americans during the revolution. Yet on the whole the Loyalists proved a weak and unreliable support for British efforts. Any defeat made many Loyalist militiamen ready to renounce their allegiance and become stalwart Whigs, at least until the next British victory. British hopes for the Loyalists also suffered a serious blow in October 1780, when over 1,000 Loyalists under Major Patrick Ferguson were defeated at King's Mountain. Limited strength also hampered British efforts to reassert political control in the South; they never had sufficient men to defeat Whig armies in the field and at the same time protect Loyalist civilians from Whig reprisals. Though many fought well, the Loyalists simply lacked the numbers and organization to provide the basis for reconquering the South.

From a military point of view, British employment of the Loyalists presented a classic example of misuse of resources. Before the French intervention — when the British had the best chance of defeating the Whigs — they made little use of the Loyalists. After France entered the war — when the British task became much more difficult — they placed too great a reliance on the Loyalists. Even in the best of circumstances, of course, refugees are notoriously weak elements out of which to make an army. During the French Revolution some British leaders expected great things from antirevolutionary forces on the European continent, but those experienced in the American conflict refused to have anything to do with organizing an internal European opposition to the French Revolution. Their dealings with the Loyalists had convinced them that such groups were hopelessly divided among themselves and almost impossible to mold into an effective fighting force.

Even if the British had employed the Loyalists in the best possible manner, their contribution probably could not have won the war. The British ordinarily could defeat Whig armies in the field. With certain exceptions British forces and generals showed themselves time and time again superior to their Whig counterparts. Yet, though the British had the men and skills to defeat their opponents, they lacked the men and skills to conquer the American continent. To subdue a coastline of 1,000 miles, with settled territory running 200 miles into the interior, required more resources than Britain had available. Then, too, the British failed in fighting a world war because they possessed an insufficient margin of superiority over France. In certain ways the Whigs did not defeat the British, but the American continent and the French did.

In spite of their limited contribution to the British potential for victory, the Loyalists did prove valuable to the British in various ways. Some served as militiamen and as soldiers in the regular army, others manned privateers that preyed on Whig shipping, and civilians worked for the British forces as pioneers, carters, and the like. In fact, the British could never have dispensed with native Americans as a source of labor. In occupied areas — such as Charleston, Philadelphia, or New York — the Loyalists undertook much of the organization of government and also manned the defenses of the cities when necessary. As best they could in essentially garrison towns, they led normal lives, sponsoring balls and theatrical performances, and even publishing newspapers.

Some Loyalists occupied themselves in seemingly more exciting ways. Both sides had highly organized spy operations, and numerous Loyalists performed that service for the British. To weaken the Whig economy, the British counterfeited Continental currency, and Loyalists did much of the printing and distributing of this imitation money. In performing work that took them behind Whig lines, the Loyalists had the advantage in that no language barrier separated the wartime opponents. Loyalist animosity toward the Whigs also inspired them to undertake, independently of the British, some limited fighting against their native enemies. As a result of their raids on the Whigs they turned those parts of New Jersey near the British lines guarding New York into something of a waste land. Probably the Loyalist expeditions proved more of a nuisance than a serious impediment to the Whig war effort. In all likelihood they sufficiently annoyed the Whigs to push them into greater exertions against the British.

In serving the British cause the Loyalists suffered from several handicaps. The British tended to treat them as inferiors. Loyalist officers never received all the perquisites of their British counterparts and ranked below them as well. Countless Loyalists met rebuffs from the British in the form of a senseless snobbery against anyone or anything colonial. Loyalist dependence on the British reinforced this almost inevitable equation between provincial and inferior. In occupied areas Loyalists could not have survived without the military presence of the British nor without their food and other essentials. The fact of dependence did not produce a feeling of gratitude among the Loyalists. They discovered that the British also plundered their property as ruthlessly as the Whigs. Loyal merchants had their ships seized by the vessels of the Royal Navy, and loyal householders had their houses raided by passing British patrols. Those who lost property to the British — as many Loyalists did — undoubtedly discovered new limits on their willingness to make future sacrifices for the British.

By ending in defeat for the British, the revolution also brought about the downfall of the Loyalists. For the majority of Loyalists the personal cost of their defeat was probably relatively small, provided, of course, that they had escaped much loss of property or significant physical injury during the fighting. Most Loyalists had little desire to leave their homes after the collapse of their cause, and the states allowed many of them to remain. Whether a Loyalist had to depart depended on many factors. In general, states that had experienced little bitter fighting did not banish many Loyalists. And moderate or passive Loyalists — those who had not actively aided the British or fled at some time into British lines — were accepted as citizens of the new governments with little difficulty. As early as 1779 Connecticut provided for the rehabilitation of Loyalists who would take an oath of allegiance to the state. Those accepted back into American society in 1783 disappeared as a separate element; they never inspired the legends or emotion after the revolution that the "Lost Cause" of the Confederacy did after the Civil War.

Some Loyalists who stayed behind did encounter hostility and personal violence. At the end of the revolution the victors in certain instances settled personal scores with their opponents. Ordinarily these acts of revenge occurred in areas of extremely bitter fighting or where neither side had ever clearly dominated. Whigs sometimes accorded Loyalists the formality of a legal trial, but possibly just as often made them the victims of mob justice. As late as 1785 North Carolina recorded the hanging of a former Loyalist.

For yet other Loyalists their allegiance meant exile from their homes. As a rule those who had fled to the British or had been banished could not return, at least not immediately. Some Loyalists did try to make their way back without permission, but paid for their attempt by being put in jail or tarred and feathered by a mob. Most refugees had no alternative but to stay with the British at the end of the war. As a consequence the British government organized large-scale evacuations of its supporters from America. Since most Loyalists were concentrated near Charleston or New York at the conclusion of the fighting, these cities were the most important ports of embarkation. To evacuate the Loyalists from New York, for example, took most of 1782 and 1783. These departures were not always permanent, however, for some refugees did manage to get back. Peter Van Schaack, a New York lawyer, had sided with the British in 1778 but had his American citizenship restored in 1784. After his return to New York, Van Schaack never again became active in politics. Other Loyalists, however, accomplished even that feat. Henry Cruger, another member of a leading New York family, had been a member of Parliament and in 1781 mayor of Bristol. Later he returned to the United States and in 1792 won election to the New York Senate.

Fate held a harder end for other Loyalists. Many could not return and had to spend their lives in an unwanted exile. Joseph Galloway, Speaker of the Pennsylvania Assembly from 1766 to 1775, became a prominent Loyalist leader during the war. When he petitioned the Pennsylvania legislature to return to America in 1793, it denied his request; his position among the Loyalists had earned him too much hatred. In certain ways Galloway's life illustrated the burden of exile for many Loyalists. When he left Philadelphia with the retreating British forces in 1778, his wife stayed behind to try to save some of the family's fortune. She died in 1789 before they could ever be reunited. Her efforts, however, did secure some of the family's property for their children, though the Pennsylvania government confiscated the part that specifically belonged to her husband. Unfortunately, the number of Loyalists who went into enforced permanent exile cannot be determined. Approximately 100,000 Americans left with the British during the war, but for how many the exile was permanent and for how many merely temporary, cannot be calculated.

Many Loyalists found a new home in England; their number probably totaled five to six thousand. These refugees faced many difficulties in adjusting to their new environment. They landed in an unfamiliar country which offered them few opportunities to earn a living. Most Loyalists did not have easily marketable skills, and even those that did often found the English economy closed to them. Loyalists also encountered in abundance the familiar English prejudice against provincials, an attitude reinforced by the fact that many Englishmen had sympathized with the Whigs in the revolution. By 1781 most politically significant Englishmen thought the war a needless extravagance and considered any attempt to prolong it futile. Of course, Loyalists in certain instances wore out their own welcome. As is the case with all refugee groups, they devoted much of their time to planning and plotting their return. Their English hosts could be excused for not having much sustained interest in the topic, except possibly as a way of getting rid of increasingly tiresome guests.

Most refugees did not go to England because of its distance and because they sensed that it held few opportunities for them. The largest body of American emigrants settled in Canada. Approximately 30,000 located in the Maritime provinces and another 10,000 in Quebec and Ontario. The modern history of the Maritimes largely began with the arrival of the Loyalists, for they substantially outnumbered the earlier inhabitants and quickly established their political control. Canada offered a new start to those Loyalists who knew something about farming, for land was available for clearing and cultivation. Professional men, however, found little market for their skills in an essentially wilderness society. Even with easy access to land, many Loyalist settlers became disenchanted with Canada in later years and returned to the United States. Most of the Negro refugees from America settled in Canada, but dissatisfaction with their treatment led over 1,000 of them to emigrate to Sierra Leone in 1792. Despite these departures the Loyalist presence in the Maritimes has remained strong, even into the twentieth century. The Ontario and Quebec exiles met a more ironic fate. Many of them settled in the path of later immigrant groups from the United States. By the nineteenth century Upper Canada lay across the natural course of advance for American agriculture. Many pioneers crossed the border and exchanged their United States citizenship for the opportunity offered by Canada. These later settlers overwhelmed much of the Loyalist element in their new homeland.

The West Indies also provided a haven for some Loyalists, though the path there was often somewhat circuitous. Some, for example, first moved to East or West Florida, only to move again when Spain recovered these territories from the British as a result of the revolution. Ordinarily the West Indies proved most attractive to those Loyalists who owned slaves and wanted to continue a staple agriculture. Over 10,000 Loyalists, including slaves, settled in Jamaica. Their later history is obscure, for as a small proportion of the island's total population, they became lost in its masses. The Loyalist element in the Bahamas can be more easily identified because of the islands' small population. The roughly 8,000 Loyalists – a figure that once again included slaves – who settled there quickly dominated their new home.

For most exiles the central economic fact of their departure from America was their loss of property. Some, of course, had good connections in their new environments and in later years more than recovered their losses. Others prospered in the revolution from the opportunities that war always offers to a few strategically placed individuals. Some Loyalists saved at least part of their fortunes and took it with them – first into the British lines, and then on board the ships that carried them into exile. But most suffered some kind of loss, if for no other reason than Whig confiscation of the property of their proscribed opponents. At the end of the war the British government did its best to insist on articles in the 1782 Treaty of Paris that permitted Loyalists to recover their property in America. Unfortunately, the provisions never had any effect, since the state governments refused to honor them and the American national government possessed neither the will nor the means to compel obedience.

Loyalist property losses caused the creation by the Parliament in 1783 of a claims commission to offer some compensation. Two commissioners sat in London, while two went to Canada and one to New York. As a result of their work, the British government distributed approximately £3,000,000 to over 4,000 Loyalists. Not surprisingly in a hierarchical society such as that of eighteenth-century England, upper-class Loyalists received more adequate rewards than the more lowly. Sir John Johnson, for example, received reimbursement for approximately one-half of his claimed loss of £100,000. By contrast former slaves were often informed that receiving their freedom from the British government was sufficient reward for their loyalty. Yet, within the limits of class and race prejudice the commissioners performed their task well and honestly. They conscientiously grappled with such diverse problems as assessing the worth of an abandoned piece of furniture, a lost Crown office, or a confiscated house lot.

The proceedings of the claims commissioners have great value for the student of Loyalism. They permit easy identification of numerous Loyalists, record their experiences in the revolution, and offer some measure of the damages they suffered. Undoubtedly, Loyalists sometimes exaggerated the tales of loss and suffering, yet the commissioners had some test of the accuracy of claims through the willingness of other Loyalists to catch one of their fellows in a lie. The commission proceedings supply ample evidence of what the revolution meant for many Americans.

Historians have traditionally tried to measure the change that the departure of the Loyalists produced in American society. Often their studies have focused on land records and have involved calculations of the amount of land that changed hands as a result of the Whig confiscations. The claims records made clear that, though the turnover in land was considerable, some Loyalists lost equally significant quantities of other possessions — livestock, household furniture, or goods used in trade. Possibly these represented the maximum amount of property that most eighteenth-century Americans could hope to acquire in a lifetime. Conversely, the claims records indicated that for some Whigs the only economic gain derived from exiling the Loyalists was the plow, horse, or bedstead that they took from some departing neighbor.

Economic loss, however, was often not the most significant sacrifice for numerous Loyalists. At the beginning of the revolution many had thought themselves fighting for Britain. With their departure from America they discovered that they had erred in their calculations. When Thomas Hutchinson sought a new home in England, he chose to live in Bristol because it reminded him of his beloved Boston in Massachusetts. The wife of Edward Chandler could not quite convince herself that the hams of England equalled those of New Jersey. Hutchinson, Mrs. Chandler, and other Loyalists discovered in exile that they had to some extent deluded themselves about the locus of their loyalty. When they sided with Britain, they had really fought for America — at least for the kind of American society they wanted. Exile often taught them that their real allegiance had been to America all along.

FOR FURTHER READING

Brown, Wallace. *The King's Friends: The Composition and Motives of the American Loyalist Claimants*. Providence: Brown University Press, 1966.
————. *The Good Americans: The Loyalists in the American Revolution*. New York: William Morrow & Co., Inc., 1969.
Labaree, Leonard Woods. *Conservatism in Early American History*. New York: Cornell University Press, 1945.
Leder, Lawrence H., ed. *The Colonial Legacy, vol. I: Loyalist Historians*. New York: Harper & Row Torchbooks, 1971.
Nelson, William H. *The American Tory*. New York: Oxford University Press, 1962.
Smith, Paul H. *Loyalists and Redcoats: A Study in British Revolutionary Policy*. Chapel Hill: University of North Carolina Press, 1964.

1

The Coming of the Revolution

In 1779 Joseph Galloway, a prominent Pennsylvania Loyalist, was examined before the House of Commons by Lord
Germain, the Secretary of State for America. In this selection from his testimony Galloway advances his explanation of
the origins of the revolution. His comments indicate the
slowness with which it gained momentum and the existence
of substantial numbers of Americans who opposed it. Galloway's excessive optimism about the willingness of the
majority of Americans to accept British rule once again is
also important evidence of the kind of advice that inspired
British planning about the reconquest of America.

SOURCE: *The Examination of Joseph Galloway, Esq; Late
Speaker of the House of Assembly of Pennsylvania, before
the House of Commons, in a Committee on the American
Papers, with Explanatory Notes* (London, 1779), 2-7, 11-12.

Q. At the beginning of the present rebellion, when the inhabitants
first took up arms, had the people, in general, independence in view?
A. I do not believe, from the best knowledge I have of the state of
America at that time, that one-fifth of the people had independence in
view. I wish when I give an opinion, always to give my reasons for it.
The progress of the spirit of independence was very gradual. So early
as the year 1754, there were men in America, I may say in the towns of
Boston, New York, Philadelphia, and Williamsburg, who held independence in prospect, and who were determined to seize any opportunity that
offered to promote it, by procuring additional persons to their number.
These men, when the Stamp Act was passed, made a stalking-horse, or
skreen, of the gentlemen of the law in every part of America, to cover
their designs, and to sound the trumpet of opposition against Government; but avowed, that their conduct was on the ground of obtaining a
redress of American grievances, and not with a design to separate the
two countries. Upon this ground, I am confident, the gentlemen of the
law acted. When the Tea Act was passed, they made the same use of the
merchants who were smugglers in America, as they had done the lawyers
before, still declaring, that they meant not independence. So late as the
sitting of the Congress in 1774, the same men when charged with it in
Congress, and whilst they held it tenaciously and religiously in their
hearts, they almost to a degree of profanity denied it with their tongues

— and all this was done on their knowledge, that the great bulk of the people of North America was averse to independence. If we look at the resolves of Congress, down almost to the very period of their declaration of independence, we shall find the same language, the same pretence of obtaining a redress of grievances, held out to the people. And for the same reason, at the very time they declared independence they gave out, that it was not with a view to a total separation of the two countries, but from necessity; because, unless they declared independence, the powers of Europe would not trade with them, and they were in great distress for want of a great many foreign necessaries. So that, from all circumstances, I am convinced, that not one fifth part of the people had independence in view!

Q. If so large a proportion of the people of America were so averse to independence, why have they suffered their present rulers to obtain so much power over them as to prevent any effectual exertion in support of their principles?

A. The Congress having prevailed upon a very small part of the people to take up arms, under the pretence of obtaining a redress of grievances; and having an army composed of those people under their command, and subject to military discipline, they disarmed, or caused to be disarmed, all persons whom they thought disaffected to their measures, or wished to be united to this country, contrary to their scheme of Independence. I have the resolves of Congress, dated 2d January, 1776, at my house to that purpose. They went so far as to disarm (by sending two battalions into Queen's county, in the province of New York, for that purpose) a large number of the people of that district, for no other reason but because they voted against sending a member to the Convention of New York; they totally, as I may say, disfranchised them; and they would not suffer them to trade, or be traded with; they suffered them to be sued, but would not let them sue in their courts of justice; they would not suffer them to pass out of their district on any account. By these means the well-affected part of America to this government became disarmed, and the arms were put into the hands of those on whom the Congress could rely — a small part of the people.

•   •   •   •   •

Q. From your knowledge of the people of America, what proportion of the inhabitants do you think at this time would prefer a reconciliation with Great Britain, rather than assist in supporting American independence?

A. From the experience which the people have had of the superlative and excessive tyranny of their new rulers; from the distresses they have felt by the ravages of war, and the loss of their trade; from an aversion which they have to an attachment and connection with France, which they are fearful will terminate in the loss of their liberties, civil as well as religious; and from the old attachment, and I believe an earnest desire to be united with this country, I think I may venture to say, that many more than four-fifths of the people would prefer an union with Great Britain, upon constitutional principles, to that of Independence.

Many of the people, who at first took part in the opposition to Government, and were deluded by the Congress and its adherents, have severely felt every degree of distress. From those feelings they now reason, and that reason has prevailed on them to compare their old happy situation with their present misery, and to prefer the former.

2

The Whig Use of Violence

Ann Hulton was the sister of one of the Commissioners of Customs in Boston from 1767 to 1776 and also a regular correspondent of Mrs. Adam Lightbody, the wife of a merchant in Liverpool, England. In this letter to Mrs. Lightbody, Ann Hulton describes the violence the Whigs employed against their opponents in Boston after the arrival of the tea of the East India Company. In addition to suggesting the reasons that might have kept some Loyalists silent or passive in the revolution, the letter makes clear the willingness of others to defy their opponents openly. The Castle referred to is Castle William, a fort in the Boston harbor, and "Malcolm" is John Malcolm, a British customs official.

SOURCE: Ann Hulton, *Letters of a Loyalist Lady* (Cambridge, Mass.: Arne Press, 1927), 69-71. Reprinted with permission from Harvard University Press. Copyright 1927 by the President and Fellows of Harvard College; 1955 by Kenneth Ballard Murdock.

January 31st 1774

You will perhaps expect me to give you some Account of the State of Boston & late proceedings here but really the times are too bad & the Scenes too shocking for me to describe. I suppose you will have heard long before this arrives of the fate of the Tea — Whilst this was in suspence. The Commissioners of the Customs & the Tea Consignees were obliged to seek refuge at the Castle. My Brother happened to be there on a vissit of a long engagement to Colonel Lessley when those other Gentlemen came over. He continued there about twenty days, in the mean time vissiting his own House (about 8 Miles from the Castle) several times. The Colonel & the Gentlemen of his Choir rendered the retreat as agreable as possible by their polite Attention to every Refugee.

After the destruction of the Tea, my Brother returned Home & the other Commissioners Left the Castle. The violent fury of the People having subsided a little. One would have thought before that all the Malice that Earth & Hell could raise were pointed against the Governor. Mr. Paxton (one of the Commissioners) & the Tea Consignees, two of whom are the Governors Sons, the others are Mr. Clark a respectable Old Gentleman & his Sons, with two other Merchants Mr. Haliwell another Commissioner & likewise of this Country was an object of their threats.

The Tea Consignees remain Still at the Castle. Six weeks since the Tea was destroyed, and there is no prospect of their ever returning & residing in Boston with Safety. This place, & all the Towns about entered into a written agrement not to afford them any Shelter or protection, so that they are not only banished from their families & homes, but their retreat is cut off, & their interest greatly injured by ruining their Trade.

It is indeed a severe case, & can hardly be credited, I think, that the Governors Sons should be treated as fugitives & outlaws in their own Country. One of them lately went from the Castle, & with his Wife to her Fathers House, a Gentleman at Plymouth 40 Miles from Boston. They had no sooner arrived there, but the Bells tolled and the Town Assembling instantly went to the House, demanded that Mr. Hutchinson should depart immediately out of the Town. Colonel Watson his father in law, spoke to them, saying that it was so late at Night, & the Weather so severe, that Mr. H. & his wife could not without great inconvenience remove from his house that night, but promised them, they should go in the Morning by 9 o'Clock. The time came, and they were not gone, when the Town bells tolled again, & the people gathered about the house. Upon which the Young Couple Sett off in a great snow storm, & nobody knows since where they are.

But the most shocking cruelty was exercised a few Nights ago, upon a poor Old Man a Tidesman one Malcolm he is reckoned creasy, a quarrel was picked with him, he was afterward taken, & Tarred, & feathered. Theres no Law that knows a punishment for the greatest Crimes beyond what this is, of cruel torture. And this instance exceeds any other before it he was stript Stark naked, one of the severest cold nights this Winter, his body covered all over with Tar, then with Feathers, his arm dislocated in tearing off his cloaths, he was dragged in a Cart with thousands attending, some beating him with clubs & Knocking him out of the Cart, then in again. They gave him several severe whipings, at different parts of the Town. This Spectacle of horror & sportive cruelty was exhibited for about five hours.

The unhappy wretch they say behaved with the greatest intrepidity, & fortitude all the while. Before he was taken, defended himself a long time against Numbers, & afterwards when under Torture they demanded of him to curse his Masters the King Governor etc. which they could not make him do, but he still cried, Curse all Traitors. They brought him to the Gallows & put a rope about his neck saying they would hang him he said he wished they would, but that they could not for God was above the Devil. The Doctors say that it is imposible this poor creature can live. They say his flesh comes off his back in Stakes.

3

A Decision Is Made

William Eddis was a British customs official in Annapolis, Maryland. In this letter to a friend he details the reasons that made him side with the Crown. The occasion that made it necessary for him to take a public stand was the passage of the Continental Association.

SOURCE: William Eddis, *Letters from America, Historical and Descriptive; Comprising Occurrences from 1769, to 1777, Inclusive* (London, 1792), 220-225.

Annapolis, Aug. 24, 1775

On the fourteenth instant, the Convention concluded their deliberations. If their proceedings are published before I have an opportunity to transmit this, I will enclose them for your information. You will then be enabled to form an opinion of the disposition of this province.

When you have perused the association of the freemen of Maryland, you will, I presume, acknowledge the propriety of my objecting to subscribe to it, and acknowledge that such conduct would be inconsistent with my principles, and the station under government, in which I am situated. I verily believed some regard would have been paid to the particular circumstances of revenue officers, but our present rulers entertain different sentiments, and all persons, without exception, must associate and enrol; the Governor, and his household, *only* excepted.

His Excellency, ever attentive to my interest, has generously made me an offer to become one of his family, immediately after the embarkation of Mrs. Eddis, who is now anxiously preparing for her approaching voyage. We had firmly determined, that no circumstances, however adverse to our hopes, should induce us again to consent, even to a temporary separation; but the cruel necessity of our once more submitting to it, has of late appeared too evident. She is perfectly convinced, that I must speedily avow my political sentiments, in the most explicit manner; and that my refusal to join in the popular measures, will subject me to inconveniences which may better be supported, when my family is removed to some secure asylum. Influenced by such forcible considerations, she has acknowledged the expediency of what is so distressing to our domestic happiness! and early in the ensuing month, we must bid farewell! — a painful farewell to each other!

The Governor's humane and generous offer impresses my mind with the most lively gratitude: yet am I greatly embarrassed how to conduct myself on the occasion. Considering the wild, unsettled times, he is uncommonly popular; but how long he may continue so is a matter of great uncertainty. It is highly probable he may speedily think it necessary to express his decided approbation of the present proceedings, which step, I am fearful, would effectually cancel his past merits; subject him to calumny and censure: and render his longer continuance in Maryland impossible. Should the event prove these conjectures to be well-founded, I cannot possibly expect protection from the friendly attention of my worthy patron; on the contrary, I must either bid adieu to America, and every pleasing prospect, or meanly comply with the requisitions of the Convention, in direct opposition to the sentiments of my heart. Let me weigh both evils, with a settled determination to make that election which will hereafter be attended with the most salutary effects, and the most pleasing reflections.

If I abandon this country, in consequence of a steady adherence to my principles and duty, I must unavoidably be subjected to a precarious life of uncertainty and dependence; and instead of enjoying a comfortable asylum in my native land, I may only experience a variety of misfortunes and disappointments, and drink yet deeper draughts of the cup of affliction. I am, however, perfectly assured, if I preserve my integrity unblemished, though I should thereby be subjected to "the spurns that patient merit of the unworthy takes," yet, hereafter, I shall receive an adequate reward.

On the other hand, should I act in opposition to the dictates of my mind, by subscribing to the assocation, and taking arms, I shall not only be subject to those painful feelings which accompany a consciousness of doing wrong; but be justly despised by every brave and honest man; detested and avoided by every respectable society; and when tranquillity is happily restored, deservedly cast out, to encounter a complication of miseries, without one chearing thought to support such a reverse of fortune.

I have now fairly stated my situation; and believe, from your knowledge of my principles, you will readily determine how I shall regulate my conduct; and whenever I am unhappily necessitated to quit this country, where I have experienced great blessings, this pleasing reflection will accompany me, that I have left behind me a fair and unblemished reputation.

4

British Plans for the Loyalists

Sir Banastre Tarleton was the commander of the British Legion. In this selection he discusses the British plans for the use of the Loyalists in South Carolina after the capture of Charleston.

SOURCE: Sir Banastre Tarleton, *History of the Campaigns of 1780 and 1781, in the Southern Provinces of North America* (Dublin, 1787), 24-27.

After the surrender of the town, the commander in chief, without loss of time, adopted measures which appeared both judicious and necessary. He returned thanks to the army in general, and expressed himself in the language of gratitude when he particularized those officers and men, whose attention, toils, and courage, had contributed to his success. He dispatched the Earl of Lincoln to Europe, with intelligence of the important advantage which had attended His Majesty's arms; and he circulated proclamations amongst the inhabitants of South Carolina, well calculated to induce them to return to their allegiance, and to manifest their loyalty by joining the King's troops. It was stated, that the helping hand of every man was wanted to re-establish peace and good government: And that as the commander in chief wished not to draw the King's friends into danger, while any doubt could remain of their success; so now that this was certain, he trusted that one and all would heartily join, and, by a general concurrence, give effect to such necessary measures for that purpose as from time to time might be pointed out. Those who had families were to form a militia to remain at home, and occasionally to assemble in their own districts, when required, under officers of their own chusing, for the maintenance of peace and good order. Those who had no families, and who could conveniently be spared for a time, it was presumed, would chearfully assist His Majesty's troops in driving their oppressors, acting under the authority of Congress and all the miseries of war, far from that colony. For this purpose it was said to be necessary, that the young men should be ready to assemble when required, and to serve with the King's troops for any six months of the ensuing twelve that might be found requisite, under proper regulations. They might chuse officers to each company to command them, and were to be allowed, when on service, pay, ammunition, and provisions, in the same manner as the King's troops. When they joined the army, each man was to be furnished with a certificate, declaring that he was not only engaged to serve as militiaman for the time specified; that he was not to be marched beyond North Carolina and Georgia; and than when the time was out, he was freed from all claims whatever of military service, excepting the common and usual militia duty at the place of his residence: He would then, it was said, have paid his debt to his country, and be entitled to enjoy, undisturbed, that peace, liberty, and property, at home, which he had contributed to establish.

The proclamations issued by the general produced great effect in South Carolina: In most of the districts adjoining to Charles town, great numbers offered to stand forth in the defence of the British government, and many did voluntarily take up arms, and place themselves under the direction of Major Ferguson, who was appointed to receive and command them. A general revolution of sentiment seemed to take place, and the cause of Great Britain appeared to triumph over that of the American Congress. Two hundred and ten of the inhabitants of the town, signed an address to the commander in chief and the admiral, soliciting to be re-admitted to the character and condition of British subjects, the citizens having been hitherto considered as prisoners on parole, declaring their disapprobation of the doctrine of American independency, and expressing their regret, that, after the repeal of those statutes which gave rise to the troubles, the overtures made by His Majesty's commissioners had not been regarded by the general assembly of the United States of America. Sir Henry Clinton, in one of the manifestoes issued at this period, declared, that if any persons should thenceforward appear in arms, in order to prevent the establishment of His Majesty's government in that country, or should, under any pretence or authority whatsoever, attempt to compel any other person or persons so to do, or who should hinder the King's faithful and loyal subjects from joining his forces, or otherwise performing those duties their allegiance required, such persons should be treated with the utmost severity, and their estates be immediately seized for confiscation.

5

British Disappointments

Lord Cornwallis was the commander of the British forces in the South for most of 1780-81. These letters to Cornwallis from two Loyalist officers explain the disappointment of British plans and the difficulties they faced in trying to use the Loyalists to reconquer the South.

SOURCE: Public Record Office. Cornwallis Papers. Transcripts in the Manuscript Division, Library of Congress.

My Lord,

I am sorry to acquaint your Lordship that the 7th Instant Major Ferguson was attack near King mountain by a Body of the enemy. Their numbers enabled them to surround our post, & ours was only sufficient to form a Single line on the top of the hill.

The Action lasted an hour & five minutes, when the North Carolina militia who were intyrly Commanded by their own Officers on the right gave way, which not only discouraged the other Regiments; but drove them down the hill before them. Our little Detachment of soldiers Charged the enemy with success, & Drove the right wing of them back in Confusion; but unfortunately Major Ferguson made a Signal for us to retreat, being afraid that the enemy would get possession of the heighth from the other side: the Militia being ignorant of the cause of our retreat; it threw the few that Stood their post under the officers from 96, in disorder though the officers cut some of them down: they intermixed themselves with our Detachment, & broke us in such a manner that, we could no longer Act, being then reduced to 2 Serjeants & 20 Rank & file.

The Left on seeing us broke gave way, got all in a croud on the Hill, & though every Officer used his endeavours to rally the men, as nothing now offered but to make a Breach through the enemy; I am sorry to say was not able to get a man to follow them, the Chief part being without amunition, excepting four men that followed Major Ferguson while the other Officers were doing their best amongst the croud, to collect more to follow them; but I am sorry to say that Major Ferguson was killed before he advanced 20 yards. Ensign Mac Ginnes of Col. Allan's Corps was also killed soon after the Action commenced which rendered the Militia he Commanded almost useless. In this situation, the small body of soldiers we had being cut up, and finding it impossible to rally the Militia I thought proper to surrender as the only means of saving the lives of some brave men still Left.

In justice to the Officers and men I must beg leave to acquaint your Lordship that they behaved with the greatest Gallantry & attention, even to a wish; as to the Militia, there was many of them, both Officers & men, who, when, there; the enemy was within a hundred yards round us, that behaved with a Degree of Gallantry.

Our wounded are left at one Wilsons, 4 Miles this side of the place of Action: They are without Body Cloths or Blankets, and I am now afraid the man who attends them without mediciens, & not sufficiently Capable.

I am not allowed to make myself acquainted with the State of the Militia so that I have not it in my power to furnish your Lordship with a State of them.

I inclosed a State of our Detachment, & I cannot help mentioning to your Lordship that the few of them that remain, both officers and men are without Cloaths & shoes, & not a Blanket amongst us all.

As this Letter is to be read by the Commanding Officer, & I am not allowed to mention particulars, I have only to wish your Lordship may be pleased to think of us, particularly of the poor soldiers who have been a suffering for some time past. I have the honor to be with due respect

> My Lord
> Your Lordships Most
> Obedient Servant
> A De Peyster Captain
> Royal American Regiment

Camp near Gilbert Town
11th October 1780

Camp at Colonel Williams's October 12, 1780

My Lord,

In Deep distress in Many respects I write your Lordship to give an Idea of our much Distressed Frontiers. You were pleased to Confer the Command of the Late Colonel Thomas's Regiment upon me, Pursuant to which Colonel Ferguson arrived in Our back parts, as Inspector General of Militia and Called upon Me. I accordingly Raised the Subjects and Joined him with sometimes Upwards of three hundred Seldom less than two and remained during the Summer and Cooperated with his Majestys troops Almost Thro North Carolina at last retreated back to the verge of South Carolina where Colonel Ferguson met his Unhappy Defeat and death. I had near One hundred brave Men killed and taken. I was at the same time Sent into my Regiment to Raise My Regiment to be ready to act with him When he should fall back — which he never did to me. I am fallen back to Colonel Cruger & Colonel Cunningham not having Men to Stand in My Regiment. I never Received part nor parcell of Your Lordships Money sent the Militia. My Regiment in the front of the province has Suffered Much the Most from Rebel depradations then Any Other Regiment. Having the Indian Country & North Carolinians both to Suffer from has Caused me never to have it in my Power to Answer the full Contents of your Lordship's Order Respecting the Rebel Confiscated property Except By Ordering Each Captain to give Orders to Each Respective Officer or private in their Companys to hold in their Possession any property taken from forfeited by or brought into the District of that Species Since I received Your Lordships Orders for that Purpose. As the Summer has been Little Else but Merching and Countermerching never two days Calm space to mind our farms or any Domestick Comfort. I had my dwelling houses burnt on two plantations. My property of every kind taken even to a Spoon; which renders my Case very Extreme. Still doubt not but I shall be on an Equal footing with Other back woods field Officers. I hope your Lordship will Consider the much distressed backwood Militia as Naked & in every Respect Unfit for Service. Major Plummer's regiment Lost One hundred Men Or more with Colonel Ferguson killed and taken, himself wounded & Left in the field. I think from Every Circumstance and it the General Opinion of the Most Experienced men that the Militia Cannot hold the back Country as Long as Holstein's River Nolachuckky and the Western Water People remain Unconquered.

I am Your Lordships Obedient
Humble Servant
Zachariah Gibbs Major

6

The Price of Allegiance

Not all Loyalists fled to the British. Although her family took refuge with the British, Grace Galloway, the wife of Joseph Galloway, stayed behind in Philadelphia. In this letter to her daughter in England, she reveals the cost of the revolution in human terms to many Loyalists.

SOURCE: Joseph Galloway Papers, Manuscript Division, Library of Congress.

Philadelphia October the 15 1781 forget not to date your Letters. Nothing would have induced me to have took up my pen again, till I dare write with freedom, but to Relieve the Anxiety of my beloved & darling Daughter & all I can now say is to beg you not to expect me to write often, for I am not in the way of Opportunitys, & my health often prevents me from stooping. My health Daily grows worse. England Alone could give me Relief. But that now is out of the question. My nerves are to weak to undertake the Voyage, & I have no hopes of ever haveing

one days health more. Yet at times I go down & Appears so Chearfull
that people think little Ails me. Your pappa knows I talked of going to
england many years ago but now it is too late. A box of things you sent
Arrived last Aprile but I have received none of them. Yet some were on
the Road two Months since, but whether taken or not I cannot Learn.
The difficulty of getting them is so great that I desire you to send no
more. I am extremely Uneasy that I can't hear from you. I was told
Letters was seen for me in New York but on enquiry none were to be
found. Allways enclose to Mr. Shoemaker. From him is all I receive & I
have been ten Months without one line & now near six. This is a Double
Affliction to me. I was very solicitous to know how you was situated but
can hear Nothing but from common Report. Your pappas letter just as
you ware going to Bath but without a Date Alarmed me very much for
fear his health was the inducement, & many times I thought he may
want my Care & Assiduity who never forsook him & though incapable of
Nurseing myself I saw every Necessary care taken & that with an affection & Anxiety no servant could attend to. Do you my dear now Act for
me. I have no expectation of ever seeing you here & wish you to be content
to stay where you are. Could I be with You it would be happiness
supreme; you never can like America again. Things are now Drawing
to a Crises. How they will Terminate we must leave "War is the Business but to whome tis Given/ To Fall or conquer that Depends on
heaven." I am far from being sanguin & I wish others ware not so much
so. I mean on your side of the water. My being so long seperated from
you has allmost broke my heart & I am ready to Use the words of Milton
"that hope which comes to all comes not to me." Indeed my dear I am
not like your mamma. My spirits are all gone. I am turned out amonge
the herd of mankind, & left to sink. This I could bear had I but health
but all the Accumalated ills of Life would shake a stoughter spirited
then mine. I have sent in a Memorial to the Assembly for the reversion
of the Lands given to Mrs Grawdon for Dower, & my Moiety of Lang-
horn, Park, & the house in town. I must not let hope have to much possession for fear of a Disapointment. Give my dear love to your pappa &
may the Great God who alone can extricate us, look down on our present
Sufferings, & may we submit to his severe Chastisments as becomes the
Christian & the Phylosopher. Then let what will happen we may stand
like Rocks of Ademint, Unmoved, at all this World can threaten or
Confer. May he pour down his blessings on the head of my dearest
betsay & teach her to depend on him alone who never forsakes those who
Rely on Him. I can say no more but that my soul & all it's faculties are
too much engrossed by My dear betsay for her to doubt but I am her

Affectionate Mother G Galloway

7

Departure

Richard Wyvill was a British officer in New York. In this selection he describes the evacuation of the Loyalists from New York in 1783.

SOURCE: Memoir of Richard August Wyvill, Peter Force Papers, Manuscript Division, Library of Congress.

Most of the Loyalists, in New York, are embarking, for Nova Scotia, taking their wood dwellings, with them, which gives the streets, a strange appearance leaving large openings, in many of them: A number of half pay Officers, and discharged men, are also going there, where, they are to have land given them, implements of Husbandry, and rations, for ten Years. It was, a most affecting scene, when the Inhabitants embarked, quitting, their friends forever, to whom they were attached, both, by ties of blood, and friendship, and many of our rough soldiers, felt the sympathetic tear, on their cheeks, on leaving their old Comrades. The prospect before them, was, also, most distressing, going, to a distant, and strange Country, where their success was extremely doubtfull, and their future prospects, in life, perfectly uncertain.

8

Exile

The Loyalists met varying fates in exile. These petitions to the British government from Thomas Peters describe the reception of the Negro Loyalists in Nova Scotia and detail the treatment that led many of them to decide to emigrate to Sierra Leone in 1792.

SOURCE: Public Record Office, Foreign Office 4, vol. 1.

To the Right Honourable Lord Grenville one of his Majesty's principal Secretaries of State.

The humble Memorial and Petition of Thomas Peters a free Negro and late a Serjeant in the Regiment of Guides and Pioneers serving in North America under the Command of General Sir Henry Clinton on Behalf of himself and others the Black Pioneers and loyal Black Refugees hereinafter described.

Sheweth

That your Memorialist and the said other Black Pioneers having served in North America as aforesaid for the Space of seven Years and upwards during the War afterwards went to Nova Scotia under the Promise of obtaining the usual Grant of Lands and Provision.

That notwithstanding they have made repeated Applications to all Persons in that Country who they conceived likely to put them in Possession of their due Allotments, the said Pioneers with their Wives and Children amounting together in the whole to the number of 102 People now remain at Annapolis Royal have not yet obtained their Allotments of Land, except one single Acre each for a Town Lot, and though a farther Proportion of 20 Acres each (vizt. about half the Allowance of Land that is due to them) was actually laid out and located for them agreeable to the Governor's Order it was afterwards taken from them on Pretence that it had been included in some former Grant and they have never yet obtained other Lands in Lieu thereof and remain destitute and helpless.

That besides the said 102 People at Annapolis who have deputed your Memorialist to represent their unhappy Situation there is also a number of free Black Refugees consisting of about 100 Families or more at New Brunswick in a like unprovided and destitute Condition for though some of them have had a part of their Allowance of Land offered to them it is so far distant from their Town lots (16 or 18 Miles back) as to be entirely useless to them and indeed worthless itself from its remote Situation.

That the said two Descriptions of People having authorized and empowered Your Memorialist to act for them as their Attorney he has at much Trouble and risk made his Way into this Country in the Hope that he should be able to procure for himself and his Fellow Sufferers some Establishment where they may attain a competent Settlement for themselves and be enabled by their industrious Exertions to become useless [*sic*] Subjects to his Majesty.

That some Part however of the said Black People are earnestly desirous of obtaining their due Allotment of Land and remaining in America but others are ready and willing to go wherever the Wisdom of Government may think proper to provide for them as free Subjects of the British Empire.

Your Memorialist therefore humbly prays your Lordship, that your Lordship will humanely consider the Case of your Memorialist and the said other Black People and by laying the same before his Majesty or otherwise as your Lordship shall deem most proper that they may be afforded such Relief as shall appear to be best adapted to their Circumstances & Situation.

And your Memorialist shall ever pray, etc.

The Mark of Thomas Peters

To the Right Honourable Lord Grenville one of His Majesty's principal Secretaries of State.

The humble Petition of Thomas Peters, a Negro, late Serjeant in the Regiment of Guides & Pioneers serving in North America in the late War under the Command of General Sir Henry Clinton, and now deputed by his Fellow Soldiers and by other Free Negroes and People of Colour Refugees, settled at Annapolis, Digby and St. John's (New Brunswick) in Nova Scotia.

Humbly sheweth

That the Situation of your Memorialist and of the other free Negroes and People of Colour above mentioned is rendered extremely irksome and disadvantageous not only by the Want of the promised Allotments of Land which they cannot yet obtain (as represented in another Memorial) though seven Yeares are elapsed since their Arrival in the Province appointed for their Settlement but more especially they are injured also by a public and avowed Toleration of Slavery in Nova Scotia as if the happy Influence of his Majesty's free Government was incapable of being extended so far as America to "maintain Justice and Right" in affording the Protection of the Laws & Constitution of England.

That even the King's Courts in Nova Scotia have publicly decided in Favour of Slavery, and refused the Protection of the Laws to the poor negroes in that unhappy State which has occasioned such a degrading and unjust Prejudice against People of Colour in general that even those that are acknowledged to be free Inhabitants and Settlers in the Province are refused the common Rights and Privileges of the other Inhabitants, not being permitted to vote at any Election nor to serve on Juries whereby it is become very difficult for them to obtain ordinary

Justice in the Recovery of Debts due to them for Labor performed or even to obtain common Protection from Violence and personal Ill Usage, insomuch that several of them through this notorious Partiality or "Respect of Persons" (which is absolutely forbid and even deemed odious in the Laws of England) have already been reduced to Slavery without being able to obtain any Redress from the King's Courts, And that one of them thus reduced to Slavery did actually lose his Life by the Beating and Ill Treatment of his Master and another who fled from the like Cruelty was inhumanly shot and maimed by a Stranger allured thereto by the public Advertisement of a Reward for such unnatural Violence who "delivered him up to his Master" in that deplorable wounded state although the Laws of God (and of Course also the Common Law of England) have absolutely prohibited "the delivery up to his Master the Servant" (or Slave) "that has escaped from his Master" (Deut. 23.15). And as the poor friendless Slaves have no more Protection by the Laws of the Colony (as they are at present misunderstood) than the mere Cattel or brute Beasts, their Treatment of Course is also similar or even worse than the Treatment of Cattle, as the Caprice & Passions of wicked Men are more liable to be excited against human Beings than against dumb Animals; and that the oppressive Cruelty and Brutality of their Bondage is in General shocking to human Nature but more particularly shocking irritating and obnoxious to their Brethern of the same Kindred the free People of Colour who cannot conceive that it is really the Intention of the British Government to favour Injustice, or tolerate Slavery in Nova Scotia where the Nature of the Climate does not afford even the false Pretence of Necessity for Evil (so frequently alledged for the Evil of Slavery in the West Indies) as it is less congenial to Blacks then Whites, and therefore they humbly and earnestly implore Protection and Redress.

                                        The Mark of Thomas Peters

9

A Calculation of Loss

In this statement to the Loyalist claims commissioners
Arthur Thomas accounts for his losses in the revolution. In
addition to providing a calculation of property damage, the
statement indicates the kind of evidence that the proceedings
of the claims commissioners offer to the student of Loyalism.

SOURCE: Proceedings of Commissioners on Loyalist Claims
for Canada, Manuscript Division, Library of Congress.

Case of Arthur Thomas late of Philadelphia
May 6, 1786.

Claimant affirms he is a Native of Pennsylvania, settled at Philadelphia
when Troubles broke out, in Trade. At first Took part with the British
Government. Declared his Sentiments publicly. Was called upon to sign
an Association in 1775 — which he refused. Afterwards called upon to
give Gold for Paper Money, in order to support the Expences of an
Expedition against Canada which Claimant refused. This Conduct made
him particularly obnoxious. From these parts of his Conduct having
made him offensive to the Rebels, in June 1776 a Mob collected, & beset
his House. They had just before attacked the House of another Loyalist,
Solomon, whom they took Prisoner, & carried about the Town. This
Mob came against the Claimant as he imagines merely on Account of
his Loyalty. It was, he thinks, about the time when they were urgent
with people for a public Declaration of Independence.
   Claimant was endeavoring to prevail with the officers of Militia to
save Solomon from the fury of the Mob — when his own house was
attacked. His two Sons were forced to run away. Claimant staid in the
house of different friends several Days, but made his Escape in the
Night, & fled into the Country & kept himself concealed for some time
in July. Was afterwards taken & brought before Council of Safety in
August & imprisoned 5 or 6 Weeks, in close Confinement, & then discharged on Bail. In November or December he fled to New York. He
afterwards went to Philadelphia when British were in possession. Staid
as long as the British Army did. Assisted in barracking & quartering
the Troops. Returned with the Army to New York. Staid till after the
Peace. Then went, but without his family, to Bermudas in Aug. 1783.
Returned from Bermudas to New York, then came to Nova Scotia. Now
lives at Wilmington on the Delawar in Delawar State. He went thither

from this Province better than a Year ago, in Consequence of a request from his Son, now settled at Philadelphia, who could better assist him when in the Delawar State.

Produces Copies of Certificates as to Loyalty and Losses from J Galloway.

Produces Copy of Certificate as to Loyalty & Suffering, from S. Shoemaker.

When the Mob broke into his house they rifled and plundered it. Lost the chief of his furniture to value of above 60 £ Sterling. Lost articles in his Trade such as Leather. Thinks there was near 500 £ lawful in Cash or old paper money. Thinks his whole loss equal to £1200 Pennsylvania Currency.

The house has been confiscated & sold. Claimant values his Interest at 600 £ after Incumbrances. Produces Valuation of House & Lot, after deducting Ground Rent & Mortgage, at 600 £ Pennsylvania Currency by Abel James & Henry Drinker. They also say that the said house & Lot had been sold, in Consequence of Attainder of Claimant for adhering to the Enemies of the State.

Explains the reason of Claim being made for his Son — which was done by his friends in England that in Case of Accident happening to the Claimant the Son might be secured, but though there was Money intended for the Son, Claimant looked upon it as his own.

Claimant says he never took Oaths to American States. He could not remove his family. Had Thought of going to England. Does not admit himself to be a Subject of the States.

10

The Return of a Loyalist

Samuel Curwen was a merchant of Salem, Massachusetts, who eventually took refuge in England. In these letters to his business associates and Loyalist friends in England, he describes his return to Massachusetts, his property losses, and the changes he found in American society after the revolution. Curwen did manage to salvage some of his property and, instead of carrying out his threat to go to Nova Scotia, remained in Salem until his death in 1802.

SOURCE: George Atkinson Ward, ed., *Journal and Letters of the late Samuel Curwen, Judge of Admiralty, etc., An American Refugee in England, from 1775 to 1784* (New York, 1842), 415-417.

To Capt. Michael Coombs, London

Salem, Mass., Oct. 9, 1784.

Dear Sir,

This day fortnight, at half past three P.M., I landed on the head of the Long-wharf, in Boston, being the first American ground I had touched since May 12, 1775, when I departed from Philadelphia. It is no less strange than unaccountable, how low, mean and diminutive every thing on shore appeared to me. On Sunday, being the day following, I left for this place, where I alighted at the house of my former residence, and not a man, woman, or child, but expressed a satisfaction at seeing me, and welcomed me back. Thus much for myself.

The few things for your *widow* I have delivered into her hands, and I find her a woman of uncommon vigor and equanimity, nor do I think one to be met with who has better acquitted herself in the late trying times. By her resolution she has preserved the household furniture from confiscation and waste, and your account-books from inspection, though menaced and flattered by the state agents. The melancholy derangement of my own affairs has so entirely unsettled me, that I can scarce attend to any thing. I think it very unlikely my house can be saved. It shall be among my first engagements to attend to your affairs.

With real regard, your friend,

S. Curwen.

To Jonathan Smith, Esq., Philadelphia

Salem, Oct. 9, 1784.

Dear Sir:

A few days since I returned to the place of my nativity, after an absence of more than nine years, in which interval I find great revolutions to have taken place, not only with regard to the civil and political state of America in general, but also with respect to the property of individuals. Whilst some from the narrowest and basest condition have arisen to high honors and great wealth, others from comfortable, reputable, and even respectable and affluent, have fallen into indigent and distressed circumstances; and although the latter is not exactly my case, I confess myself verging to that point; my affairs are sadly deranged, but I hope time and application will cure the disorder. For that purpose, I beg you will forward to me a box containing my account-books left in your father's hands for security during my absence.

Your most obedient servant,
S. Curwen.

To Capt. Michael Coombs, London.

Salem, Nov. 15, 1784.

Dear Sir:

I have waited on Mr. Sewall, a lawyer of your town; from him I learn he has undertaken to procure the necessary papers, and will, at my pressing instance, set about it immediately; my argument being constantly, *delay is almost as fatal to my friend as total neglect.*

I am now to congratulate you on the salvation of your wharf and warehouse from the villainous hands of the rapacious harpies, the commissioners; that part of your real estate, by great luck was neglected in the libel by which your other was seized and confiscated, and therefore it still remains your property. What debts are claimed and proved, must, by the law that confiscated, be levied on and taken out of the estate sold, the remainder escheats to the public treasury. But so infamously knavish has been the conduct of the commissioners, that though frequent attempts have been made to bring them to justice, and respond for the produce of the funds resting in their hands, so numerous are the defaulters in *that august body,* the General Court, that all efforts have hitherto proved vain. Not twopence in the pound have arrived to the public treasury of all the confiscations!

Mr. Sewall says, were you disposed, he would advise you not to come here, until the act respecting refugees or absentees be passed, which will be, it is thought, this session.

The triumphant here look down with contempt on the vanquished; their little minds are not equal to the astonishing success of their feeble arms. God bless the worthy and blast the villainous of every party.

Very truly yours,
S. Curwen.

To Hon. Judge Sewall, Bristol, England.

Salem, Nov. 22, 1784.

Dear Sir:

I find myself completely ruined. I confess I cannot bear to stay and perish under the ruins of my late ample property, and shall, therefore, as soon as I can recover my account-books, left in Philadelphia on my departure from America, and settle my deranged affairs, retreat to Nova Scotia, unless my allowance shall be taken from me. I am ignorant whether it may be prudent to make application to the commissioners on American refugees' affairs; but being here by their indulgence, I wish my allowance may continue. And if in this representation you can afford me any assistance by yourself, or in concert with Mr. Danforth, to whom I have also written, I shall thankfully acknowledge your counsel and aid, as a kind endeavor to rescue from want your old and faithful friend,

S. Curwen.